# THE ADDRESS BOOK

# THE
# ADDRESS
# BOOK

## How to Reach Anyone Who *Is* Anyone

### MICHAEL LEVINE

A Perigee Book

Every effort has been made to provide the most current mailing addresses. Addresses, however, do change, and neither publisher nor author is responsible for misdirected or returned mail.

*We regret that when this book went to press,
it was too late to include the names of the recently
elected United States public officials.*

Perigee Books
are published by
The Putnam Publishing Group
200 Madison Avenue
New York, NY 10016

Library of Congress Cataloging-in-Publication Data

Levine, Michael.
    The address book : how to reach anyone who is anyone / Michael Levine.
        p.   cm.
    ISBN 0-399-51793-6 (alk. paper)
    1. United States—Directories.   2. Social registers—United
States.   3. Celebrities—United States—Directories.
    4. Associations, institutions, etc.—United States—Directories.
    5. Associations, institutions, etc.—Directories.   I. Title.
    E154.5.L48   1993                92-31749 CIP
    917.3′0025—dc20

Cover design by Richard Rossiter

Photo of the author © 1993 by Darren Michaels

Printed in the United States of America

1  2  3  4  5  6  7  8  9  10

This book is printed on acid-free paper.

Dedicated to
my agent and friend
Alice Martell
for her encouragement,
tenacity and constant
belief in me.

# Acknowledgments

*With lovers and friends, I still can recall.*
*Some are dead and some are living.*
*In my life, I've loved them all.*

Saying thank you to my friends and family somehow seems so inadequate. It's what I say to people who hold the elevator door open for me.

So, to the following loyal friends and family I send my love and deepest appreciation through these words.

My brilliant literary agent and good friend, Alice Martell, and her assistant Paul Plunkett.

My encouraging friends at Putnam Publishing Company (where I've been published since 1984): my dynamic editor Laura Shepherd, John Duff, Rena Wolner and Christine DelRey.

My dedicated and loving father Arthur O. Levine, stepmother Marilyn, and sister Patty.

My special friends: Keith Atkinson, Rana Bendixon and Sorrell, Ken Bostic, Leo Buscaglia, Ron Byrd, Bill Calkins, Susan Gauthier, Karen L'Heureux, Heather Lawrence, Richard Imprescia, Bette Geller Jackson, Lori and Lisa Kleinman, Robert Kotler, Bonnie and Gordon Larson, Richard Lawson, Nancy Mager, John McKillop, Lynn Novatt, David Newman, Dennis Prager, Steven Short, Peter Smaha, Joshua Trabulus, Earlene White.

My wonderful business partners Mitchell Schneider and Monique Moss.

My office family Amanda Cagan, Todd Brodginski, Marla Capra, Katherine Caulfield, Vivianna Ceballos, Naomi Goldman, Kim Kaiman, Matt Labov, Julie Nathanson, Robert Pietranton, Kelly Reichard, Tresa Redburn-Cody, Julie Rona, Marcee Rondan, Rhonda Saenz, Jane Singer, Kimberley Smith, Melissa Spraul, Brigid Walsh, Julie Wheeler, Allison Whyte, Staci Wolfe, Lesley Zimmerman.

My business associates Bob and Lori Bernstein, Laura Herlovich, Barry Langberg, Matt Lichtenberg, Dan Pine, Joy Sapieka.

My special thanks to Kathleen Conner for her incredible commitment to excellence in the researching of this book.

# The Guilt:
# Garrison Keillor on Letter Writing

The first step in writing a letter is to get over the guilt of not writing. You don't "owe" anybody a letter. Letters are a gift. The burning shame you feel when you see unanswered mail makes it harder to pick up a pen and makes for a cheerless letter, too. I feel bad about not writing, but I've been so busy, etc. Skip this. Few letters are obligatory, and they are *Thanks for the wonderful gift* and *I am terribly sorry to hear about George's death* and *Yes, you're welcome to stay with us next month*, and not many more than that. Write those promptly if you want to keep your friends. Don't worry about others, except love letters, of course. When your true love writes, *Dear Light of My Life, Joy of My Heart, O Lovely Pulsating Core of My Sensate Life*, some response is called for.

From *We Are Still Married*
by Garrison Keillor
(Viking Press, 1989)

# Operation Address Book

There are several million names not appearing in this address book, but they may be among the most important people of all: the countless dedicated men and women serving in our armed forces around the world. There's nothing that means more to our troops than a letter from home, and though most of them certainly correspond with their families, they also enjoy hearing from other Americans as well. This year, more than 200,000 servicemen and servicewomen will participate in the America Remembers Campaign, which delivers letters, packages, baked goods, and other precious reminders of home.

You can participate. The following are several addresses you can write to that guarantee your letter or package will reach our defenders of freedom at their lonely outposts. Please take the time to write them.

**America Remembers the Army**
c/o Commander
2nd ACR
ATTN: S-5/PAO
APO New York, NY 09093

**America Remembers Enterprise (CVN-65)**
c/o Commander Enterprise
(CVN-65)
ATTN: PAO
FPO San Francisco, CA
96636-2610

**America Remembers the Forrestal (CV-59)**
c/o Commander, Forrestal
(CV-59)
ATTN: PAO
FPO Miami, FL 34080-2730

**America Remembers 435th Tactical Air Wing**
c/o 435th TAW
Rhein-Main Air Base
APO New York, NY 09057

**America Remembers the Marines**
c/o Camp Foster USO
P.O. Box 743
FPO Seattle, WA 98774

**America Remembers U.S. Forces in Korea**
c/o Chaplain
APO San Francisco, CA 96202

# Introduction

A couple of years ago, I proudly accepted an invitation to deliver a speech at the Harvard Business School. Never having visited an Ivy League school, I wasn't quite sure what to expect.

The audience of America's best and brightest took me completely by surprise—and damn near gave the faculty a collective heart attack—when they stood and cheered my concluding observation: "Some ideas are so stupid, only intellectuals can believe them."

I came to appreciate this truism about twelve years ago when I first approached New York's publishing elite with my admittedly simple idea to create a series of address books. One by one, they peered down from their thrones, rejecting the idea as "far too simple," and suggesting that in this hurry-up world, only fools would be naive enough to write to people they didn't know.

Finally, Putnam saw its worth, and today, it is estimated over 2,000,000 letters have been successfully delivered, thanks to the best-selling series of address books.

I've heard from desperate medical patients who have received help from blood donors thanks to the book, from lost lovers reunited, from consumers battling and beating corporate villains, and, of course, from fans hearing from their heroes.

By the way, two years ago I visited the White House, and never in my life did I feel prouder than when I saw *The Address Book* on the desks in several executive offices.

Yes, the address book was a simple idea; an idea that works. But, how can you make it work for you?

* How can you make sure the notable receives your letter? The number-one reason mail to notables is left unanswered is that it is addressed improperly and never reaches its intended destination. A letter addressed simply to "Barbra Streisand, Hollywood, California" will find its way only to the dead-letter file of the post office. The complete, accurate addresses in this book will get your mail to the offices, agents, studios, managers, or even homes of the addressees, and I have been unable to find one notable, no matter how busy or important, who doesn't personally read some of his or her mail—

even the president of the United States. That doesn't mean notables read and answer every single piece, but it should offer encouragement to people who write to them.

* Politicians have a standard rule of thumb: for every letter they receive, they estimate that one hundred people who didn't take the time to write are thinking the same thought as the letter expresses. So you can calculate the effect of your single letter by multiplying it by one hundred! And all entertainment figures keep a close watch on their mail. It is a real indication of what people are thinking and feeling. Often, the notable is surrounded by a small group of associates who tend to isolate the star from the public. Your letter helps break down this barrier. Amazing things have been accomplished with letters as long as they have the proper mailing address.

* Here are several important things to remember in writing notables: always include a self-addressed stamped envelope. This is the single most important factor in writing a letter if you want a response. Because of the unusually high volume of mail notable people receive, anything you can do to make it easier for them to respond is going to work in your favor. Keep your letters short and to the point. Notables are usually extremely busy people, and long letters tend to be set aside for "future" consideration. For instance, if you want an autographed picture of your favorite TV personality, don't write three pages of prose to explain your request.

* Make your letters as easy to read as possible. This means type it or, at the very least, handwrite it very neatly. Avoid crayons, markers, or even pencils. And don't forget to leave some margins on the paper.

* And, be sure to include your name and address (even on all materials that you include with your letter) in the event the materials are separated from your letter. You would be amazed how many people write letters without return addresses and then wonder why they never hear from the person to whom they wrote.

* Never send food to notables. Due to spoilage and security matters, it cannot be eaten anyway. (Would you eat a box of homemade brownies given to you by a total stranger?) If you send gifts, don't wrap them in large boxes with yards of paper, string, and tape around them. (They may not have a crowbar on hand.) Again, don't forget to include your name and address on all material you send. Of course, don't send—or ask for—money.

* In writing to corporation heads, remember most of them rose to their lofty positions because they were better problem-solvers than their company peers. Good corporation heads are zealous about finding solutions to written complaints (especially if you have sent copies of your complaint letters to appropriate consumer organiza-

tions). A recent survey of corporation heads showed that 88 percent of all letters of complaint were resolved. Therefore, the old adage, "When you have a problem, go to the top," appears to be accurate. Likewise, corporation executives greatly appreciate hearing good news (satisfaction, extra service, helpful employees, and so forth).

But nowhere is it written that mail should only be filled with praise and congratulations. You may enjoy shaking a fist at your favorite villain, so I have included infamous people in my book.

Most people are usually very kind and sincere in their letters. They write what they would say or ask if they had the opportunity to do so in person. This is especially true of children, who are extremely honest. On the other hand, infamous people and others who are out of favor with the public predictably receive hostile and angry letters

Most of the people, famous and infamous, listed in *The Address Book* are movers and shakers, and thus highly transient, changing their addresses far more often than the average person. Their mail is usually forwarded to them, but occasionally a letter may be returned to the sender. If this should happen to your letter, first check to make sure that you have copied the address correctly. If you wish to locate another address for the person to whom you are writing, begin your search by writing to him or her in care of the company or association with which they may have been most recently associated. For example, if a musician or singer has last recorded an album with a specific record company, write in care of that company; a sports figure might be contacted through the last team he or she was associated with; an author through his most recent publisher; and so forth.

According to 1987 statistics, about 90 million pieces of mail land in the dead-letter pile because the carrier couldn't make out the address, so write clearly.

Remember, *a person who writes to another makes more impact than ten thousand who are silent.*

—Michael Levine
Los Angeles, CA

And none will hear the postman's knock without a quickening of the heart. For who can bear to feel himself forgotten?

—W. H. AUDEN, from "Night Mail"

**A & E
(Arts and Entertainment
    Network)**
555 Fifth Avenue
New York, NY 10017
Nick Davatzes, CEO
*Cable network*

**A & M Records, Inc.**
1416 North LaBrea Avenue
Hollywood, CA 90028
Herb Alpert, Chairman
*Record company*

**A & W Restaurants**
17197 North Laurel Park Drive,
    Suite 500
Livonia, MI 48152
E. Dale Mulder, CEO/Chairman
    of the Board
*Fast food chain*

**A. C. Nielsen Company**
Nielsen Plaza
Northbrook, IL 60062
N. Eugene Harden, President
*Television ratings company*

**A Special Wish Foundation**
4300 Amalgamated Pl., #101
Groveport, OH 43125
Ramona Fickle, Executive
    Director
*Grants wishes of children with life-
    threatening ailments*

**Aaron, Hank (Henry)**
P.O. Box 4064
Atlanta, GA 30302
*Baseball home-run king*

**Abba**
Box 26072 S-100 41
Stockholm, Sweden
*Pop group*

**Abbey of Regina Laudis
Order of St. Benedict—
    Library**
Bethlehem, CT 06751
Mother Agnes Shaw, O.S.B.,
    Librarian
*Special collection of medieval
    mystics/patristic writings*

**Abbott and Costello Fan Club**
P.O. Box 262
Carteret, NJ 07008
Billy Wolfe, President

**Abbott, George**
1270 Ave. of the Americas
New York, NY 10020
*Director, author*

**Abbott, Jim**
c/o California Angels
P.O. Box 2000
Anaheim, CA 92803
*Professional baseball player*

**Abbott Laboratories**
One Abbott Park Road
Abbott Park, IL 60064   .
Duane L. Burnham, Chairman
and CEO
*Pharmaceutical company (Murine,
Selsun Blue, etc.)*

**ABC Television Network**
a division of Capitol Cities/ABC
Inc.
77 West 66th St.
New York, NY 10023
Thomas S. Murphy, Chairman

**Abdul, Paula**
30 West 21st Street
New York, NY 10010
*Dancer, choreographer, singer*

**Abdul-Jabbar, Kareem
(Lew Alcindor)**
1875 Century Park E., #1200
Los Angeles, CA 90067
*All-time leading basketball scorer*

**About Face/Let's Face It**
123 Edward St.
Toronto, Ontario M5G 1E2
Canada
Betty Bednar, Director
*Facial disfigurement support group*

**Abraham, F. Murray**
9301 Wilshire Blvd., #312
Beverly Hills, CA 90210
*Actor*

**Abzug, Bella**
2 5th Ave.
New York, NY 10011
*Activist*

**Academy of American Poets**
177 E. 87th St.
New York, NY 10128
Alex Thorburn, Program
Director

**Academy of Country Music**
6255 Sunset Blvd., #923
Hollywood, CA 90028
Fran Boyd, Executive Director

**Academy of Family Films
and Family Television**
334 West 54th St.
Los Angeles, CA 90037
Dr. Donald A. Reed, Executive
Director
*TV watchdog organization*

**Academy of Model
Aeronautics**
1810 Samuel Morse Drive
Reston, VA 22090
Geoffrey Styles, Director of
Public Relations

**Academy of Motion Picture
Arts and Sciences**
8949 Wilshire Blvd.
Beverly Hills, CA 90211
Karl Malden, President
*Oscar's parents*

**Academy of Natural Sciences
of Philadelphia**
19th and the Parkway
Philadelphia, PA 19103
Keith S. Thomson, CEO

**Academy of Science Fiction,
Fantasy & Horror Films**
334 W. 54th St.
Los Angeles, CA 90037
Dr. Donald A. Reed, President

**Academy of Television Arts
and Sciences**
3500 W. Olive Ave., #700
Burbank, CA 91505
James L. Loper, Executive
Director

**ACA Joe, Inc.**
148 Townsend St.
San Francisco, CA 94107
Alice Wany Lam, CEO/
Chairman of the Board
*Chain of clothing stores*

**ACCESS: A Security
Information Service**
1730 M St., NW, #605
Washington, DC 20036
Bruce Seymore, information
specialist
*Library of international security,
arms control and military affairs*

**Accidental Nuclear War
Prevention Project**
1187 Coast Village Rd., #123
Santa Barbara, CA 93108
Dean Babst, Coordinator

**AC/DC**
11 Leonminster Road, Morden
Surrey SM4 England
*Rock band*

**Ace Hardware Corp.**
2200 Kensington Ct.
Oak Brook, IL 60521
Theodore Costoff, Chairman

**Acheson, James**
c/o Sandra Marsh Mgmt.
14930 Ventura Blvd., #200
Sherman Oaks, CA 91403
*Award-winning costume designer*

**Acid Rain Foundation, Inc.,
The**
1410 Varsity Dr.
Raleigh, NC 27606
Dr. Ellis B. Cowling, President

**ACT UP (AIDS Coalition to
Unleash Power)**
496 A Hudson St., #G4
New York, NY 10014
Tom Cunningham,
Administrator
*Angry AIDS activists*

**Action Comics**
DC Comics, Inc.
355 Lexington Avenue
New York, NY 10017
Julius Schwartz, Editor
*Comic book*

**Actors and Others for
Animals**
5510 Cahuenga Blvd.
N. Hollywood, CA 91607
Cathy Singleton, Executive
Officer

**Adams, A. John Bertrand**
1825 K St., NW
Washington, DC 20006
*Public affairs consultant*

**Adams, Brock**
513 Senate Hart Office Bldg.
Washington, DC 20510
*Senator from Washington*

**Adams, Bryan**
1416 North LaBrea Ave.
Hollywood, CA 90028
*Singer*

**Adams, Cindy**
*New York Post*
210 South St.
New York, NY 10002
*Entertainment columnist*

**Adams, Mark**
c/o John Berggruen Gallery
228 Grant Ave.
San Francisco, CA 94108
*Artist*

**Adams, Michael**
c/o Denver Nuggets
1635 Clay St.
Denver, CO 80204
*Professional basketball player*

**Adams, Richard George**
26 Church St.
Whitchurch, Hampshire,
   England
*Author*

**Adams & Rinehart, Inc.
Information Center**
708 Third Ave.
New York, NY 10017
Jennifer Farrar, Director of
   Information Services
*Library and databases for business
   and finance*

**Adato, Perry Miller**
WNET
356 W. 58th St.
New York, NY 10019
*Documentary producer, writer,
   director*

**ADC Band**
17397 Santa Barbara
Detroit, MI 48221
*Rock group*

**Adidas USA, Inc.**
15 Independence Blvd.
Warren, NJ 07060
Ann Occi, Director of Creative
   Services and Public Relations
*Sneaker manufacturer*

**Adler, Charles Spencer**
955 Eudora St., #1605
Denver, CO 80220
*Headache psychiatrist*

**Adler, Lee**
Lime Kiln Farm
Climax, NY 12042
*Artist, educator, marketing
   executive*

**Adler, Mortimer Jerome**
Institute for Philosophical
   Research
101 E. Ontario St.
Chicago, IL 60611
*Author*

**Adliss, Brian Wilson**
Woodlands Foxcombe Rd.
Boars Hill, Oxford OX1 5DL
   England
*Author*

**Adobe Systems, Inc.**
1585 Charleston Rd.
Mountain View, CA 94039
John E. Warnock, Chairman
   and CEO
*Computer software company*

**Adoptees' Liberty Movement
   Association**
P.O. Box 154
Washington Bridge Station
New York, NY 10033
*Search organization*

**Adult Video Association**
270 N. Canon Dr., #1370
Beverly Hills, CA 90210
Ron Sullivan, Co-Chairman
*Trade organization*

**Adults Molested as Children
United**
P.O. Box 952
San Jose, CA 95108
Henry Giarretto, Executive
Director
*Support group*

**Adulyadej, King Bhumibol**
Chitralada Villa
Bangkok, Thailand
*Ruler of Thailand*

**Advance Publications, Inc.**
350 Madison Ave.
New York, NY 10017
Samuel I. Newhouse, Jr.,
Chairman and CEO
*Publishes newspapers, magazines,
and books* (Vanity Fair,
Ballantine Books, etc.)

**Advanced Nuclear Fuels
Corp. Library**
2101 Horn Rapids Rd.
Box 130
Richland, WA 99352
Joan Okrent, Librarian
*Nuclear energy library*

**Advertising Research
Foundation Library**
3 E. 54th St.
New York, NY 10022
Roslyn Arnstein, Manager,
Information Center
*Market research and advertising
library*

**Advocate, The**
P.O. Box 4371
Los Angeles, CA 90078
Bruce Murray, Editor
*National gay newsmagazine*

**Aerosmith**
c/o Fan Club
P.O. Box 4668
San Francisco, CA 94101
*Rock group*

**Aerospace Corporation**
Charles C. Lauritsen Library
Box 92957, Sta. M1-199
Los Angeles, CA 90009
Susan B. Crowe, Manager of
Library Services
*Aerospace library*

**Aesthetic Realism
Foundation, Inc. Library**
141 Greene St.
New York, NY 10012
Richita Anderson, Librarian
*Library collection based on Eli
Siegel's principles of Aesthetic
Realism*

**Aetna Life and Casualty Co.**
151 Farmington Ave.
Hartford, CT 06156
James T. Lynn, Chairman and
CEO
*Insurance company*

**Affair De Coeur**
1555 Washington Ave., Suite B
San Leandro, CA 84577
Louise Snead, Editor
*Magazine for romance readers and
writers*

**AFL-CIO**
815 16th St., NW
Washington, DC 20006
Lane Kirkland, President
*Union of unions*

**African American Institute**
Africa Policy Information
 Center
833 United Nations Plaza
New York, NY 10017
Daphne Toporzis, Assistant
 Editor
*Special collection of news clippings
 on African/American policy*

**African Methodist Episcopal
Zion Church**
Box 19039, E. Germantown
 Station
Philadelphia, PA 19138
John H. Adams, Senior Bishop
*Religious group*

**African Wildlife Foundation**
1717 Massachusetts Ave., NW
Washington, DC 20036
John H. Hemingway, Chairman
 of the Board

**AFTRA
(American Federation of TV
and Radio Artists)**
260 Madison Ave.
New York, NY 10016
John C. Hall, Jr., Executive
 Secretary

**Aga Khan IV, H.H. Prince
Karim**
Aiglemont
60270 Gouvieux, France
*Spiritual leader and Imam of
 Ismaili Muslims*

**Agassi, Andre**
c/o Andre's Court Club
Dept. DA, P.O. Box 4297
Portland, OR 97208
*Tennis star*

**Agee, Warren Kendall**
University of Georgia, Henry W.
 Grady College of Journalism
 and Mass Communications
Athens, GA 30602
*Journalism educator*

**Aiello, Danny**
10000 Santa Monica Blvd.,
 #305
Los Angeles, CA 90067
*Actor*

**Aiken Thoroughbred Racing
Hall of Fame and Museum**
P.O. Box 2213
Aiken, SC 29802
William Post, Director

**Ailes, Roger**
440 Park Ave., 13th Fl.
New York, NY 10016
*Political communications executive*

**Ainge, Danny**
c/o Portland Trail Blazers
700 NE Multnomah St.
Portland, OR 97232
*Professional basketball player*

**Air and Waste Management
Association**
P.O. Box 2861
Pittsburgh, PA 15230
Charles D. Pratt, President

**Air Jordan Flight Club**
P.O. Box 2300
Dept. SI
Portland, OR 97208
*Club for Michael Jordan fans*

**Air Supply**
1990 S. Bundy Dr., #590
Los Angeles, CA 90025
*Rock group*

**Airline Pilots Association Engineering and Air Safety Resource Center**
535 Herndon Pkwy.
Herndon, VA 22070
John O'Brien, Director
*Library of aviation safety and regulations*

**Akaka, Daniel K.**
720 Senate Hart Office Bldg.
Washington, DC 20501
*Senator from Hawaii*

**Akido Federation, Internationale**
c/o Dr. Peter Goldsbury
Secretary General Adjoint FIA
Ushita Honmachi 3129
4–Chome Higashi-ku
Hiroshima 732, Japan
Doshu K. Uishiba, Honorary President
*International governing body for the sport of Akido*

**Akihito**
The Imperial Palace
1–1 Chiyoda-ku
Tokyo, Japan
*Emperor of Japan*

**ALA Gay & Lesbian Task Force—Clearinghouse**
c/o American Library Association
Office of Library Outreach Services
50 E. Huron
Chicago, IL 60611
*Information on homosexuality, lesbianism/feminism and gay rights*

**Al-Anon Family Group Headquarters, Inc.**
P.O. Box 862
Midtown Station
New York, NY 10018
Myrna Hammersley, Executive Director

**al-Assad, Lieutenant General Hafiz**
Office of the President
Damascus, Syria
*President of Syria*

**al-Khalifa, Sheikh Isa bin-Sulman**
Rifa's Palace
Manama, Bahrain
*Emir of Bahrain*

**Al-Nahayan, Sheikh Zayed Bin Sultan**
Amiti Palace
Abu Dhabi, United Arab Emirates
*President of United Arab Emirates*

**al-Sabah, Sheikh Jaber al-Ahmad**
Sief Palace
Amiry Diwan, Kuwait
*Emir of Kuwait*

**al-Thani, Sheikh Khalifa bin Hamad**
The Royal Palace
Doha, Qatar
*Emir of Qatar*

**Alabama**
Box 529
Ft. Payne, AL 35967
*Country music group*

**Alabama Space and Rocket Center**
**Library/Archives**
One Tranquility Base
Huntsville, AL 35807
James Hagler, Director
*Space library with special collection of Dr. Wernher Von Braun's papers*

**Alaska Air Group, Inc.**
19300 Pacific Hwy. South
Seattle, WA 98188
Raymond J. Vecci, Chairman, President and CEO
*Alaska Airlines and Horizon Air Industries*

**Alaska State Museum**
395 Whittier
Juneau, AK 99801
Bruce Kato, Director

**Albany Institute of History and Art**
**McKinney Library**
125 Washington Ave.
Albany, NY 12210
Prudence Backman, Chief Librarian
*Special collection of early New York history*

**Albee, Edward**
14 Harrison St.
New York, NY 10013
*Playwright*

**Alberto-Culver Co. Research Library**
2525 Armitage Ave.
Melrose Park, IL 60160
Jo Rathgerber, Research Librarian
*Library on toiletries, household and grocery products*

**Albertson's**
P.O. Box 20, 250 Parkcenter Blvd.
Boise, ID 83726
Gary G. Michael, Chairman and CEO
*Sixth largest food retailer in the U.S.*

**Albright, Dr. Tenley**
2 Commonwealth Ave.
Boston, MA 02117
*Retired ice skating champion*

**Alcoholics Anonymous**
P.O. Box 459, Grand Central Station
New York, NY 10163

**Alda, Alan**
151 El Camino
Beverly Hills, CA 90212
*Actor, writer, director*

**Aldredge, Theoni Vachliotis**
35 W. 90th St.
New York, NY 10024
*Costume designer*

**Alexander, Jane**
151 El Camino
Beverly Hills, CA 90212
*Actress*

**Alexander, Jason**
151 El Camino
Beverly Hills, CA 90212
*Actor*

**Alexander, Shana**
c/o Joy Harris Lantz
888 7th Ave.
New York, NY 10106
*Journalist, author, lecturer*

**Alfa Candy Corporation**
P.O. Box 344
New York, NY 10034
George Atstaedter, President
*Manufactures "healthy" candy*

**Alfonso, Kristian**
1530 Ventura Blvd., #345
Sherman Oaks, CA 91403
*Actress*

**Alhadeff, Morris Jerome**
2025 1st Ave., Penthouse A
Seattle, WA 98121
*Organization (various) executive*

**Ali, General Zine al-Abidine Ben**
Présidence de la République
Tunis, Tunisia
*President of Tunisia*

**Ali, Muhammad (Cassius Clay)**
Box 187
Berrien Springs, MI 49103
*Retired champion*

**Alia, Ramiz**
Office of the President
Tirana, Albania
*President of Albania*

**Alicea, Luis**
c/o St. Louis Cardinals
Busch Stadium
St. Louis, MO 63102
*Professional baseball player*

**All-American Amateur Baseball Association**
340 Walker Drive
Zanesville, OH 43701
Tom J. Checkush, Executive Director

**All Star Sporting Goods**
Subsidiary of Ampac Enterprises, Inc.
1 Main Street
P.O. Box 1356
Shirley, MA 01464
David J. Holden, President
*Manufactures baseball equipment*

**Allen, Debbie**
PMK
955 S. Carrillo Dr., #200
Los Angeles, CA 90048
*Actress, director, producer, dancer, choreographer and L.A. Library angel*

**Allen, Marcus**
c/o Los Angeles Raiders
332 Center St.
El Segundo, CA 90245
*Professional football player*

**Allen, Woody**
930 Fifth Ave.
New York, NY 10021
*Actor/writer/director*

**Allende, Fernando**
Box 4232
Aspen, CO 81612-4232
*Actor*

**Alley, Kirstie**
9320 Wilshire Blvd., 3rd Fl.
Beverly Hills, CA 90212
*Actress*

**Alliance for Environmental Education, Inc.**
10751 Ambassador Dr., #201
Manassas, VA 22110
Steven C. Kussmann, Chairman

**Alliance of Resident Theatres/New York Library**
325 Spring St., Rm. 315
New York, NY 10013
Stephen N. Butler, Director of Member Services
*Nonprofit theater collection*

**Allied-Signal, Inc.**
101 Columbus Road, P.O. Box 4000
Morristown, NJ 07962
Edward L. Hennesey, Jr., Chairman
*Aerospace, automotive and chemical company*

**Allman, Gregg**
P.O. Box 4332
Marietta, GA 30061
*Musician*

**Allred, Gloria**
6380 Wilshire Blvd., #1404
Los Angeles, CA 90048
*Feminist attorney*

**Alonso, Maria Conchita**
Box 537
Beverly Hills, CA 90213
*Actress*

**Alpha Flight**
New World Entertainment/ Marvel
387 Park Ave. S.
New York, NY 10016
Stan Lee, Publisher
*Comic book*

**Alpo Petfoods, Inc.**
P.O. Box 2187
Lehigh Valley, PA 18001
Franklin Krum, CEO
*Pet food manufacturer*

**Alston & Bird Law Library**
One Atlantic Center
1201 W. Peachtree St.
Atlanta, GA 30309
Patricia G. Strougel, Library Manager

**Alternative Press Center Library**
Box 33109
Baltimore, MD 21218
Bill Wilson, Coordinator
*Liberation, Third World Movements, etc.*

**Altman, Robert**
502 Park Ave., #15G
New York, NY 10022
*Director*

**Altura, Burton Myron**
450 Clarkson Ave.
Brooklyn, NY 11203
*Physiologist, educator*

**Aluminum Company of America**
1501 Alcoa Bldg.
Pittsburgh, PA 15219
Paul H. O'Neill, Chairman and CEO
*World's largest producer of aluminum*

**Alvin and the Chipmunks**
4400 Coldwater Canyon, #300
Studio City, CA 91604

**Amalgamated Clothing & Textile Workers Union, AFL-CIO**
**Research Department Library**
15 Union Sq.
New York, NY 10003
Deborah Fulker, Librarian
*Union and textile library*

**Amateur Athletic Foundation
of Los Angeles Library**
2141 W. Adams Blvd.
Los Angeles, CA 90018
Wayne Wilson, Library Director
*Olympic Games Official Reports
1896–1984*

**Amateur Hockey Association
of the United States**
2997 Broadmoor Valley Rd.
Colorado Springs, CO 80906
Robert Johnson, Executive
Director

**Amateur Skating Union of
the United States**
1033 Shady Lane
Glen Ellyn, IL 60137
Shirley Yates, Executive
Secretary

**Amateur Softball Association**
2801 NE 50th St.
Oklahoma City, OK 73111
Don E. Porter, Executive
Director

**Amax, Inc.**
200 Park Ave.
New York, NY 10166
Allen Born, Chairman and CEO
*Sixth largest U.S. metals company*

**Amazing Spider Man**
New World Entertainment/
Marvel
387 Park Ave. S.
New York, NY 10016
Stan Lee, Publisher
*Classic superhero comic book*

**Ambler, Eric**
c/o Campbell, Thomson &
McLaughlin
31 Newington Green
London N16 9PY England
*Author*

**AMC Entertainment Inc.**
106 W. 14th St.
Kansas City, MO 64105
Stanley H. Durwood, CEO
*Movie theater chain*

**Amdahl Corporation**
1250 E. Arquest Ave.
Sunnyvale, CA 94088
John C. Lewis, Chairman and
CEO
*Computer manufacturer*

**Amen, Irving**
90 SW 12th Terrace
Boca Raton, FL 33486
*Artist*

**AMEND Network
(Abusive Men Exploring New
Directions)**
8000 E. Prentic Ave., D-1
Englewood, CO 80111
Courtney Pullen, Executive
Officer

**America**
8730 Sunset Blvd., Penthouse
Los Angeles, CA 90069
*Rock group*

**America the Beautiful Fund**
219 Shoreham Bldg.
Washington, DC 20005
Joshua Peterfreund, President

**America West Airlines, Inc.**
51 W. 3rd St.
Tempe, AZ 85281
Edward R. Beauvais, Chairman

**American Academy and
Institute of Arts & Letters
Library**
633 W. 155th St.
New York, NY 10032
Nancy Johnson, Librarian

**American Accordion Musicological Society**
334 S. Broadway
Pitman, NJ 08071
Stanley Darrow, Secretary

**American Advertising Museum**
9 NW Second Ave.
Portland, OR 97209
Jan Krutz, Program Coordinator
*Advertising, media, marketing, library/museum*

**American Alliance for Health, Physical Education and Recreation and Dance**
1900 Association Dr.
Reston, VA 22091
Joel Meier, President

**American Amateur Baseball Congress, Inc.**
215 E. Green St., P.O. Box 467
Marshall, MI 49069
Joseph R. Cooper, President

**American Amateur Karate Federation**
1930 Wilshire Blvd.
Suite 1208
Los Angeles, CA 90057
Hidetaka Nishiyama, President

**American Ambulance Association Resource Library**
3814 Aubrun Blvd., Suite 70
Sacramento, CA 95821
David A. Nevins, Division of Publications

**American Anorexia/Bulimia Association**
133 Cedar Lane
Teaneck, NJ 07666
Caaron Belcher Willinger, Executive Director

**American Association for Artificial Intelligence**
445 Burgess Dr.
Menlo Park, CA 94025
Claudia C. Mazzetti, Executive Director
*Proponents of self-thinking computers*

**American Association for the Advancement of Science**
1333 H St., NW
Washington, DC 20005
Richard C. Atkinson, Chairman of the Board

**American Association of Aardvark Aficionados**
P.O. Box 200
Parsippany, NJ 07054
Robert L. Bogart, President

**American Association of Botanical Gardens and Aboreta, Inc.**
786 Church Rd.
Wayne, PA 19087
Hadley Osborn, President

**American Association of Retired Persons**
601 E Street, NW
Washington, DC 20049
Horace B. Deets, Executive Director

**American Association of Suicidology**
2459 South Ash
Denver, CO 80222
Julie Perlman, Executive Officer

**American Association of Zookeepers, Inc.**
SW Gage Blvd.
Topeka, KS 66606
Oliver Claffey, President

**American Association of Zoological Parks and Aquariums**
Oglebay Park
Wheeling, WV 26003
David G. Zucconi, President

**American Atheist**
P.O. Box 140195
Austin, TX 78714
R. Murray-O'Hair, Editor
*Magazine*

**American Audio Prose Library, Inc.**
1015 E. Broadway
Box 842
Columbus, MO 65205
Kay Bonetti, Director
*Readings and interviews of American authors on tape*

**American Baby Magazine**
475 Park Ave. S.
New York, NY 10016
Judith Nolte, Editor

**American Ball Manufacturing Corporation**
1225 Tappan Circle
Carrollton, TX 75006
William V. Brown, President
*Sporting goods manufacturer*

**American Banker's Association Center for Banking Information**
1120 Connecticut Ave., NW
Washington, DC 20036
Joan Gervino, Director
*Law, banking and finance library*

**American Bass Association**
886 Trotters Trail
Wetumpka, AL 36092
Bob Parker, President
*Fishing group*

**American Bible Society Library**
1865 Broadway
New York, NY 10023
Dr. Peter J. Walsh, Director of Archives
*Collection of 50,000 copies of the Bible and related reference works*

**American Bicycle Association**
P.O. Box 718
Chandler, AZ 85244
Clayton John, President
*Promotes the sport of off-road bicycling (BMX)*

**American Birding Association**
P.O. Box 6599
Colorado Springs, CO 80934
Allan R. Keith, President
*Promotes recreational birding*

**American Blimp Corporation**
1900 NE 25th Ave., Suite 5
Hillsboro, OR 97124
James R. Thiele, President
*Blimp manufacturer*

**American Bowling Congress**
5301 S. 76th St.
Greendale, WI 53129
Boyd M. Rexton, President
*Governing body for amateur bowling*

**American Brands, Inc.**
1700 E. Putnam Ave.
Old Greenwich, CT 06870
William J. Alley, Chairman and CEO
*Cigarette and alcohol manufacturer*

**American Bread Company**
P.O. Box 100390
Nashville, TN 37210
Charles K. Evers, CEO
*Cookie and cracker manufacturer*

**American Bugatti Club, Inc.
Archives**
400 Buckboard Lane
Persimmon Hill
Ojai, CA 83023
Leo A. Keoshian, Chief
Archivist
*Photos and blueprints of the Bugatti
car*

**American Camping
Association**
Bradford Woods
5000 Street Rd., 67N
Martinsville, IN 46151
Chuck Ackenbom, President

**American Canal Society, Inc.**
908 Rathton Rd.
York, PA 17403
William E. Trout III, President
*Preservation of canals*

**American Cancer Society**
1599 Clifton Rd., NE
Atlanta, GA 30329
John R. Seffrin, Chairman

**American Carpatho—
Russian Orthodox Greek
Catholic**
312 Garfield St.
Johnstown, PA 15906
Bishop Nicholas (Smisko),
Primate
*Religious group*

**American Cave Conservation**
131 Main and Cave Sts.
P.O. Box 409
Horse Cave, KY 42749
David G. Foster, Executive
Director

**American Center of the
Quality of Work Life**
37 Tip Top Way
Berkeley Heights, NJ 07922
Andrew Ezzell, President

**American Cetacean Society**
P.O. Box 2639
San Pedro, CA 90731
Susan Lafferty, President
*Marine animal protection society*

**American Checker
Foundation**
1345 North Van Pelt Ave.
Los Angeles, CA 90063

**American Chemical Society**
1155 16th St., NW
Washington, DC 20036
Joseph A. Dixon, Chairman of
the Board

**American Chewing Gum Inc.**
Eagle and Lawrence Rd.
Havertown, PA 19083
Edward L. Fenimore, President

**American Chicle Group**
810 Main St.
Cambridge, MA 02139
Donald R. Eberhart, Manager
*Candy and confectionery
manufacturer*

**American Clock & Watch
Museum**
**Edward Ingraham Library**
100 Maple St.
Bristol, CT 06010
Joyce Stoffers, Managing
Director
*Largest known collection of
American clock trade catalogs*

**American College Testing Program**
P.O. Box 168
Iowa City, IA 52243
Richard L. Ferguson, President
*Designs achievement tests*

**American Committee for International Conservation**
c/o Secretary, Roger McManus
Center for Marine Conservation, Rm. 500
1725 De Sales St., NW
Washington, DC 20036
George Rabb, Chairman

**American Conference of Therapeutic Self-Help/Self-Health/Social Action Clubs**
710 Lodi St.
Syracuse, NY 13203
Shirley Mae Burghard, R.N., Executive Director
*Provides information and materials on self-help groups nationwide*

**American Conservation Association, Inc.**
30 Rockefeller Plaza, Rm. 5402
New York, NY 10112
Laurance Rockefeller, Chairman of the Board

**American Correctional Association Library**
8025 Laurel Lakes Ct.
Laurel, MD 20707
Diana Travisono, Librarian
*Penal codes and practices*

**American Cyanamid Company**
One Cyanamid Plaza
Wayne, NJ 07470
George J. Sella, Jr., Chairman and CEO
*Produces vaccines, surgical equipment and chemicals*

**American Donkey and Mule Society Information Office**
2901 N. Elm St.
Denton, TX 76201
Betsy Hutchins, Information Officer
*Donkey and mule library*

**American Double Dutch League**
P.O. Box 776
Bronx, NY 10451
David Walker, Founder
*Organization for rope jumpers*

**American Egg Board**
1460 Renaissance Dr., #301
Park Ridge, IL 60068
Louis B. Rafel, President
*The "what cholesterol?" group*

**American Electric Power Company, Inc.**
1 Riverside Plaza
Columbus, OH 43215
Willis S. White, Jr., Chairman
*Serves portions of the Midwest and South*

**American Express Company**
American Express Tower
World Financial Center
New York, NY 10285
James D. Robinson III, Chairman and CEO

**American Farm Bureau Federation**
225 Touhy Ave.
Park Ridge, IL 60068
Dean Kleckner, President

**American Farmland Trust**
1920 N. St., NW, #400
Washington, DC 20036
Ralph E. Grossi, President

**American Federation of Mineralogical Societies, Inc.**
920 SW 70th St.
Oklahoma City, OK 73139
Diane Dare, President

**American Federation of Police**
**Research Center and Library**
1100 NE 125th St.
North Miami, FL 33161
Gerald Arenberg, Executive Director
*Law enforcement and crime prevention library*

**American Film Institute**
**Louis B. Mayer Library**
2021 N. Western Ave.
Box 27999
Los Angeles, CA 90027
Jean Firstenberg, Director and CEO
Ruth Spencer, Librarian
*Film school and library with special script collections*

**American Financial Corporation**
One E. Fourth St.
Cincinnati, OH 45202
Carl H. Lindner, Chairman and CEO
*Great American Life Insurance, Hunter Savings and Loan, etc.*

**American Fisheries Society**
5410 Grosvenor Ln., #110
Bethesda, MD 20814
Dr. Richard Gregory, President

**American Floral Art School**
**Floral Library**
539 S. Wabash Ave.
Chicago, IL 60605
James Morestz, Director
*4000 books on floral arrangement*

**American Forest Council**
1250 Connecticut Ave., NW, #320
Washington, DC 20036
Laurence D. Wiseman, President

**American Forestry Association, The**
1516 P St., NW
Washington, DC 20005
Richard M. Hollier, President

**American Foundation for the Blind**
**Helen Keller Archives**
15 W. 16th St.
New York, NY 10011
Alberta J. Lonergan, Archivist
*Helen Keller and Anne Sullivan Macy's papers*

**American Genealogical Lending Library**
Box 244
Bountiful, UT 84010
Bradley W. Stewart, President

**American Geographical Society**
156 Fifth Ave., #600
New York, NY 10010
John E. Gould, President

**American Gladiators**
Four Point Entertainment
3575 Cahuenga Blvd., #600
Los Angeles, CA 90068
Ron Ziskin, Executive Producer
*Syndicated sports competition*

**American Greetings Corporation**
10500 American Rd.
Cleveland, OH 44144
Morry Weiss, CEO/President
*Greeting card manufacturer*

**American Heritage**
60 Fifth Ave.
New York, NY 10011
Richard Snow, Editor
*History magazine*


**American Hiking Society**
1015 31st St., NW
Washington, DC 20007
Charles Sloan, President


**American Home Products
Corporation**
685 Third Ave.
New York, NY 10017
John R. Stafford, Chairman and
CEO
*Producer of Advil, Anacin, Chap
Stick, etc.*


**American Horse Protection
Association, Inc.**
100 29th St., NW, #T-100
Washington, DC 20007
William L. Blue, Chairman


**American Humane
Association—American
Association for Protecting
Children, National
Resource Center on Child
Abuse and Neglect**
9725 E. Hampden Ave.
Denver, CO 80231
Robyn Alsop, Research Center
Librarian


**American Humane
Association, The**
9725 E. Hampden
Denver, CO 80231
Donald H. Anthony, President


**American Hypnotists'
Association
Hypnosis Technical Center**
Glanworth Bldg, Suite 6
1159 Green St.
San Francisco, CA 94109
Dr. Angela Bertuccelli,
Librarian


**American Institute of
Biological Sciences, Inc.**
730 11th St., NW
Washington, DC 20001
Paul R. Ehrlich, President


**American Institute of Fishery
Research Biologists**
c/o Dr. J. W. Rachlin
Lehman College
Bedford Park Blvd.
Bronx, NY 10468
John H. Helle, President


**American International
Group, Inc.**
70 Pine St.
New York, NY 10270
Maurice R. Greenberg,
Chairman, President, CEO
*U.S.'s largest international insurer*


**American Irish Historical
Society**
991 Fifth Ave.
New York, NY 10028
Kevin M. Cahill, M.D., President


**American Kidney Fund**
6110 Executive Blvd., Suite
1010
Rockville, MD 20852
Francis J. Soldovere, Executive
Director
*Support and information for all
patients who have kidney disease,
need dialysis or transplants*

**American Kitefliers Association**
1559 Rockville Pike
Rockville, MD 10852
Jim Miller, President
*Organization for anyone interested in kite flying*

**American League of Anglers and Boaters**
1331 Pennsylvania Ave., NW, #726
Washington, DC 20004
Michael Sciulla, President

**American League of Professional Baseball Clubs, The**
350 Park Ave.
New York, NY 10022
Dr. Robert W. Brown, M.D., President

**American Library Association**
50 E. Huron St.
Chicago, IL 60611
Linda L. Crismond, Executive Director

**American Littoral Society**
Sandy Hook
Highlands, NJ 07732
Harold Nils Pelta, President
*Studies wetland, estuary and coastal habitats*

**American Lung Association**
1740 Broadway
New York, NY 10019
John R. Garrison, Managing Director

**American Mime, Inc. Library**
61 Fourth Ave.
New York, NY 10003
Paul Curtis, Director
*History of the American Mime Theatre*

**American Motorcyclist**
P.O. Box 6114
Westerville, OH 43081
Greg Harrison, Executive Editor
*Magazine*

**American Museum of Magic**
107 E. Michigan
Box 5
Marshall, MI 49068
Robert Lund, Owner

**American Museum of Natural History**
Central Park West at 79th St.
New York, NY 10024
George D. Langdon, Jr., President

**American Museum of the Moving Image**
36–01 35th Ave.
Astoria, NY 11106
Rochelle Slovin, Director
*Film, TV and video museum*

**American Name Society Place Name Survey of the U.S.—Library**
James Gilliam Gee Library
East Texas State University
Commerce, TX 75428
Dr. Fred Tarpley, National Director
*U.S. geographical names*

**American Nature Study Society**
5881 Cold Brook Rd.
Homer, NY 13077
Paul Spector, President

**American Numismatic Association**
818 North Cascade Ave.
Colorado Springs, CO 80903
James Taylor, Education Director
Robert Hoge, Museum Curator

**American Ornithologists' Union, Inc.**
**National Museum of Natural History**
Smithsonian Institution
Washington, DC 20560
Glen E. Woolfenden, President

**American Pedestrian Association**
P.O. Box 624, Forest Hills Station
Forest Hills, NY 11375
Joan Vickies, Founder

**American Petroleum Institute**
1220 L St., NW
Washington, DC 20005
Charles DiBona, President

**American Philatelic Research Library**
Box 8338
State College, PA 16803
Gini Horn, Librarian
*Stamp collector's heaven*

**American Planning Association**
1776 Massachusetts Ave., NW
Washington, DC 20036
Stuart Mick, President
*Association of city planners*

**American Players Theatre, Inc. Library**
Route 3
Spring Green, WI 53588
Michael R. Whaley, Library Director
*Extensive/rare drama collection*

**American President Companies, Ltd.**
1111 Broadway
Oakland, CA 94607
W. Bruce Seaton, Chairman and CEO
*Ocean, rail and truck transportation*

**American Recreation Coalition**
1331 Pennsylvania Ave., NW, #726
Washington, DC 20004
Derrick A. Crandall, President

**American Red Cross**
Program and Services Department
17th and D Sts., NW
Washington, DC 20006
Susan B. Walter, Youth Associate

**American Resources Group**
Suite 210, Signet Bank Bldg.
374 Maple Ave., E.
Vienna, VA 22180
Dr. Keith A. Argow, President
*Monitors natural resources*

**American Rivers**
801 Pennsylvania Ave., SE,
#303
Washington, DC 20003
Kevin J. Coyle, President
*Protects rivers*

**American Sammy
Corporation**
2421 205th St., Suite D-104
Torrance, CA 90501
*Manufactures software for electronic
games*

**American Society for
Environmental History**
Center for Technology Studies
New Jersey Institute of
Technology
Newark, NJ 07102
William Cronon, President

**American Society for the
Prevention of Cruelty to
Animals**
441 E. 92nd St.
New York, NY 10128

**American Society of Dowsers**
Danville, VT 05828
Donna Robinson, Director
*Water finders*

**American Society of
Ichthyologists and
Herpetologists**
Section of Ecology and
Systematics
Corson Hall, Cornell University
Ithaca, NY 14853
Dr. F. Harvey Pough, President
*Studies fish and snakes*

**American Society of
Landscape Architects**
4401 Connecticut Ave., NW,
5th Fl.
Washington, DC 20008
David Bohardt, Executive Vice-
President

**American Society of
Limnology and
Oceanography**
Biological Oceanography
Division
Bedford Institute of
Oceanography
P.O. Box 1006
Dartmouth NS B2Y 4A2
Canada
Trevor Platt, President

**American Society of
Zoologists**
104 Sirius Cir.
Thousand Oaks, CA 91360
Albert F. Bennett, President

**American Squaredance**
Burdick Enterprises
P.O. Box 488
Huron, OH 44839
Stan and Cathie Burdick,
Editors

**American Standard Inc.**
1114 Ave. of the Americas
New York, NY 10036
Emmanuel A. Kampouris,
President and CEO
*World's largest producer of
plumbing products*

**American Stores Company**
P.O. Box 27447, 709 E. South
Temple
Salt Lake City, UT 84127
L. S. Skaggs, Chairman
*Largest U.S. food retailer (Alpha
Beta, Jewel, Lucky, Osco Drug,
etc.)*

**American Survival Guide**
McMullen Publishing, Inc.
2145 W. La Palma Ave.
Anaheim, CA 92801
Jim Benson, Editor
*Survivalist magazine*

**American Taekwondo
Association**
6210 Baseline Rd.
Little Rock, AR 72209
H. U. Lee, President
*Sponsors competitions*

**American Telephone &
Telegraph Company**
550 Madison Ave.
New York, NY 10022
Robert E. Allen, Chairman and
CEO
*Largest U.S. telecommunications
company*

**American Theatre Organ
Society
Archives/Library**
1393 Don Carlos Ct.
Chula Vista, CA 92010
Vernon P. Bickel, Curator

**American Trails**
1400 16th St., NW
Washington, DC 20036
Charles Flink, Chairman
*Supports and maintains hiking
trails*

**American Water Resources
Association**
5410 Grosvenor Ln., #220
Bethesda, MD 20814
Peter E. Black, President

**American Wildlands Alliance**
7500 E. Arapahoe Rd., #355
Englewood, CO 80112
Sally A. Ranney, President

**Americans Combatting
Terrorism**
P.O. Box 370
Telluride, CO 81435
Thomas P. O'Connor, Director

**Americans for the
Environment**
1400 16th St., NW
Washington, DC 20036
Betsy Loyless, Chair

**Amerind Foundation, Inc.,
The**
P.O. Box 248, Dragoon Rd.
Dragoon, AZ 85609
William Duncan Fulton,
President
*Archaeology, ethnology museum and
art gallery*

**Ameritech Corporation**
30 S. Wacker Dr.
Chicago, IL 60606
William L. Weiss, Chairman and
CEO
*A telephone holding company,
mostly Midwestern Bell
companies*

**Ames Department Stores, Inc.**
2418 Main St.
Rocky Hill, CT 06067
Stephen L. Pistner, Chairman
  and CEO
*Operates general merchandise
  discount stores*

**Amgen Inc.**
1840 Dehavilland Dr.
Thousand Oaks, CA 91320
Gordon M. Binder, Chairman
  and CEO
*Largest independent biotechnology
  concern in the U.S.*

**Amigos de las Americas**
5618 Star Ln.
Houston, TX 77057
Cedie Sencion, Director of
  Recruiting
*Leadership development for Latin
  America*

**Amin, Idi**
Box 8948
Jidda 21492, Saudi Arabia
*Former Ugandan dictator*

**Amoco Corporation**
200 E. Randolph Dr.
Chicago, IL 60601
H. Laurance Fuller, Chairman,
  President and CEO
*Second largest U.S. natural gas
  producer*

**Amory, Cleveland**
200 W. 57th St.
New York, NY 10019
*Author*

**Amp Inc.**
P.O. Box 3608
Harrisburg, PA 17105
Harold A. McInnes, Chairman
  and CEO
*World's largest supplier of electrical
  connectors*

**Amputee Shoe and Glove
  Exchange**
P.O. Box 27067
Houston, TX 77227
Dr. Richard E. Wainerdi,
  Director

**AMR Corporation**
4333 Amon Carter Blvd.
Fort Worth, TX 76155
Robert L. Crandall, Chairman,
  President and CEO
*American Airlines*

**Amway Corporation**
7575 E. Fulton Rd.
Ada, MI 49355
Jay Van Andel, Chairman
*Direct sales organization*

**Ancestral Home of James
  Knox Polk**
301 W. 7th St.
Columbia, TN 38401
John Holtzapple, Director

**Anchorage Museum of
  History and Art**
121 W. Seventh Ave.
Anchorage, AK 99501
Patricia B. Wolf, Director

**Ancient and Honourable
  Order of Small Castle
  Owners of Great Britain**
900 McKay Tower
Grand Rapids, MI 49503
Hollis M. Baker, Secretary
*Motto: "Tax Vobiscum"*

**Ancona, George Ephraim**
Rte. 10, Box 94G
Santa Fe, NM 87501
*Photographer, film producer, author*

**Anderson, David Poole**
*The New York Times*
229 W. 43rd St.
New York, NY 10036
*Sportswriter*

**Anderson, Harry**
9830 Wilshire Blvd.
Beverly Hills, CA 90212
*Actor, magician, comedian*

**Anderson, Jack**
1531 P Street, NW
Washington, DC 20005
*Investigative journalist*

**Anderson, Loni**
9830 Wilshire Blvd.
Beverly Hills, CA 90212
*Actress*

**Anderson, Melody**
9169 Sunset Blvd.
Los Angeles, CA 90069
*Actress*

**Anderson, O. J.**
c/o New York Giants
Giants Stadium
East Rutherford, NJ 07073
*Professional football player*

**Anderson, Richard Dean**
RR 1 North
Jefferson, NH 03583
*Actor*

**Anderson, Robert Woodruff**
Roxbury, CT 06783
*Playwright, novelist, screenwriter*

**Anderson, Theodore Wilbur**
Stanford University Department
of Statistics
Stanford, CA 94304
*Statistics educator*

**Andersonville National
Historic Site**
Rte. 1, Box 85
Andersonville, GA 31711
Bill Burnett, President
*Civil War POW camp*

**Andre the Giant
(Roussimoff)**
P.O. Box 3859
Stamford, CT 06905
*Professional wrestler*

**Andretti, Mario**
53 Victory Ln.
Nazareth, PA 18064
*Race car driver and racing
patriarch*

**Andrews, Anthony**
Peters, Fraser & Dunlop
The Chambers
Lots Rd.
London SW10 OXF England
*Actor*

**Andrews, Bart**
7510 Sunset Blvd., #L
Los Angeles, CA 90046
*"I Love Lucy" expert*

**Andrews, Julie**
P.O. Box 666
Beverly Hills, CA 90213
*Singer, actress*

**Andrews, V. C.**
c/o Pocket Books
1230 Ave. of the Americas
New York, NY 10020
*Author*

**Andrus, Cecil D.**
State Capitol
Boise, ID 83720
*Governor of Idaho*

**Angelou, Maya**
c/o Random House
201 E. 50th St.
New York, NY 10022
*Writer*

**Anglers for Clean Water, Inc.**
P.O. Box 17900
Montgomery, AL 36141
Helen Sevier, President

**Anheuser-Busch Companies, Inc.**
One Busch Pl.
St. Louis, MO 63118
August A. Busch III, Chairman
and President
*Budweiser beer, Eagle Snacks and theme parks*

**Animal Protection Institute of America**
P.O. Box 22505
6130 Freeport Blvd.
Sacramento, CA 95822
Duf Fischer, Executive Director

**Animal Welfare Institute**
P.O. Box 3650
Washington, DC 20007
Christine Stevens, President

**Anka, Paul**
P.O. Box 100
Carmel, CA 93921
*Singer*

**Annenberg, Walter**
Box 98
Rancho Mirage, CA 92270
*VIP*

**Annenberg Research Institute Library**
420 Walnut St.
Philadelphia, PA 19106
Avira Astrinsky, Library Director
*Extensive collection*

**Ann-Margret (Olsson)**
10100 Santa Monica Blvd., 16th Fl.
Los Angeles, CA 90067
*Actress, performer*

**Annette Funicello Fan Club**
Box 134
Nestleton, Ontario LOB 1LO
Canada
Mary Lou Fitton, President

**Ant, Adam**
Box 866
London SE1 3AP England
*Musician*

**Anti-Defamation League of B'nai B'rith**
823 United Nations Plaza
New York, NY 10017
Abraham Foxman, Director

**Antiochian Orthodox Christian Archdiocese of North America**
358 Mountain Rd.
Englewood, NJ 07631
Metropolitan Archbishop Philip (Saliba), Primate
*Religious group*

**Antique Automobile Club of America**
**AACA Library & Research Center, Inc.**
501 W. Governor Rd.
Box 417
Hershey, PA 17033
Kim Miller, Librarian
*Blueprint collection*

**Antique Phonograph**
**Monthly Archives**
**APM Library of Recorded**
**Sound**
502 E. 17th St.
Brooklyn, NY 11226
Allen Koenigsberg, Director
*Collection of over 5000 cylinders*

**Apollonia**
**(Patty Kotero)**
8271 Melrose Ave., #110
Los Angeles, CA 90046
*Actress*

**Appalachian Trail**
**Conference**
P.O. Box 807
Harpers Ferry, WV 25425
Margaret C. Drummond, Chair

**Apple Computer Inc.**
20525 Mariami Avenue
Cupertino, CA 95014
John Sculley, CEO/Chairman of
the Board
*Manufacturer of Apple and*
*MacIntosh computer hardware*
*and software*

**Applegate, Christina**
9744 Wilshire Blvd., #309
Beverly Hills, CA 90212
*Actress*

**Appomattox Court House**
**National Historical Park**
P.O. Box 218
Appomattox, VA 24522
John B. Montgomery,
Superintendent

**APSCO Enterprises**
50th St. and First Ave.
Building Number 57
Brooklyn, NY 11232
Rudy DiPietro, President
*Manufactures official sports*
*clothing/penants*

**Aptidon, Hassan Gouled**
Présidence de la République
Dijibouti, Republic of Dijibouti
*President of the Republic of*
*Dijibouti*

**Aquino, Amy**
10100 Santa Monica Blvd.,
16th Fl.
Los Angeles, CA 90067
*Actress*

**Ara Group, Inc., The**
1101 Market St.
Philadelphia, PA 19107
Joseph A. Neubauer, Chairman,
President and CEO
*Largest food service company in the*
*U.S.*

**Arab Gulf States Information**
**Documentation Center**
P.O. Box 5063
Baghdad, Iraq
Dr. Jasim M. Jirjees, Director
General

**Arafat, Yassir**
Arnestonconseil 17 Belvedere
1002 Tunis, Tunisia
*PLO leader*

**Aralle-Arce, Juan Bautista**
University of California
4823 Phelps Hall
Santa Barbara, CA 93106
*Language educator*

**Arbitron Company**
3333 Wilshire Blvd.,
  Suite 712
Los Angeles, CA 90012
Rick Aurichio, President
*T.V. ratings company*

**Archaeological Conservancy,
  The**
415 Orchard Dr.
Santa Fe, NM 87501
Stewart L. Udall, Chairman of
  the Board

**Archer, Jules**
404 High St.
Santa Cruz, CA 95060
*Writer*

**Archer-Daniels-Midland
  Company**
4666 Faries Pkwy., Box 1470
Decatur, IL 62525
Dwayne O. Andreas, Chairman
  and CEO
*Agricultural products*

**Archie Comics**
Archie Comic Publications,
  Inc.
325 Fayette Avenue
Mamaroneck, NY 10543
John L. Goldwater, Publisher
*Comic book*

**Architectural Digest**
Knapp Communications
5900 Wilshire Blvd.
Los Angeles, CA 90036
Thomas P. Losee, Jr., Publisher
*Magazine*

**Archive of Contemporary
  Music**
110 Chambers St.
New York, NY 10007
Robert George, Director

**Arena U.S.A., Inc.**
Subsidiary of Adidas
28 Engelhard Dr.
Cranbury, NJ 08512
Peter Tannenbaum, Vice-
  President of Merchandising
*Sporting goods*

**Arista Records, Inc.**
6 W. 57th St.
New York, NY 10019
Clive Davis, President
*Record company*

**Arizona Condors**
4210 N. Brown Ave.
Scottsdale, AZ 85251
Adrian Webster, General
  Manager
*Soccer team*

**Arizona State Museum**
University of Arizona
Tucson, Arizona 85721
R. G. Vivian, Associate Director

**Arizona-Sonora Desert
  Museum**
2021 N. Kinney Rd.
Tucson, AZ 85743
David Honcocks, Director

**Arkansas Arts Center, The**
P.O. Box 2137
Little Rock, AR 72203
Townsend Wolfe, Director and
  Chief Curator

**Arkansas State University Museum**
Continuing Education/Museum Blvd., Box 490
Jonesboro, AR 72467
Dr. Eugene Smith, President and CEO

**Arkansas Territorial Restoration**
3rd & Scott
Little Rock, AR 72201
William B. Worthen, Jr., Director

**Arkin, Adam**
121 N. San Vicente Blvd.
Beverly Hills, CA 90211
*Actor*

**Armstrong World Industries, Inc.**
P.O. Box 3001
Lancaster, PA 17604
William W. Adams, Chairman and President
*Tile company*

**Arnaz, Desi, Jr.**
P.O. Box 60684
Boulder City, NV 89006
*Actor*

**Arness, James**
P.O. Box 49003
Los Angeles, CA 90049
*Actor*

**Arnold, Roseanne (Barr)**
151 El Camino
Beverly Hills, CA 90212
*Comedienne, actress*

**Arnold's Archives**
1106 Eastwood, SE
East Grand Rapids, MI 49506
Arnold Jacobsen, Archivist
*Rare Broadway show and musical comedy records and memorabilia*

**Arquette, Rosanna**
8899 Beverly Blvd.
Los Angeles, CA 90048
*Actress*

**Art Institute of Chicago, The**
Michigan Ave. and Adams St.
Chicago, IL 60603
Marshall Field, President

**Arthur, Bea**
151 El Camino
Beverly Hills, CA 90212
*Actress*

**Arthur, Rebeca**
9255 Sunset Blvd., #515
Los Angeles, CA 90069
*Actress*

**Arthur Andersen & Co.**
Societé Cooperative
18, quai General-Guisan
1211 Geneva 3, Switzerland
Gerard Van Kemmel, Chairman
*Fourth largest accounting firm in the world*

**Artists Space**
**Artists File**
223 W. Broadway
New York, NY 10013
Susan Wyatt, Director
*Slide files of 2800 New York artists*

**Asarco Inc.**
180 Maiden Ln.
New York, NY 10038
Richard de J. Osborne, Chairman, President and CEO
*Mines, smelts and refines metals*

**Ashcroft, John D.**
State Capitol
Jefferson City, MO 65101
*Governor of Missouri*

**Ashland Oil, Inc.**
1000 Ashland Dr.
Russell, KY 41169
John R. Hall, Chairman and
    CEO
*Independent petroleum refiner;*
    *produces Valvoline*

**Ashley, Elizabeth**
232 N. Canon Dr.
Beverly Hills, CA 90210
*Actress*

**Ashley, Merrill**
New York City Ballet, Inc.
Lincoln Center Plaza
New York, NY 10023
*Ballerina, author*

**Ask a Silly Question**
P.O. Box 1950
Hollywood, California 90078
Kathleen Conner, President
*Research and information company*

**Asner, Edward**
P.O. Box 7407
Studio City, CA 91604
*Actor*

**Assante, Armand**
RD #1, Box 561
Campbell Hall, NY 10916
*Actor*

**Assassination Archives &**
    **Research Center**
918 F St., NW, Suite 510
Washington, DC 20004
David Lovett, Contact
*Extensive materials on JFK*
    *assassination*

**Associated Milk Producers,**
    **Inc.**
6609 Blanco Rd., P.O. Box
    790287
San Antonio, TX 78279
Irvin J. Elkin, President
*Largest milk cooperative in the U.S.*

**Association for Voluntary**
    **Surgical Contraception**
122 E. 42nd St.
New York, NY 10168
Hugo Hoogenboom, Executive
    Director

**AST Research, Inc.**
16215 Alton Pkwy., P.O. Box
    19658
Irvine, CA 92713
Safi U. Qureshey, Co-Chairman,
    President and CEO
*PC producer*

**Astin, Sean**
9830 Wilshire Blvd.
Beverly Hills, CA 90212
*Actor*

**Astroturf Industries Inc.**
Subsidiary of Balsam
    Corporation
809 Kenner St.
Dalton, GA 30720
E. M. Milner, President
*Manufactures Astroturf*

**Atari Corporation**
1196 Borregas Ave.
Sunnyvale, CA 94086
Sam Tramiel, CEO/President
*Video game manufacturer*

**Atchison County Historical**
    **Society**
200 Main St.
Atchison, KS 66002
Rev. Angelus Lingenfelser, CEO
*Museum with special Amelia*
    *Earhart exhibit*

**ATEC**
115 Post Street
Santa Cruz, CA 95060
Jack Shepard, CEO
*Sporting goods*

**Athletic Congress of the**
**U.S.A., The**
P.O. Box 120
Indianapolis, IN 46206
Ollan Cassell, Executive
Director
*Track and field regulators*

**Atkins, Cholly**
**(Charles Atkinson)**
5102 Stampa Ave.
Las Vegas, NV 89102
*Choreographer*

**Atlanta Braves**
P.O. Box 4064
Atlanta, GA 30302
Robert J. Cox, Vice-President/
General Manager
*Professional baseball team*

**Atlanta Falcons**
Suwanee Road at I-85
Suwanee, GA 30174
Rankin Smith, Jr., President
*Professional football team*

**Atlanta Hawks**
One CNN Center, Suite 405
South Tower
Atlanta, GA 30303
Stan Kasten, President/General
Manager
*Professional basketball team*

**Atlanta Historical Society,**
**Inc.**
3101 Andrews Dr., NW
Atlanta, GA 30305
John Harlow, Executive Director

**Atlantic Center for the**
**Environment, The**
39 S. Main St.
Ipswich, MA 01938
Lawrence B. Morris, Director

**Atlantic Monthly, The**
745 Boylston St.
Boston, MA 02116
William Whitworth, Editor
*Magazine*

**Atlantic Records**
75 Rockefeller Plaza
New York, NY 10019
Ahmet M. Ertegun, Chairman/
CEO
*Record company*

**Atlantic Richfield Company**
515 S. Flower St.
Los Angeles, CA 90071
Lodwrick M. Cook, Chairman
and CEO
*Eighth largest U.S. petroleum*
*refiner*

**Attenborough, Sir Richard**
**(Samuel)**
Old Friars
Richmond Green, Surrey
England
*Actor, producer, director*

**Audubon Naturalist Society**
**of the Central Atlantic**
**States**
8940 Jones Mill Rd.
Chevy Chase, MD 20815
Anthony White, President
*Bird watchers*

**Austin, Tracy Ann**
c/o Advantage International
1025 Thomas Jefferson, NW
Washington, DC 20007
*Tennis player*

**Austin Athletic Equipment Corp.**
705 Bedford Ave., Box 423
Bellmore, NY 11710
Jonathan Austin, President
*Sporting goods*

**Automatic Data Processing, Inc.**
One ADP Blvd.
Roseland, NJ 07068
Josh S. Weston, Chairman and CEO
*Largest U.S. independent information processing company*

**Autry, Gene**
P.O. Box 710
Los Angeles, CA 90078
*Actor*

**Avedon, Richard**
407 E. 75th St.
New York, NY 10021
*Photographer*

**Avengers**
New World Entertainment/ Marvel
387 Park Ave. S.
New York, NY 10016
Stan Lee, Publisher
*Comic book*

**AVIA**
Subsidiary of Reebok International, Ltd.
16160 SW Upper Boones Ferry Rd.
Portland, OR 97224
William Dragon, Jr., President/ CEO
*Manufactures sports shoes*

**Avis Inc.**
900 Old Country Rd.
Garden City, NY 11530
Joseph V. Vittoria, Chairman and CEO
*Employee-owned rental car company*

**Avon Products, Inc.**
9 W. 57th St.
New York, NY 10019
James E. Preston, Chairman, President and CEO
*Direct sales cosmetic company*

**Aylesworth, Thomas Gibbons**
48 Van Rensselaer Ave.
Stamford, CT 06902
*Author, editor*

**Aylwin, Paricio**
Oficina de Presidente
Palacio de la Moneda
Santiago, Chile
*President of Chile*

**Aziz, King Fahd Ibin Abdul**
Royal Diwan
Riyadh, Saudi Arabia
*Ruler of Saudi Arabia*

**Aznavour, Charles**
4 Avenue De Lieulee
78, Galluis, Montfort-l'Amaury, France
*Singer*

**B**

If you want to know your true opinion of someone, watch the effect produced in you by the first sight of a letter from him.

—SCHOPENHAUER

**Babangida, General Ibrahim Badamasi**
Office of the President
Dodan Barracks
Ikoyi, Lago, Nigeria
*President of Nigeria*

**Bacall, Lauren**
151 El Camino
Beverly Hills, CA 90212
*Actress*

**Bacon, Kevin**
9830 Wilshire Blvd.
Beverly Hills, CA 90212
*Actor*

**Badd, Johnny B.**
P.O. Box 105366
Atlanta, GA 30348
*Professional wrestler*

**Badham, John M.**
10100 Santa Monica Blvd.,
16th Fl.
Los Angeles, CA 90067
*Film director*

**Baez, Joan Chandos**
P.O. Box 818
Menlo Park, CA 94026
*Folk singer, activist*

**Bailey, F. Lee (Francis)**
One Center Plaza
Boston, MA 02108
*Attorney, author*

**Baio, Scott**
P.O. Box 5617
Beverly Hills, CA 90210
*Actor*

**Baker, Mark Linn**
10100 Santa Monica Blvd.,
16th Fl.
Los Angeles, CA 90067
*Actor*

**Baker, Russell (Wayne)**
Observer
*The New York Times*
229 W. 43rd St.
New York, NY 10036
*Writer*

**Baker, William Oliver**
AT&T Bell Labs
600 Mountain Ave.
Murray Hill, NJ 07974
*Oft-honored research chemist*

**Baker & McKenzie**
One Prudential Plaza
130 E. Randolph Dr.
Chicago, IL 60601
Robert Cox, Chairman of the
    Executive Committee
*Largest law firm in the world*

**Baker Hughes Inc.**
3900 Essex Ln.
Houston, TX 77027
James D. Woods, Chairman,
    President and CEO
*Services oil wells*

**Bakker, Jim**
Federal Medical Center
2110 Center St., E.
Rochester, MN 55901
*Defrocked evangelist*

**Bakker, Tammy Faye**
P.O. Box 690788
Orlando, FL 32869
*Evangelist*

**Bakula, Scott**
131 S. Rodeo Dr., #300
Beverly Hills, CA 90212
*Actor*

**Baldessari, John Anthony**
Sonnabend Gallery
420 W. Broadway
New York, NY 10012
*Artist*

**Baldridge, Leticia**
P.O. Box 32287
Washington, DC 20007
*Writer, management training
    consultant*

**Baldwin, Alec**
9200 Sunset Blvd., #710
Los Angeles, CA 90069
*Actor*

**Baldwin, William**
9200 Sunset Blvd., #710
Los Angeles, CA 90069
*Actor*

**Bale, Christian**
Langham House
308 Regent St.
London W1R 5AL England
*Actor*

**Balin, Marty
(Martyn Jerel Buchwald)**
P.O. Box 347008
San Francisco, CA 94134
*Founder of Jefferson Airplane*

**Bally Manufacturing
    Corporation**
8700 W. Bryn Mawr Ave.
Chicago, IL 60631
Arthur M. Goldberg, Chairman
    and CEO
*World's largest operator of casino
    hotels*

**Balser, Rev. Glennon**
Advent Christian Church
P.O. Box 23152
Charlotte, NC 28212
*Religious group president*

**Baltimore Orioles**
Memorial Stadium
Baltimore, MD 21218
Roland D. Hemmond, Vice-
    President of Baseball
    Operations
*Professional baseball team*

**Baltimore Streetcar Museum,
    Inc.**
P.O. Box 4881
Baltimore, MD 21211
John J. O'Neill, President

**Banc One Corporation**
100 E. Broad St.
Columbus, OH 43271
John B. McCoy, Chairman
*Bank holding company*

**Banda, Hastings Kamuzu**
Office of the President
Private Bag 388
Capital City, Lilongwe 3, Malawi
*President of Malawi*

**Bangerter, Norman H.**
210 State Capitol
Salt Lake City, Utah 84114
*Governor of Utah*

**Bank of Boston Corporation**
100 Federal St.
Boston, MA 02110
Ira Stepanian, Chairman and
   CEO
*18th largest U.S. banking
   organization*

**Bank of New York Company,
   Inc., The**
48 Wall St.
New York, NY 10286
J. Carter Bacot, Chairman and
   CEO
*15th largest bank holding company
   in the U.S.*

**BankAmerica Corporation**
Bank of America Center
San Francisco, CA 94104
Richard M. Rosenberg,
   Chairman and CEO
*Second largest banking institution
   in the U.S.*

**Bankers Trust New York
   Corporation**
280 Park Ave.
New York, NY 10017
Charles S. Sanford, Jr.,
   Chairman
*Global merchant bank*

**Banks, Ernie
(Ernest)**
New World Van Lines
615 W. Victoria
Compton, CA 90220
*Mr. Cub*

**Banks, James Albert**
University of Washington
122 Miller Hall DQ-12
Seattle, WA 98195
*Educator's educator*

**Barad, Jill Elikann**
Mattel Inc.
5150 Rosecrans Ave.
Hawthorne, CA 90250
*Barbie's boss*

**Barbeau, Adrienne**
P.O. Box 1334
N. Hollywood, CA 91604
*Actress*

**Barber, Skip (John)**
Route 7
Canaan, CT 06018
*Former race car driver, racing
   teacher*

**Barbie and Ken**
5150 Rosecrans Ave.
Hawthorne, CA 90250
*Famous doll and famous doll
   boyfriend*

**Bardis, Panos Demetrios**
University of Toledo
Bancroft St.
Toledo, OH 43606
*Sociologist, editor, author, poet,*
*  educator*

**Bardwick, Judith M.**
1389 Via Tabara
La Jolla, CA 92037
*Business management consultant*

**Barkley, Charles**
c/o Philadelphia 76ers
P.O. Box 25040
Philadelphia, PA 19147
*Professional basketball player*

**Barnard, Scott Henry**
Joffrey Ballet
130 W. 56th St.
New York, NY 10019
*Ballet artistic director*

**Barnet, Will**
15 Gramercy Park S.
New York, NY 10003
*Artist, educator*

**Barnett, Arthur Doak**
Johns Hopkins School of
  Advanced International
  Studies
1740 Massachusetts Ave., NW
Washington, DC 20036
*Political scientist, educator*

**Barnett Banks, Inc.**
100 Laura St., P.O. Box 40789
Jacksonville, FL 32203
Charles E. Rice, Chairman and
  CEO
*Florida's largest financial*
*  institution*

**Barnum Museum, The**
820 Main St.
Bridgeport, CT 06604
Linda A. Altshuler, President
*Circus museum with special Tom*
*  Thumb and Jenny Lind exhibits*

**Barrett, Majel**
1800 N. Highland Ave., #405
Los Angeles, CA 90028
*Actress, original and Next*
*  Generation "Star Trek"*

**Barron's National Business**
**  and Financial Weekly**
Dow Jones and Co. Inc.
200 Liberty St.
New York, NY 10281
Alan Abelson, Editor
*Publication*

**Baryshnikov, Mikhail**
9830 Wilshire Blvd.
Beverly Hills, CA 90212
*Dancer, choreographer, actor*

**Barzun, Jacques**
1170 Fifth Ave.
New York, NY 10029
*Author, literary consultant*

**Bashir, Brigadier Omar**
**  Hassam Ahmed**
Revolutionary Command
  Council
Khartoum, Sudan
*Prime Minister of Sudan*

**Baskin-Robbins USA**
**  Company**
P.O. Box 1200
Glendale, CA 91209
Jim Earnhardt, President
*31 flavors ice-cream company*

**Bat Conservation International**
P.O. Box 162603
Austin, TX 78716
Verne R. Read, Chairman

**Bateman, Jason**
P.O. Box 333
Woodland Hills, CA 91365
*Actor*

**Bateman, Justine**
3960 Laurel Canyon Blvd., Suite 193
Studio City, CA 91604
*Actress*

**Bates, Kathy D.**
121 N. San Vicente Blvd.
Beverly Hills, CA 90212
*Actress*

**Batman**
DC Comics Inc.
355 Lexington Avenue
New York, NY 10017
Julius Schwartz, Editor
*Superhero comic book*

**Batterers Anonymous**
1269 NE Street
San Bernardino, CA 92405
Jerry M. Goffman, Ph.D., Founder
*Help for families of battered spouses*

**Battle, Kathleen**
165 W. 57th St.
New York, NY 10019
*Opera singer*

**Baucus, Max S.**
706 Senate Hart Office Bldg.
Washington, DC 20510
*Senator from Montana*

**Bausch & Lomb**
42 East Ave.
P.O. Box 743
Rochester, NY 14603
Norman D. Salik, Vice-President
*Manufactures sunglasses*

**Baxter, Meredith**
10100 Santa Monica Blvd., 16th Fl.
Los Angeles, CA 90067
*Actress*

**Baxter International, Inc.**
One Baxter Pkwy.
Deerfield, IL 60015
Vernon R. Loucks, Jr., Chairman and CEO
*World's largest producer of health care products and services*

**Bay City Rollers**
27 Preston Grange Road
Lothian, Scotland
*Rock band*

**Bayh, Evan**
Room 206, Statehouse
Indianapolis, IN 46204
*Governor of Indiana*

**Beach, "Sexy" Sonny**
1692 Sprinter St., NW
Atlanta, GA 30318
*Professional wrestler*

**Beach Boys**
101 Mesa Lane
Santa Barbara, CA 93109
*Perennial pop group*

**Bear Stearns Companies, Inc.**
245 Park Ave.
New York, NY 10167
Alan C. Greenberg, Chairman and CEO
*Investment banking, securities trading and brokerage firm*

**Beastie Boys, The**
1750 N. Vine St.
Hollywood, CA 90028
*Rap group*

**Beatty, Patricia Jean**
5085 Rockledge Rd.
Riverside, CA 92506
*Children's author*

**Beatty, Warren**
1849 Sawtelle Ave., #500
Los Angeles, CA 90069
*Actor*

**Beau, Si**
8147 Melrose Ave.
Los Angeles, CA 90046
*Tailor to the movie stars*

**Beauty and the Beast**
c/o Disney Studios
500 South Buena Vista St.
Burbank, CA 91521
*Cartoon heroine and her hero*

**Bechtel Group, Inc.**
Fifty Beale St.
San Francisco, CA 94105
Stephen D. Bechtel, Jr.,
   Chairman Emeritus
*Engineering and construction firm*

**Becker, Boris**
Nusslocher Strasse 51, 6906
   Leiman
Baden, Germany
*Tennis star*

**Becton, Dickinson, and
   Company**
One Becton Dr.
Franklin Lakes, NJ 07417
Wesley J. Howe, Chairman
*World's largest producer of syringes*

**Bee Gees
(Maurice, Barry and Robin
   Gibb)**
P.O. Box 8179
Miami, FL 33139
*Pop group*

**Begley, Ed, Jr.**
151 El Camino
Beverly Hills, CA 90211
*Actor*

**Bell Atlantic Corporation**
1600 Market St.
Philadelphia, PA 19103
Raymond W. Smith, Chairman
   and CEO
*Third largest provider of local
   phone service in the U.S.*

**Bell Bicycle, Inc.**
Subsidiary of Echelon Sports
   Corporation
15301 Shoemaker Ave.
Norwalk, CA 90650
Phil Mathews, President/CEO
*Wholesaler of bicycle helmets*

**Bellow, Saul**
University of Chicago
1126 E. 59th St.
Chicago, IL 60637
*Writer*

**Bellsouth Corporation**
1155 Peachtree St. NE
Atlanta, GA 30367
John L. Clendenin, Chairman,
   President and CEO
*Second largest U.S. utility*

**Belushi, James**
9830 Wilshire Blvd.
Beverly Hills, CA 90212
*Actor*

**Ben and Jerry's Homemade Ice Cream**
P.O. Box 240
Waterbury, VT 05676
Ben Cohn
Jerry Greenfield

**Benevolent and Loyal Order of Pessimists**
P.O. Box 1945
Iowa City, IA 52244
Jack Duvall, President
*"In front of every silver lining, there's a dark cloud."*

**Bening, Annette**
232 N. Canon Drive
Beverly Hills, CA 90210
*Actress and the one who finally got Warren Beatty*

**Bennett, William J.**
Hudson Institute
1015 18th St., NW
Washington, DC 20410
*Author, former Secretary of Education*

**Bennington Museum, The**
W. Main St.
Bennington, VT 05201
Laura C. Luckey, Director
*History museum*

**Benson, Ezra T.**
Church of Jesus Christ, Administration Bldg.
47 E. S. Temple
Salt Lake City, UT 84415
*Religious leader*

**Benson, Robby**
822 S. Robertson Blvd., #200
Los Angeles, CA 90035
*Actor, voice of the Beast*

**Bentley, Ray**
c/o Buffalo Bills
One Bills Dr.
Orchard Park, NY 14127
*Professional football player and author of children's books*

**Bentsen, Lloyd**
703 Senate Hart Office Bldg.
Washington, DC 20501
*Senator from Texas*

**Berenger, Tom**
Box 1842
Beaufort, SC 29901
*Actor*

**Berenstain, Stan and Jan**
c/o Random House Children's Books
201 East 50th St.
New York, NY 10022
*Authors*

**Beresford, Bruce**
151 El Camino
Beverly Hills, CA 90212
*Film director*

**Bergen, Candace**
4000 Warner Blvd.
Burbank, CA 91522
*Actress*

**Bergen, Polly**
151 El Camino
Beverly Hills, CA 90212
*Actress*

**Bergman, Alan**
c/o Lantz Office
888 7th Ave., #2501
New York, NY 10016
*Writer, lyricist*

**Bergman, Sandahl**
9300 Wilshire Blvd., #410
Beverly Hills, CA 90212
*Comedienne, actress*

**Berko, Ferenc**
P.O. Box 360
Aspen, CO 81612
*Photographer*

**Berkshire Hathaway, Inc.**
1440 Kiewit Plaza
Omaha, NE 68131
Warren E. Buffett, Chairman
and CEO
*World Book Encyclopedia, See's Candies, etc.*

**Bernard, Crystal**
10100 Santa Monica Blvd.,
#1600
Los Angeles, CA 90067
*Actress*

**Bernsen, Corbin**
9000 Sunset Blvd., #1200
Los Angeles, CA 90069
*Actor*

**Berra, Yogi
(Lawrence Peter)**
P.O. Box 288
Houston, TX 77001
*Baseball coach*

**Berry, Chuck**
Buckner Road—Berry Park
Wentzbille, MO 63385
*Musician*

**Bertinelli, Valerie**
151 El Camino
Beverly Hills, CA 90212
*Actress*

**Bertolucci, Bernardo**
8899 Beverly Blvd.
Los Angeles, CA 90048
*Film director*

**Bessell, Ted**
8899 Beverly Blvd.
Los Angeles, CA 90048
*TV director, actor*

**Bethlehem Steel Corporation**
701 E. 3rd St.
Bethlehem, PA 18016
Walter P. Williams, Chairman
and CEO
*Second largest U.S. steel producer*

**Better Homes and Gardens**
1716 Locust St.
Des Moines, IA 50336
Joan McCloskey, Editor
*Magazine*

**Bettmann, Otto Ludwig**
Florida Atlantic University
Wimberly Library
Boca Raton, FL 33431
*Picture archivist, graphic historian*

**Beverly Brothers**
P.O. Box 3857
Stamford, CT 06905
*Professional "tag team" wrestlers*

**Beverly Hills 90210**
Spelling Entertainment Inc.
5700 Wilshire Blvd., Suite 575
Los Angeles, CA 90036
Charles Rosen, Executive
Producer
*Fox television series*

**B-52's, The**
P.O. Box 506
Canal St. Station
New York, NY 10013
*Rock group*

**Bialik, Mayim**
c/o Booh Schut Agency
11350 Ventura Blvd., Suite 206
Studio City, CA 91604
*Actress*

**Bic Pen Corporation**
500 Bic Dr.
Milford, CT 06460
Bruno Bich, President
*Ball-point pen manufacturer*

**Biden, Joseph R.**
221 Senate Russell Office Bldg.
Washington, DC 20510
*Senator from Delaware*

**Big Brothers/Big Sisters of America**
230 N. 13th St.
Philadelphia, PA 19108
Thomas McKenna, National
   Executive Director

**Big Thunder Gold Mine**
Box 706
Keystone, SD 57751
James Hersrud, Corporation
   President
*Actual working gold mine*

**Bike Athletic Company**
Susidiary of Kazmaier
   International
P.O. Box 666
Knoxville, TN 37901
James R. Corbett, President
*Jock strap manufacturer*

**Bingaman, Jeff**
524 Senate Hart Office Bldg.
Washington, DC 20510
*Senator from New Mexico*

**Binney & Smith, Inc.**
P.O. Box 431
Easton, PA 18044
Richard Guren, CEO
*Manufacturers of Crayola Crayons*

**Bird, Larry**
c/o Boston Celtics
150 Causeway St.
Boston, MA 02114
*Former professional basketball
   player, basketball executive*

**Bird Talk**
Fancy Publications
Box 6050
Mission Viejo, CA 92690
Karyn New, Editor
*Pet magazine*

**Birmingham Museum of Art**
2000 8th Ave., N
Birmingham, AL 35203
William M. Spencer III, CEO

**Birnholz, Jack**
420 Lincoln Rd. #384
Miami Beach, FL 33139
*International real estate expert*

**Bisset, Jacqueline**
8899 Beverly Blvd.
Los Angeles, CA 90038
*Actress*

**Bixby, Bill**
c/o DGA
7020 Sunset Blvd.
Los Angeles, CA 90046
*Actor, director*

**Biya, Paul**
Office of the President
Yaounde, Cameroon
*President of Cameroon*

**Black, Shirley Temple**
American Embassy Prague
Unit 25302
APO 09213-5630
*Ambassador, former child actress*

**Black & Decker Corporation, The**
701 E. Joppa Rd.
Towson, MD 21204
Nolan D. Archibald, Chairman,
President and CEO
*World's largest power-tool company*

**Black Crowes, The**
75 Rockefeller Plaza, 20th Fl.
New York, NY 10019
*Rock group*

**Blackman, Rolando**
c/o Dallas Mavericks
777 Sports St.
Dallas, TX 75207
*Professional basketball player*

**Blackmun, Harry A.**
U.S. Supreme Court Building
1 First St., NE
Washington, DC 20543
*Associate Justice of the Supreme Court*

**Blades, Ruben**
1999 Ave. of the Stars, #2850
Los Angeles, CA 90067
*Actor*

**Blair, Linda**
8228 Sunset Blvd., #212
Los Angeles, CA 90046
*Actress*

**Blair, Nicky**
8730 Sunset Blvd.
Los Angeles, CA 90069
*Famed restaurateur*

**Blake, Mike**
3530 Pine Valley Dr.
Sarasota, FL 34239
*Baseball expert*

**Blanchard, Dr. Tim**
Conservative Baptist Association
of America
Box 66
Wheaton, IL 60189
*General director, religious organization*

**Block, Lawrence**
Knox Burger Assoc.
39½ Washington Sq. S.
New York, NY 10012
*Author of literate Burglar books, etc.*

**Blockbuster Entertainment Corp.**
901 E. Olas Blvd.
Ft. Lauderdale, FL 33301
H. Wayne Huizenga, Chairman
and CEO
*U.S. leader in video rentals*

**Blood Sweat & Tears**
9200 Sunset Blvd., #822
Los Angeles, CA 90069
*Pop group*

**Bloomfield, Clara Derber**
Roswell Park Cancer Institute
Elm and Carlton Sts.
Buffalo, NY 14263
*Oncologist*

**Blossom, Lady**
P.O. Box 105366
Atlanta, GA 30348
*Professional wrestler*

**Blue Cross and Blue Shield Association**
676 N. St. Clair St.
Chicago, IL 60611
Bernard R. Tresnowski,
President and CEO
*Oldest and largest U.S. health insurance company*

**Blume, Judy**
E. P. Dutton
375 Hudson St.
New York, NY 10014
*Author*

**BMG**
1133 Ave. of the Americas
New York, NY 10036
Michael Dornemann,
Chairman/CEO
*Record company*

**B.M.X. Products**
1250 Avenida a Caso, Suite H
Camarillo, California 93010
Skip Hess, President
*Bicycle manufacturer*

**Bode, Roy Evan**
Dallas Times Herald
1101 Pacific
Dallas, TX 75202
*Newspaper editor*

**Boeing Company, The**
7755 E. Marginal Way S.
Seattle, WA 98108
Frank A. Shrontz, Chairman
and CEO
*World's largest commercial aircraft maker*

**Boers, Terry John**
Chicago Sun-Times Inc.
401 N. Wabash, Rm. 110
Chicago, IL 60601
*Sports columnist*

**Bogdanovich, Peter**
c/o William Pfeiffer
2040 Ave. of the Stars
Century City, CA 90067
*Film director, writer, producer*

**Boise Cascade Corporation**
One Jefferson Sq., P.O. Box 50
Boise, ID 83728
John B. Fery, Chairman and
CEO
*Paper product producer*

**Boitano, Brian**
Brian Boitano Enterprises
101 First St., Suite 370
Los Altos, CA 94024
*Ice skater*

**Bol, Manute**
c/o Philadelphia 76ers
P.O. Box 25040
Philadelphia, PA 19147
*Professional basketball player*

**Bolan, Thomas Anthony**
36 W. 44th St., 6th Fl.
New York, NY 10036
*Lawyer, conservative politician*

**Bolcom, William Elden**
University of Michigan School
of Music
1339 Moore Hall
Ann Arbor, MI 48109
*Musician, composer, educator*

**Bolger, James Brendan**
Prime Minister's Office
Parliament Buildings
Wellington, New Zealand
*Prime Minister of New Zealand*

**Bolton, Michael**
c/o Contemporary
Communications
155 E. 55th St.
New York, NY 10022
*Pop singer*

**Bolton Institute for a Sustainable Future, Inc.**
4 Linden Sq.
Wellesley, MA 02181
Elizabeth and David Dodson Gray, Co-Directors

**Bombeck, Erma Louise**
c/o Universal Press Syndicate
4900 Main St.
Kansas City, MO 64112
*Author, columnist*

**Bon Jovi**
c/o Fan Club
P.O. Box 4843
San Francisco, CA 94101
*Rock group*

**Bond, Christopher S.**
293 Senate Russell Office Bldg.
Washington, D.C. 20510
*Senator from Missouri*

**Bond, Julian**
6002 34th Pl., NW
Washington, DC 20015
*Civil rights leader*

**Bond, Victoria Ellen**
Roanoke Symphony Orchestra
P.O. Box 2433
Roanoke, VA 24010
*Conductor, composer*

**Bonet, Lisa**
151 El Camino
Beverly Hills, CA 90212
*Actress*

**Bongo, Omar (Albert-Bernard)**
Présidence de la République
Boite Postale 546
Libreville, Gabon
*President of Gabon*

**Bono, Sonny**
250 W. Camino Buena Vista Park
Palm Springs, CA 92262
*Mayor of Palm Springs, former singer*

**Bono, Steve**
c/o San Francisco 49ers
711 Nevada St.
Redwood City, CA 94061
*Professional football player*

**Boone's Lick State Historic Site**
State Road 187
Boonesboro, MO 65233
Michael Dickey, Site Administrator
*Salt manufacturing site*

**Boorman, John**
8899 Beverly Blvd.
Los Angeles, CA 90048
*Film director*

**Boosler, Elayne**
800 S. Robertson Blvd., #5
Los Angeles, CA 90035
*Comedienne*

**Boot Hill Museum**
Front St.
Dodge City, KS 67801
Ben Zimmerman III, Chairman

**Booth, George**
P.O. Box 1539
Stony Brook, NY 11790
New Yorker *cartoonist*

**Booth, Shirley**
Box 103
Chatham, MA 02633
*Actress*

**Boothbay Theatre Museum**
Corey Lane/Lenthall
Box 297
Boothbay, ME 04537
Franklin Lenthall, Curator
*Theater collection from the 18th
century to the present*

**Borden, Inc.**
277 Park Ave.
New York, NY 10172
R. J. Ventres, Chairman
*Nation's largest dairy product
company*

**Boren, David L.**
453 Senate Russell Office Bldg.
Washington, DC 20501
*Senator from Oklahoma*

**Borg, Bjorn**
International Management
Group
One Erieview Plaza, #1300
Cleveland, OH 44114
*Retired tennis player*

**Borge, Victor**
Fieldpoint Park
Greenwich, CT 06830
*Comic pianist*

**Borg-Warner Corporation**
200 S. Michigan Ave.
Chicago, IL 60604
James F. Bere, Chairman and
CEO
*Leading provider of protective and
security services*

**Boris, Ruthanna**
Center for Dance Development
and Research
555 Pierce St., #1033
Albany, CA 94706
*Dancer, choreographer, dance
therapist, educator*

**Borland International, Inc.**
1800 Green Hills Rd.
Scotts Valley, CA 95066
Philippe Kahn, Chairman,
President and CEO
*Third largest maker of PC software*

**Borman, Frank**
Patlex Corporation
250 Cotorro Ct.
Las Cruces, NM 88005
*Laser patents executive, former
astronaut and Eastern airlines
executive*

**Bosley, Tom**
1999 Ave. of the Stars, #2850
Los Angeles, CA 90067
*Actor*

**Boston Bruins**
Boston Garden
150 Causeway St.
Boston, MA 02114
Harry Sinden, President/
General Manager
*Professional hockey team*

**Boston Celtics**
Boston Garden at North Station
150 Causeway St.
Boston, MA 02114
Jan Volk, Executive Vice-
President/General Manager
*Professional basketball team*

**Boston Red Sox**
Fenway Park
24 Yawkey Way
Boston, MA 02215
James "Lou" Gorman, Senior
Vice-President/General
Manager
*Professional baseball team*

**Bostwick, Barry**
8899 Beverly Blvd.
Los Angeles, CA 90048
*Actor*

**Bosworth, Brian**
230 Park Ave.
New York, NY 10169
*Former football player, aspiring*
*actor*

**Boulding, Kenneth Ewart**
University of Colorado Institute
of Behavioral Sciences
Campus Box 483
Boulder, CO 80309
*Economist, educator*

**Boxleitner, Bruce**
151 El Camino
Beverly Hills, CA 90212
*Actor*

**Boy Scouts of America**
1325 Walnut Hill Ln.
Irving, TX 75038
Ben H. Love, Executive Director

**Boyle, Lara Flynn**
606 N. Larchmont Blvd., #309
Los Angeles, CA 90004
*Actress*

**Boys and Girls Clubs of**
**America**
771 First Ave.
New York, NY 10017
Thomas Garth, National
Director

**Boyz II Men**
729 7th Ave., 12th Fl.
New York, NY 10019
*Singing group*

**Bozo the Clown**
**(Larry Harmon)**
5455 Wilshire Blvd., #2200
Los Angeles, CA 90036
*Famous clown*

**Bracco, Lorraine**
P.O. Box 49
Palisades, NY 10964
*Actress*

**Bradbury, Ray**
c/o Bantam Books
666 5th Avenue
New York, NY 10103
*Fantasy, science fiction author*

**Bradley, Bill**
731 Senate Hart Office Bldg.
Washington, DC 20510
*Senator from New Jersey*

**Bradshaw, John**
2412 South Blvd.
Houston, TX 77098
*Best-selling author, lecturer*

**Braeden, Eric**
9300 Wilshire Blvd., #410
Beverly Hills, CA 90212
*Actor*

**Brain, The**
**(Bobby Heenan)**
P.O. Box 3857
Stamford, CT 06905
*Professional wrestler*

**Brando, Marlon**
P.O. Box 809
Beverly Hills, CA 90213
*Actor*

**Brandywine River Museum**
P.O. Box 141
Chadds Ford, PA 19317
James H. Duff, CEO and
  Director
*Museum of Brandywine artists,
  including the Wyeths*

**Branstad, Terry E.** ·
State Capitol
Des Moines, IA 50319
*Governor of Iowa*

**Bravo Cable Network**
150 Crossways Park W.
Woodbury, NY 11797
Joshua Sapan, President
*Cable network*

**Bread and Puppet Museum**
RD 2, Rte. 122
Glover, VT 05839
Peter Schumann, Director
*Puppet museum*

**Breaux, John B.**
516 Senate Hart Office Bldg.
Washington, DC 20510
*Senator from Louisiana*

**Bregman, Martin**
641 Lexington Ave.
New York, NY 10022
*Film producer*

**Breslin, Jimmy**
*NY Newsday*
2 Park Ave.
New York, NY 10016
*Author, columnist*

**Brethren Church**
524 College Ave.
Ashland, OH 44805
Rev. Dave Cooksey, Director,
  Pastoral Minister
*Religious group*

**Brickowski, Frank**
c/o Milwaukee Bucks
1001 N. 4th St.
Milwaukee, WI 53203
*Professional basketball player*

**Bride's**
Conde Nast Bldg.
350 Madison Ave.
New York, NY 10017
Barbara D. Tober, Editor-in-
  Chief
*Magazine*

**Bridges, Beau**
9830 Wilshire Blvd.
Beverly Hills, CA 90211
*Actor*

**Bridges, Jeff**
9830 Wilshire Blvd.
Beverly Hills, CA 90212
*Actor*

**Briggs, Everett Ellis**
State Department
U.S. Ambassador to Portugal
Washington, DC 20520
*Ambassador*

**Briggs, Joe Bob**
P.O. Box 33
Dallas, TX 75221
*Drive-in movie critic*

**Bright, John Willis**
3911 S. Juniper Circle
Evergreen, CO 80439
*Landscape architect, rancher,
  environmental planner*

**Brightman, Sarah**
9830 Wilshire Blvd.
Beverly Hills, CA 90212
*Singer, actress*

**Brisco-Hooks, Valerie**
P.O. Box 21053
Long Beach, CA 90801
*Athlete*

**Briseno, Theodore**
c/o Police Protective League
600 E. 8th St.
Los Angeles, CA 90014
*Officer involved in the Rodney King
incident*

**Brisolara, Ashton**
P.O. Box 7321
Metairie, LA 70010
*Alcoholism and drug abuse
consultant*

**Bristol-Myers Squibb
Company**
345 Park Ave.
New York, NY 10154
Richard L. Gelb, Chairman and
CEO
*Produces Bufferin, Miss Clairol,
Vanish, etc.*

**Brittany, Morgan**
10000 Santa Monica Blvd.,
#305
Los Angeles, CA 90067
*Actress*

**Broadcast Interview Source**
2233 Wisconsin Ave., NW, #540
Washington, DC 20007
Mitchell P. Davis, contact
*Media directory publishers*

**Brock, Dee Sala**
PBS
1320 Braddock Pl.
Alexandria, VA 22314
*TV executive, educator, writer*

**Broder, David Salzer**
*Washington Post*
1150 15th St., NW
Washington, DC 20071
*Author, reporter*

**Brody, Jane Ellen**
*The New York Times*
229 W. 43rd St.
New York, NY 10036
*Nutrition, health author*

**Brokaw, Tom**
c/o NBC News
30 Rockefeller Plaza
New York, NY 10012
*Television journalist*

**Bronson, Charles**
P.O. Box 2644
Malibu, CA 90265
*Actor*

**Brooks, Garth**
1750 N. Vine St.
Hollywood, CA 90028
*Singer*

**Brooks, Gwendolyn**
7248 S. Evans Ave.
Chicago, IL 60619
*Writer, poet*

**Brooks, James**
c/o Cincinnati Bengals
200 Riverfront Stadium
Cincinnati, OH 45202
*Professional football player*

**Brooks, Mel**
9830 Wilshire Blvd.
Beverly Hills, CA 90212
*Writer, director*

**Brosnan, Pierce**
9830 Wilshire Blvd.
Beverly Hills, CA 90212
*Actor*

**Brotherhood of the Jungle Cock, Inc., The**
P.O. Box 576
Glen Burnie, MD 21061
Ken Greenfield, President
*Teaches youth about conservation*

**Brothers, Dr. Joyce**
151 El Camino
Beverly Hills, CA 90212
*Psychologist-actress*

**Brown, Charlie**
One Snoopy Pl.
Santa Rosa, CA 95401
*Much put-upon "Peanuts" character*

**Brown, Edmund G., Jr. (Jerry)**
700 S. Flower St., #600
Los Angeles, CA 90017
*Politician*

**Brown, Georg Stanford**
8899 Beverly Blvd.
Los Angeles, CA 90048
*TV director*

**Brown, Hank**
717 Senate Hart Office Bldg.
Washington, DC 20510
*Senator from Colorado*

**Brown, Helen Gurley**
*Cosmopolitan* Magazine
224 W. 57th St.
New York, NY 10019
*Editor, journalist, feminist*

**Brown, James H.**
American Society of
  Mammalogists
Department of Biology
University of New Mexico
Albuquerque, NM 87131
*Mammal expert*

**Brown, Julie**
c/o MTV
1515 Broadway, 23rd Floor
New York, NY 10036
*Downtown veejay*

**Brown, Larry**
c/o Los Angeles Clippers
3939 S. Figueroa
Los Angeles, CA 90037
*Basketball coach*

**Brown Group, Inc.**
8400 Maryland Ave., P.O. Box 29
St. Louis, MO 63166
B. A. Bridgewater, Jr.,
  Chairman, President and
  CEO
*Largest domestic shoe manufacturer and retailer*

**Brown-Forman Corporation**
P.O. Box 1080
Louisville, KY 40201
W. L. Lyons Brown, Jr.,
  Chairman and CEO
*Produces Jack Daniel's Whiskey, Hartmann Luggage, Lenox Crystal, etc.*

**Browne, Jackson**
9830 Wilshire Blvd.
Beverly Hills, CA 90212
*Singer, songwriter*

**Browning-Ferris Industries, Inc.**
P.O. Box 3151, 757 N. Eldridge
Houston, TX 77253
William D. Ruckelshaus,
  Chairman and CEO
*Second largest waste services
company in the U.S.*

**Bruno's Inc.**
P.O. Box 2486, 800 Lakeshore
  Pkwy.
Birmingham, AL 35201
Angelo J. Bruno, Chairman
*Supermarket chain*

**Brunswick Corporation**
One Brunswick Plaza
Skokie, IL 60077
Jack F. Reichert, Chairman,
  President, and CEO
*World's number-one recreational
boat manufacturer*

**Bryan, Richard H.**
364 Senate Russell Office Bldg.
Washington, DC 20510
*Senator from Nevada*

**Bryant, Gay**
Mirabella Magazine
200 Madison Ave., 8th Fl.
New York, NY 10016
*Magazine writer, editor*

**Brzezinski, Zbigniew**
1800 K St., NW, #400
Washington, DC 20006
*Foreign affairs expert*

**Buckley, William F.**
150 E. 35th St.
New York, NY 10016
*Political commentator*

**Buddhist Churches of America**
1710 Octavia St.
San Francisco, CA 94109
Rt. Reverend Siegen H.
  Yamaoka, Bishop
*Religious group*

**Buddy Holly Memorial Society**
3022 56th St.
Lubbock, TX 79413

**Buffalo Bill Historical Center**
Box 1000
Cody, WY 82414
Mrs. Henry H. R. Coe,
  Chairman

**Buffalo Bills**
One Bills Dr.
Orchard Park, NY 14127
Bill Polian, Vice-President/
  General Manager
*Professional football team*

**Buffalo Inc.**
North 724 Madelia
Spokane, WA 99202
Peter Lindstrom, President
*Manufactures Fruit of the Loom*

**Buffalo Sabres**
Memorial Auditorium
140 Main St.
Buffalo, NY 14202
Gerry Meehan, General
  Manager
*Professional hockey team*

**Buffett, Jimmy**
c/o Frontline Management
80 Universal City Plaza
Universal City, CA 91608
*Singer/songwriter*

**Bullwinkle, Rocky, Boris, Natasha, Dudley Do-Right, Snidely Whiplash, etc.**
8218 Sunset Blvd.
Hollywood, CA 90046

**Bumpers, Dale L.**
229 Senate Dirksen Office Bldg.
Washington, DC 20510
*Senator from Arkansas*

**Bundys, The
(Al, Peg, Kelly, Bud, Buck)**
10201 West Pico Blvd.
Los Angeles, CA 90035
*"Married . . . With Children" family*

**Bunny, Bugs**
c/o Warner Brothers
4000 Warner Blvd.
Burbank, CA 91522
*Famous bunny*

**Bunts, Frank Emory**
15 W. 24th St., 7th Fl.
New York, NY 10010
*Artist*

**Burdick, Quentin N.**
511 Senate Hart Office Bldg.
Washington, DC 20501
*Senator from North Dakota*

**Burger King**
17777 Old Cutler Rd.
Miami, FL 33157
Barry J. Gibbons, CEO
*Fast food chain*

**Burke, Chris**
9200 Sunset Blvd., Suite 625
Los Angeles, CA 90069
*Actor*

**Burke, Delta**
c/o Martin Hurwitz
427 Canon Dr., #215
Beverly Hills, CA 90210
*Actress*

**Burke, Yvonne Watson Brathwaite**
Jones, Day, Reavis & Pogue
355 S. Grand Ave., #3000
Los Angeles, CA 90071
*Lawyer, activist, ex-congresswoman*

**Burlington Holdings, Inc.**
3330 W. Friendly Ave.
Greensboro, NC 27420
Frank S. Greenberg, Chairman and President
*Parent company of one of the world's largest textile manufacturers*

**Burlington Northern Inc.**
3800 Continental Plaza
777 Main St.
Fort Worth, TX 76102
Gerald Grinstein, Chairman, President and CEO
*Largest rail network in America*

**Burnett, Carol**
8899 Beverly Blvd.
Los Angeles, CA 90048
*Comedienne/actress*

**Burns, Conrad**
183 Senate Dirksen Office Bldg.
Washington, DC 20510
*Senator from Montana*

**Burns, James MacGregor**
Williams College Department of Political Science
Williamstown, MA 01267
*Political scientist, historian*

**Burns, Robert Ignatius**
UCLA History Department
Los Angeles, CA 90024
*Historian, educator, clergyman*

**Burr, Raymond**
15301 Ventura Blvd., #345
Sherman Oaks, CA 91403
*Actor*

**Burton, LeVar**
8428 Melrose Pl., Suite C
Los Angeles, CA 90069
*Actor*

**Burton, Tim**
151 El Camino
Beverly Hills, CA 90212
*Film director*

**Buscaglia, Dr. Leo**
P.O. Box 488
Glenbrook, NV 89413
*Author*

**Bush, Barbara Pierce**
The White House
1600 Pennsylvania Ave.
Washington, DC 20500
*Former First Lady*

**Bush, George Herbert Walker**
c/o The White House
1600 Pennsylvania Ave.
Washington, DC 20500
*Former President*

**Bushwackers, The
(Butch and Luke)**
P.O. Box 3857
Stamford, CT 06905
*Professional "tag team" wrestlers*

**Buster Brown Apparel**
2001 Wheeler Ave.
Chattanooga, TN 37406
Kent C. Robinson, CEO
*Children's clothing company*

**Butcher, Susan**
c/o Iditarod Visitors Bureau
P.O. Box 251
Nome, AL 99762
*Dogsled champion*

**Butler, Katharine Gorrell**
Syracuse University
805 S. Crouse Ave.
Syracuse, NY 13244
*Speech-language pathologist*

**Button, Dick**
250 W. 57th St., #1818
New York, NY 10017
*Skating commentator*

**Byham, William C.**
c/o DDI, Inc.
1225 Washington Pike
Bridgeville, PA 15017
*Training pioneer, author*

**Byrd, Robert C.**
311 Senate Hart Office Bldg.
Washington, DC 20501
*Senator from West Virginia*

C

A telephone call from a friend is a joy—unless you're in the middle of a meal, having a bath or on the point of going out to an engagement for which you are already late. A letter sender in effect is saying, "I am setting aside some of my time for you alone; I'm thinking of you. This is more important to me than any other thing that I am doing."

—JOHN GREENALL, *Daily Telegraph*

**C. M. Russell Museum**
400 13th St. N.
Great Falls, MT 59401
Thomas C. Brayshaw, Executive
    Director
*Western art museum, specializing in*
    *Russell*

**C. R. Bard, Inc.**
730 Central Ave.
Murray Hill, NJ 07974
George T. Maloney, Chairman
    and CEO
*Producer of medical and health care*
    *products*

**Cable News Network**
**(CNN)**
One CNN Center, P.O. Box
    105366
Atlanta, GA 30348-5366
W. Thomas Johnson, President

**Cable Satellite Public Affairs**
    **Network**
**(C-SPAN)**
400 North Capitol St., NW,
    #650
Washington, DC 20001
Brian Lamb, Chairman/CEO
*Cable channel*

**Cadaco Inc.**
4300 W. 47th St.
Chicago, IL 60632
Wayman Wittman, President
*Manufactures board games*

**Caen, Herb**
Chronicle Publications
90 Mission St.
San Francisco, CA 94103
*Newspaper columnist, author*

**Caesar, Sid**
1930 Century Park W., #403
Los Angeles, CA 90067
*Comedian, actor*

**Caine, Michael**
c/o Jerry Pam
8500 Wilshire Blvd., #801
Beverly Hills, CA 90211
*Actor*

**Caldwell, Sarah**
Opera Company of Boston
P.O. Box 50
Boston, MA 02112
*Opera producer, conductor, stage*
    *director and administrator*

**Calgary Flames**
Olympic Saddledome
P.O. Box 1540, Station M
Calgary, Alberta T2P 3B9
   Canada
Cliff Fletcher, President/General
   Manager
*Professional hockey team*

**California Angels**
P.O. Box 2000
Anaheim, CA 92803
Richard M. Brown, President
*Professional baseball team*

**California Kickers**
1755 E. Martin Luther King Jr.
   Blvd.
Los Angeles, CA 90058
Dan Foley, President
*Soccer team*

**California Museum of
   Science and Industry**
700 State Dr.
Los Angeles, CA 90037
*Jeffrey N. Rudolph, Executive
   Director*

**California Raisins**
c/o Will Vinton
1400 NW 22nd Ave.
Portland, OR 97210
*Dancing raisins*

**California State University,
   Long Beach
University Art Museum**
1250 Bellflower Blvd.
Long Beach, CA 90840
Constance W. Glenn, Director

**Call, Brandon**
9744 Wilshire Blvd., Suite 206
Beverly Hills, CA 90212
*Actor*

**Callejas, Rafael L.**
Casa Presidencial
6a Avda, la Calle
Tegucigalpa, Honduras
*President of Honduras*

**Camel, Joe**
RJR Nabisco, Inc.
1301 Ave. of the Americas
New York, NY 10019
*Controversial cigarette cartoon/logo*

**Cameron, Eleanor Francis**
E. P. Dutton
375 Hudson St.
New York, NY 10014
*Author*

**Cameron, Joanna**
P.O. Box 1011
Pebble Beach, CA 93953
*Guinness record holder, most
   national commercials for
   a performer*

**Cameron, Kirk**
9560 Wilshire Blvd., #500
Beverly Hills, CA 90212
*Actor*

**Camp Fire, Inc.
(formerly Campfire Girls)**
4601 Madison Ave.
Kansas City, MO 64112
Margaret Preska, President

**Campbell, Carroll A., Jr.**
State House
Columbia, South Carolina
   29211
*Governor of South Carolina*

**Campbell, Tony**
c/o Minnesota Timberwolves
600 First Ave. N.
Minneapolis, MN 55403
*Professional basketball player*

**Campbell Soup Company**
Campbell Place
Camden, NJ 08103
Robert J. Vlasic, Chairman
*Largest U.S. maker of canned soup*

**Canby, Vincent**
229 W. 43rd St.
New York, NY 10036
*Film critic*

**Candy, John**
8899 Beverly Blvd.
Los Angeles, CA 90048
*Comic actor*

**Cangemi, Joseph Peter**
Western Kentucky University
Department of Psychology
Bowling Green, KY 42101
*Psychologist, consultant, editor*

**Cannell, Stephen J.**
7083 Hollywood Blvd.
Hollywood, CA 90028
*TV writer/producer*

**Canseco, Jose**
c/o California Angels
P.O. Box 2000
Anaheim, CA 92803
*Professional baseball player*

**Caperton, Gaston**
State Capitol
Charleston, WV 25305
*Governor of West Virginia*

**Capriati, Jennifer**
c/o International Management
  Group
One Erieview Plaza, #1300
Cleveland, OH 44114
*Young professional tennis player*

**Capshaw, Kate**
P.O. Box 6190
Malibu, CA 90265
*Actress*

**Captain America**
New World Entertainment/
  Marvel
387 Park Ave. S.
New York, NY 10016
Stan Lee, Publisher
*Superhero comic book*

**Car and Driver**
2002 Hogback Rd.
Ann Arbor, MI 48105
William Jeanes, Editor
*Magazine*

**Carabello, Toni
(Virginia A.)**
1126 Hi-Point St.
Los Angeles, CA 90035
*Writer, editor, graphic designer*

**Carey, MacDonald**
9744 Wilshire Blvd., #308
Beverly Hills, CA 90212
*Perennial soap opera actor*

**Carey, Mariah**
51 West 52nd St.
New York, NY 10019
*Singer*

**Cargill, Inc.**
P.O. Box 9300
15407 McGinty Rd.
Minnetonka, MN 55440
Whitney MacMillan, Chairman
  and CEO
*Largest privately owned company in
  the U.S.*

**Carle, Eric**
c/o Philomel Books
200 Madison Ave.
New York, NY 10016
*Author*

**Carl's Jr.**
1200 N. Harbor Blvd.
Anaheim, CA 92801
Carl N. Karcher, Jr., Chairman
*Fast food chain*

**Carlsbad Caverns National
    Park**
3225 National Park Hwy.
Carlsbad, NM 88220
Wallace B. Elms,
    Superintendent

**Carlson, Arne**
State Capitol
St. Paul, MN 55155
*Governor of Minnesota*

**Carlson Companies, Inc.**
Carlson Pkwy.
P.O. Box 59159
Minneapolis, MN 55459
Curtis L. Carlson, Chairman
*Owns Carlson Travel Group,
    largest travel organization in
    North America*

**Carlsson, Ingvar Gosta**
Statsradsbereduingen
10333 Stockholm, Sweden
*Prime Minister of Sweden*

**Carney, Art**
RR 20, Box 911
Westbrook, CT 06498
*Actor*

**Carolco Pictures Inc.**
8800 Sunset Blvd.
Los Angeles, CA 90069
Mario F. Kassar, Chairman of
    the Board
*Movie production company*

**Caron, Glenn Gordon**
9830 Wilshire Blvd.
Beverly Hills, CA 90212
*Writer, producer, director*

**Caron, Leslie**
8899 Beverly Blvd.
Los Angeles, CA 90048
*Actress*

**Carpenter, John**
8383 Wilshire Blvd., #840
Beverly Hills, CA 90211
*Horror/suspense film director*

**Carroll, Diahann**
P.O. Box 2999
Beverly Hills, CA 90213
*Actress, singer*

**Carson, Johnny**
c/o E. Gregory Hookstratten
9489 Dayton Way, Penthouse
    Suite
Beverly Hills, CA 90210
*Ex-talk show host, comedian,
    producer*

**Carter, Benny
(Lester Bennett)**
P.O. Box 870
Hollywood, CA 90028
*Musician, composer, conductor*

**Carter, Dixie**
244 W. 54th St., #707
New York, NY 10019
*Actress*

**Carter, Hodding III**
1025 Connecticut Ave., NW
Washington, DC 20036
*Journalist*

**Carter, Jimmy**
One Woodland Dr.
Plains, GA 31780
*Former President*

**Carter, Nell**
10100 Santa Monica Blvd.,
    16th Fl.
Los Angeles, CA 90067
*Singer, actress*

**Carter, Nick**
**(Michael Angelo Avallone Jr.)**
80 Hilltop Blvd.
East Brunswick, NJ 08816
*Detective novelist*

**Carter, Rosalynn**
One Copenhill
Atlanta, GA 30307
*Former First Lady*

**Carter, Thomas**
9830 Wilshire Blvd.
Beverly Hills, CA 90212
*Director, actor, producer, writer*

**Carter Hawley Hale Stores,**
    **Inc.**
444 S. Flower St.
Los Angeles, CA 90071
Philip M. Hawley, Chairman
    and CEO
*Department store chain holding
    company*

**Carteris, Gabrielle**
8428 Melrose Pl., Suite B
Los Angeles, CA 90069
*Actress*

**Cartoon Art Museum**
665 Third St.
San Francisco, CA 94107
Malcolm Whyte, CEO and
    President

**Carvey, Dana**
30 Rockefeller Plaza, #1700
New York, NY 10019
*Comedian*

**Casals, Rosemary**
Sportswoman, Inc.
P.O. Box 537
Sausalito, CA 94966
*Tennis player*

**Cascade Holistic Economic**
    **Consultants**
14417 SE Laurie
Oak Grove, OR 97267
Randal O'Toole, Director
*Tax-exempt consulting firm to
    conservation groups*

**Casey, Robert P.**
State Capitol
Harrisburg, PA 17120
*Governor of Pennsylvania*

**Casey Jones Home and**
    **Railroad Museum**
Casey Jones Village
Jackson, TN 38305
T. Clark Shaw, Director

**Castle, Michael N.**
Legislative Hall
Dover, DE 19901
*Governor of Delaware*

**Castle Rock Entertainment**
335 North Maple Dr., #315
Beverly Hills, CA 90210
Rob Reiner, Principal and Co-
founder
*Movie production company*

**Castro, Fidel (Ruz)**
Palacio del Gobierno
Havana, Cuba
*Cuban Head of State and President
of Council of State*

**Catalina, Inc.**
Subsidiary of Kayser/Roth Inc.
6040 Bandini Blvd.
Los Angeles, CA 90040
John E. Watte, Jr., President
*Bathing suit company*

**Caterpillar Inc.**
100 NE Adams St.
Peoria, IL 61629
Donald V. Fites, Chairman,
President and CEO
*Number-one producer of earth-
moving equipment*

**Caulfield, David and Susan**
3530 Pine Valley Dr.
Sarasota, FL 34239
*Stop-smoking experts*

**Cats Magazine**
P.O. Box 290037
Port Orange, FL 32129
Linda J. Walton, Editor
*Pet magazine*

**Cave Research Foundation**
4074 W. Redwing St.
Tucson, AZ 85741
Rondal R. Bridgemon, President

**CBS Inc.**
524 W. 57th St.
New York, NY 10019
Laurence Tisch, Chairman/CEO
*Television network*

**CBS Records Inc.**
51 W. 52nd St.
New York, NY 10019
Walter Yetnikoff, President and
CEO
*Record company*

**Cedar Rapids Museum of
Art**
410 Third Ave., SE
Cedar Rapids, IA 52401
Joseph C. Czestochowski,
Director

**Centel Corporation**
O'Hare Plaza
8725 Higgins Rd.
Chicago, IL 60631
John P. Frazee, Jr., Chairman
and CEO
*Leading supplier of telephone and
cellular services*

**Center for Death Education
and Research**
University of Minnesota
Minneapolis, MN 55455
Robert L. Fulton, Ph.D.,
Director

**Center for Environmental
Information, Inc.**
99 Court St.
Rochester, NY 14604
Elizabeth Thorndike, President

**Center for Marine
Conservation, Inc.**
1725 DeSales St., NW, #500
Washington, DC 20036
Robert E. McManus, President

**Center for Plant Conservation, Inc.**
125 Arbor Way
Jamaica Plain, MA 02130
Donald A. Falk, Executive Director
*National network of botanical gardens*

**Center for Science in the Public Interest**
1875 Connecticut Ave., NW, #300
Washington, DC 20009
Michael F. Jacobson, Executive Director

**Center for Sickle Cell Diseases**
2121 Georgia Ave., NW
Washington, DC 20059
Roland B. Scott, M.D., Director

**Center for Wooden Boats**
1010 Valley St.
Seattle, WA 98109
Dick Wagner, Director

**Cevallos, Rodrigo Borja**
Office of the President
Palacio Nacional
Garcia Moreno 1043
Quito, Ecuador
*President of Ecuador*

**Chadli, Bendjedid**
Présidence de la République
El Moradia, Algiers, Algeria
*President of Algeria*

**Chafee, John H.**
567 Senate Dirksen Office Bldg.
Washington, DC 20501
*Senator from Rhode Island*

**Chamber of Commerce of the U.S.**
1615 H St., NW
Washington, DC 20062
Richard L. Lesher, President

**Chamberlain, Richard**
8899 Beverly Blvd.
Los Angeles, CA 90048
*Actor*

**Chambers, Tom**
c/o Phoenix Suns
P.O. Box 1369
Phoenix, AZ 85001
*Professional basketball player*

**Chamorro, Violeta Barrios de**
Oficina del Presidente
Managua, Nicaragua
*President of Nicaragua*

**Champion International Corporation**
One Champion Plaza
Stamford, CT 06921
Andrew C. Sigler, Chairman and CEO
*Paper, pulp and lumber producer*

**Champion Products Inc.**
Subsidiary of SaraLee Corporation
P.O. Box 850
3141 Monroe Ave.
Rochester, NY 14603
Roger Holland, President/CEO
*Manufacturer of more T-shirts and sweatshirts than anyone else*

**Champlin, Charles Davenport**
*Los Angeles Times*
Times Mirror Square
Los Angeles, CA 90053
*Television host, critic, writer*

**Chandler, Kyle**
606 N. Larchmont Blvd., #309
Los Angeles, CA 90004
*Actor*

**Chang, Michael**
c/o Advantage International
1025 Thomas Jefferson St., NW,
 #450E
Washington, DC 20007
*Professional tennis player*

**Changing Times**
**The Kiplinger Magazine**
1729 H St., NW
Washington, DC 20006
Ted Miller, Editor
*Personal finance and consumer info
 magazine*

**Chapman, Morris M.**
Southern Baptist Convention
5452 Grannywhite Pike
Brentwood, TN 37027
*Religious leader*

**Chapman, Rex**
c/o Charlotte Hornets
Hive Drive
Charlotte, NC 28217
*Professional basketball player*

**Chapman, Tracy**
c/o Lookout
506 Santa Monica Blvd.
Santa Monica, CA 90401
*Singer, songwriter*

**Charles Schwab Corporation,**
 **The**
101 Montgomery St.
San Francisco, CA 94104
Charles R. Schwab, Chairman
 and CEO
*Largest discount brokerage house in
 the U.S.*

**Charlie Daniels Band**
Rte. 6, Box 156A
Lebanon, TN 37087
*Country band*

**Charlotte Hornets**
Two First Union Center, Suite
 2600
P.O. Box 30666
Charlotte, NC 28282
Carl Scheer, Vice-President/
 General Manager
*Professional basketball team*

**Charo**
Box 1007
Hanalei, Kauai, HI 96714
*The one and only koochie-koochie
 girl*

**Chase, Chevy**
9830 Wilshire Blvd.
Beverly Hills, CA 90212
*Actor*

**Chase, Sylvia B.**
ABC News
47 W. 66th St.
New York, NY 10023
*Journalist*

**Chase Manhattan**
 **Corporation, The**
1 Chase Manhattan Plaza
New York, NY 10081
Thomas G. Labrecque,
 Chairman and CEO
*Third largest U.S. commercial
 banking concern*

**Chavez, Cesar**
Box 62
La Paz, Keene, CA 93531
*Labor leader, activist*

**Cheap Trick**
315 W. Gorham St.
Madison, WI 53703
*Musicians*

**Cheek, Molly**
9200 Sunset Blvd., #625
Los Angeles, CA 90069
*Actress*

**Chemical Banking
  Corporation**
277 Park Ave.
New York, NY 10172
Walter V. Shipley, Chairman and
  CEO
*Financial conglomerate*

**Chen Chi**
15 Gramercy Park S.
New York, NY 10003
*Artist*

**Chennault, Anna Chan**
TAC International
1511 K St., NW
Washington, DC 20005
*Aviation executive, author, lecturer*

**Cher**
c/o Bill Sammeth Organization
9200 Sunset Blvd.
Los Angeles, CA 90069
*Actress/singer*

**Cherokee Nation Youth
  Leadership Program**
P.O. Box 948
Tahlequah, OK 74465
Diane Kelley, Director,
  Department of Youth
  Leadership

**Chevron Corporation**
225 Bush St.
San Francisco, CA 84104
Kenneth T. Derr, Chairman and
  CEO
*Oil and gas producer*

**Chic Magazine**
Larry Flynt Publications
9171 Wilshire Blvd., #300
Beverly Hills, CA 90210
Doug Oliver, Executive Editor
*Men's magazine*

**Chicago**
80 Universal City Plaza, #400
Universal City, CA 91608
*Rock band*

**Chicago and North Western**
One North Western Center
Chicago, IL 60606
Robert Schmiege, Chairman,
  President and CEO
*Railroad holding company*

**Chicago Bears**
Halas Hall
250 North Washington Rd.
Lake Forest, IL 60045
Michael B. McCaskey, President/
  CEO
*Professional football team*

**Chicago Black Hawks**
Chicago Stadium
1800 W. Madison
Chicago, IL 60612
Robert Pulford, General
  Manager
*Professional hockey team*

**Chicago Bulls**
980 N. Michigan Ave.
Chicago, IL 60611
Jerry Krauss, Vice-President
*Professional basketball team*

**Chicago Cubs**
Clark and Addison Streets
Chicago, IL 60613
James G. Frey, Executive Vice-
President
*Professional baseball team*

**Chicago White Sox**
Comiskey Park
324 W. 35th St.
Chicago, IL 60616
Larry Himes, Senior Vice-
President/General Manager
*Professional baseball team*

**Chicago Zoological Park**
Brookfield Zoo
8400 W. 31st St.
Brookfield, IL 60513
George B. Rabb, Ph.D., Director

**Child Abuse Listening
Medication, Inc.**
P.O. Box 718
Santa Barbara, CA 93102
Cheryl Simmen, Executive
Director
*Child abuse prevention*

**Child Find of America**
P.O. Box 277
New Paltz, NY 12561
Carolyn Zogg, Associate
Director
*Runaway and missing children
contact group*

**Child Welfare League of
America**
440 First St., NW, #310
Washington, DC 20001
David S. Liederman, Executive
Director

**Childhelp U.S.A., Inc.**
6463 Independence Ave.
Woodland Hills, CA 91370
Sara O'Meara, Board Chairman
*Sponsors Village of Childhelp*

**Children Before Dogs**
565 W. End Ave.
New York, NY 10024
Fran Lee, Director
*Group that feels animal waste is
harming children*

**Children of the Green Earth**
Box 95219
Seattle, WA 98145
Michael Soule, Dorothy Craig,
Directors

**Children's Defense Fund**
122 C St., NW
Washington, DC 20001
Marian Wright Edelman,
President
*Child advocates*

**Children's Television
Workshop**
One Lincoln Plaza
New York, NY 10023
Joan Ganz Cooney, President
*Sesame Street producers*

**Chiles, Lawton**
State Capitol
Tallahassee, FL 32399-0001
*Governor of Florida*

**Chinoy, Helen Krich**
Smith College Center for the
Performing Arts
Northampton, MA 01060
*Theater historian*

**Chiquita Brands International, Inc.**
250 E. 5th St.
Cincinnati, OH 45202
Carl H. Lindner, Chairman and CEO
*World's number-two marketer of fresh fruits and vegetables*

**Chissano, Joaquin**
Office of the President
Avda Julius Nyerere
Maputo, Mozambique
*President of Mozambique*

**Chlumsky, Anna**
10100 Santa Monica Blvd., 16th Fl.
Los Angeles, CA 90067
*Actress*

**Chong, Rae Dawn**
Box 181
Bearsville, NY 12409
*Actress*

**Christian and Missionary Alliance, The**
P.O. Box 35000
Colorado Springs, CO 80935
David L. Rambo, President
*Religious organization*

**Christian Broadcasting Network, Inc.**
(CBN)
1000 Centerville Turnpike
Virginia Beach, VA 23463
Pat Robertson, President
*Religious cable network*

**Christian Church**
Disciples of Christ
222 S. Downey Ave., Box 1986
Indianapolis, IN 46206
John O. Humbert, General Minister and President
*Religious group*

**Christian Methodist Episcopal Church**
2805 Shoreland Dr.
Atlanta, GA 30331
W. Clyde Williams, Executive Secretary
*Religious group*

**Christian Science Monitor, The**
One Norway St.
Boston, MA 02115
*Newspaper*

**Christie, Julie**
8899 Beverly Blvd.
Los Angeles, CA 90048
*Actress*

**Chrysalis Records, Inc.**
9255 Sunset Blvd., #319
Los Angeles, CA 90069
John Sykes, President
*Recording company*

**Chrysler Corporation**
12000 Chrysler Dr.
Highland Park, MI 48288
Lee A. Iacocca, Chairman and CEO

**Church Lady, The**
c/o "Saturday Night Live"
30 Rockefeller Plaza
New York, NY 10112
*Hostess of "Church Chat"*

**Church of Christian Scientists**
175 Huntington Ave.
Boston, MA 02115
Jurgen Kurt Stark, President
*Religious group*

**Church of God**
Box 2420
Anderson, IN 46018
G. David Cox, Chairperson
*Religious group*

**Church of God in Christ**
272 S. Main St.
Memphis, TN 38101
Bishop Louis Henry Ford,
   President
*Religious group*

**Church of Jesus Christ, The
(Bickertonites)**
Sixth and Lincoln Sts.
Monongahela, PA 15063
Ezra Taft Benson, President
*Religious group*

**Church of Jesus Christ of
Latter-day Saints, The
(Mormon)**
50 E. North Temple St.
Salt Lake City, UT 84150
Ezra Taft Benson, President
*Religious group*

**Church of the Brethren**
1451 Dundee Ave.
Elgin, IL 60120
Curtis Dubble, Moderator
*Religious group*

**Church of the Lutheran
Brethren of America**
707 Crestview Dr.
W. Union, IA 52175
Rev. Robert M. Overgard, Sr.,
   President
*Religious group*

**Church of the Lutheran
Confession**
620 E. 50th St.
Loveland, CO 80537
Rev. Daniel Fleischer, President
*Religious group*

**Church of the Nazarene**
The Paseo
Kansas City, MO 64131
Jack Stone, General Secretary
*Religious group*

**Churches of Christ in
Christian Union**
Box 30
Circleville, OH 43113
Dr. Daniel Tipton, General
   Superintendent
*Religious group*

**Churches of God, General
Conference**
7176 Glenmeadow Dr.
Frederick, MD 21701
Pastor Stephen L. Dunn,
   President
*Religious group*

**Church's Fried Chicken**
1333 South Clearview Parkway
Jefferson, LA 70121
Alvin C. Copeland, Chairman
*Fast food chain*

**Cigna Corporation**
One Liberty Pl.
Philadelphia, PA 19192
Wilson H. Taylor, Chairman and
   CEO
*Insurance company*

**Cinader, Bernhard**
University of Toronto
Department of Immunology,
   Rm. 4366, Medical Sciences
   Bldg.
Toronto, Ontario M5S 1A8
   Canada
*Scientist, immunologist,
   gerontologist*

**Cincinnati Bengals**
200 Riverfront Stadium
Cincinnati, OH 45202
Paul E. Brown, General
  Manager
*Professional football team*

**Cincinnati Reds**
100 Riverfront Stadium
Cincinnati, OH 45202
Bob Quin, Vice-President/
  General Manager
*Professional baseball team*

**Cinderella Softball Leagues**
P.O. Box 1411
Corning, NY 14830
Tony Maio, President
*Girls' softball league*

**Cinemagic**
Starlog Press, Inc.
475 Park Ave. S.
New York, NY 10016
David Hutchison, Editor
*How-to publication for fantasy film
  production*

**Cinemax**
1100 Ave. of the Americas
New York, NY 10036
Michael Fuchs, Chairman/CEO
*Cable premium movie channel*

**Cineplex Odeon Corp.**
1925 Century Park E., #300
Los Angeles, CA 90067
E. Leo Kolber, Chairman of the
  Board
*Movie theater chain*

**Circle K Corporation, The**
P.O. Box 52084
1601 N. 7th St.
Phoenix, AZ 85072
Bart A. Brown, Jr., Chairman
  and CEO
*Second largest U.S. convenience
  store operator*

**Circuit City Stores, Inc.**
9950 Mayland Dr.
Richmond, VA 23233
Alan L. Wurtzel, Chairman
*Largest specialty electronics and
  appliance retailer in U.S.*

**Circus World Museum**
426 Water St.
Barbaboo, WI 53913
Fred D. Pfeming III, President

**Cirque du Soleil**
1217 Notre-Dame St. E.
Montreal, Quebec H2L 2R3
  Canada
*Circus*

**Citicorp**
399 Park Ave.
New York, NY 10043
John S. Reed, Chairman
*Largest banking enterprise in U.S.
  (prior to the finalization of other
  bank mergers)*

**Citizens Against Lawyer
  Abuse**
P.O. Box 1881
El Cajon, CA 92020
Patricia Beamon, Director

**Citizens' Committee for the
  Right to Keep and Bear
  Arms**
12500 NE Tenth Pl.
Bellevue, WA 98005
John A. Hosford, Executive
  Director

**Civil Air Patrol**
Bldg. 714
Maxwell Air Force Base,
  Alabama 36112-5570
Director, Office of Public
  Affairs

**Civil War Times Illustrated**
2245 Kohn Rd., P.O. Box 8200
Harrisburg, PA 17105
John E. Stanchak, Editor
*History magazine*

**Claiborne, Liz**
650 5th Ave.
New York, NY 10019
*Fashion designer*

**Clancy, Tom**
c/o G.P. Putnam's Sons
200 Madison Ave.
New York, NY 10016
*Thriller author*

**Clapton, Eric**
9830 Wilshire Blvd.
Beverly Hills, CA 90212
*Guitarist, film score composer*

**Clark, Dick**
3003 W. Olive Ave.
Burbank, CA 91505
*Producer*

**Clark, Mary Higgins**
210 Central Park S.
New York, NY 10019
*Author*

**Clark, Ramsey**
36 E. 12th St.
New York, NY 10003
*Former Attorney General*

**Claus, Santa**
**(also Mrs. Claus, Elves, Dancer,**
**Prancer, Donder, Vixen,**
**Cupid, Rudolph, Dasher,**
**Comet, and Blitzen)**
North Pole 30351

**Cleary, Beverly Atlee**
c/o William Morrow & Co.
1350 Ave. of the Americas
New York, NY 10020
*Author*

**Cleveland Browns**
Cleveland Stadium
Cleveland, OH 44114
Ernie Accorsi, Executive Vice-
President
*Professional football team*

**Cleveland Cavaliers**
2923 Streetsboro Rd.
Richfield, OH 44286
Wayne Embry, Vice-President/
General Manager
*Professional basketball team*

**Cleveland Indians**
Cleveland Stadium
Cleveland, OH 44114
Dennis Lehman, Senior Vice-
President
*Professional baseball team*

**Cliff, Jimmy**
c/o Victor Chambers
51 Lady Musgrave Road
Kingston, Jamaica
*Reggae singer*

**Cliffs Notes**
Box 80728
Lincoln, NE 68501
J. Richard Spellman, President
*Short cut to literacy*

**Cline, Patsy, Fan Club**
Box 244
Dorchester, MA 02125

**Clinton, Bill**
The White House
Washington, DC 20500
*President of the U.S.*

**Clinton, Hillary**
Rose Law Firm
120 E. 4th St.
Little Rock, Arkansas 72201
*Lawyer, author, political wife*

**Clorox Company, The**
1221 Broadway
Oakland, CA 94612
Charles R. Weaver, Chairman
  and CEO
*Number-one bleach producer in the
  U.S.*

**Close, Glenn**
9830 Wilshire Blvd.
Beverly Hills, CA 90212
*Actress*

**Clowns of America, Inc.**
P.O. Box 570
Lake Jackson, TX 77566
Dennis Phelps, President
*Clown association*

**Coastal Corporation, The**
Nine Greenway Plaza
Houston, TX 77046
Oscar S. Wyatt, Jr., Chairman
*Twelfth largest energy company in
  the U.S.*

**Coasters, The**
141 Dunbar Ave.
Fords, NJ 08863
*Rock and roll band*

**Coats, Dan**
407 Senate Russell Office Bldg.
Washington, DC 20510
*Senator from Indiana*

**Coca-Cola Enterprises Inc.**
1 Coca-Cola Plaza NW
Atlanta, GA 30313
Robert Goizueta, Chairman and
  CEO
*Soft drink company*

**Cochran, Thad**
326 Senate Russell Office Bldg.
Washington, DC 20510
*Senator from Mississippi*

**Cody, Iron Eyes**
999 N. Dohen Dr. W., #102
Los Angeles, CA 90069
*Actor, activist*

**Cohen, Edward**
Ammann and Whitney
96 Morton St.
New York, NY 10014
*Civil engineer*

**Cole, Joanna**
c/o Scholastic Inc.
730 Broadway
New York, NY 10003
*Author*

**Cole, Natalie**
10100 Santa Monica Blvd.,
  16th Fl.
Los Angeles, CA 90067
*Singer*

**Cole of California**
1615 Fruitland Ave.
Los Angeles, CA 90058
George Green, President
*Swimsuit manufacturer*

**Coleman, Derrick**
c/o New Jersey Nets
Meadowlands Arena
E. Rutherford, NJ 07073
*Professional basketball player*

**Coles, Robert**
Harvard University
University Health Services
75 Mount Auburn St.
Cambridge, MA 02138
*Child psychiatrist, author, educator*

**Colgate-Palmolive Company**
300 Park Ave.
New York, NY 10022
Reuben Mark, Chairman,
    President and CEO
*Second in household consumer
    products*

**Colin, Margaret**
9000 Sunset Blvd., #1200
Los Angeles, CA 90069
*Actress*

**Collins, Gary**
151 El Camino
Beverly Hills, CA 90212
*Talk show host, actor*

**Collins, Phil**
Shalford
Surrey, England
*Rock musician*

**Color Me Badd**
c/o Reprise Records
3300 Warner Blvd.
Burbank, CA 91505
*Singing group*

**Colorado Foxes**
6735 Stroh Rd.
Parker, CO 80134
Greg Todd, General Manager
*Soccer team*

**Colorado Springs Fine Arts
    Center**
30 W. Dale St.
Colorado Springs, CO 80903
David S. Wagner, CEO and
    Executive Director

**Colson, Charles**
P.O. Box 40562
Washington, DC 20016
*Former presidential adviser*

**Columbia Gas System, Inc.,
    The**
20 Montchanin Rd.
Wilmington, DE 19807
John H. Croom, Chairman,
    President and CEO
*Operates 23,000 miles of natural
    gas pipeline*

**Columbia Pictures**
Columbia Studios
10202 W. Washington Blvd.
Culver City, CA 90232
Frank Price, Chairman
*Movie production company*

**Columbia Records**
a division of CBS/Records
    Group
51 W. 52nd St.
New York, NY 10019
Don Ienner, President
*Recording company*

**Comedy Channel, The**
(An HBO Company)
120 E. 23rd St.
New York, NY 10010
Michael Fuchs, Chairman/CEO
*Cable channel*

**Comic Magazine Association
    of America**
60 E. 42nd St.
New York, NY 10017
J. Dudley Waldner, CAE,
    Executive Director

**Comics Buyers Guide**
Krause Publications
700 E. State St.
Iola, WI 54990
John Koenig, Publisher

**Commerce Clearing House, Inc.**
2700 Lake Cook Rd.
Riverwoods, IL 60015
Oakleigh B. Thorne, Chairman
*Publishes reports and books on tax and business law*

**Committee for National Arbor Day, The**
P.O. Box 38247
Olmsted Falls, OH 44138
Mrs. Edward H. Scanlon, Honorary National Chairman

**Commodore International, Ltd.**
1200 Wilson Dr.
West Chester, PA 19380
Irving Gould, Chairman and CEO
*PC manufacturer*

**Commodores, The**
3151 Cahuenga Blvd., W., #235
Los Angeles, CA 90068
*Singing group*

**Commonwealth Edison Company**
One First National Plaza, 37th Fl.
P.O. Box 767
Chicago, IL 60690
James J. O'Conner, Chairman
*Electric company that owns and operates the largest network of nuclear power plants in the U.S.*

**Compaq Computer Corporation**
20555 SH 249
Houston, TX 77070
Benjamin M. Rosen, Chairman
*Number-one maker of IBM-compatible computers*

**Compton, John George Melvin**
Office of the Prime Minister
Castries, St. Lucia
*Prime Minister of St. Lucia*

**Computer Associates International, Inc.**
711 Stewart Ave.
Garden City, NY 11530
Charles B. Wang, Chairman and CEO
*Designs and develops software*

**ConAgra, Inc.**
ConAgra Center
One Central Park Plaza
Omaha, NE 68102
Charles M. Harper, Chairman and CEO
*Major diversified food company*

**Conan the Barbarian**
New World Entertainment/ Marvel
387 Park Ave. S.
New York, NY 10016
Stan Lee, Publisher
*Comic book*

**Conant, Robert Scott**
Foundation for Baroque Music, Inc.
165 Wilson Rd.
Greenfield Center, NY 12833
*Harpsichordist*

**Concerned United Birthparents, Inc.**
2000 Walker St.
Des Moines, IA 50317
Janet Fenton, President
*Adoption rights activists*

**Cong, Vo Chi**
c/o Council of Ministers
Bac Thao, Hanoi, Viet Nam
*President of Viet Nam*

**Connecticut River Museum**
Steamboat Dock
Essex, CT 06426
*William G. Winterer, Chairman*

**Connelly, Jennifer**
8899 Beverly Blvd.
Los Angeles, CA 90048
*Actress*

**Conner, Dennis Walter**
c/o San Diego Yacht Club
1011 Anchorage Ln.
San Diego, CA 92106
*Yachtsman*

**Conner Peripherals, Inc.**
3081 Zanker Rd.
San Jose, CA 95134
Finis F. Conner, Chairman and
   CEO
*Manufactures computer disk drives*

**Connors, Jimmy**
c/o Sports Partners
   International
230 Park Ave. S.
New York, NY 10003
*Professional tennis player*

**Conomy, John Paul**
Cleveland Clinic Foundation
9500 Euclid Ave.
Cleveland, OH 44106
*Neurologist*

**Conrad, Kent**
724 Senate Hart Office Bldg.
Washington, DC 20510
*Senator from North Dakota*

**Conservation Foundation,
   The**
1250 24th St., NW
Washington, DC 20037
Russell E. Train, Chairman of
   the Board

**Consolidated Edison Co. of
   New York, Inc.**
4 Irving Pl.
New York, NY 10003
Eugene R. McGrath, Chairman,
   President, and CEO
*Fifth largest electric utility in the
U.S.*

**Consolidated Freightways,
   Inc.**
175 Linfield Dr.
Menlo Park, CA 94025
Raymond F. O'Brien, Chairman
*Full-service transportation company*

**Consolidated Rail
   Corporation**
Six Penn Center Plaza
Philadelphia, PA 19103
James A. Hagen, Chairman,
   President and CEO
*Conrail, dominant railroad in the
   Northeastern U.S.*

**Consumer Information
   Center**
P.O. Box 100
Pueblo, CO 81002
*Publisher of government info*

**Conte, Brigadier General
   Lansana**
Office du Président
Conakry, Guinea
*President of Guinea*

**Continental Airlines Holdings, Inc.**
2929 Allen Pkwy., Suite 2010
Houston, TX 77019
Carl R. Pohlad, Chairman
*Airline*

**Continental Bank Corporation**
231 S. LaSalle St.
Chicago, IL 60697
Thomas C. Theobald,
Chairman and CEO
*Recovering failed bank*

**Continental Grain Company**
277 Park Ave.
New York, NY 10172
Michel Fribourg, Chairman
*Oversees the world's second largest grain commodities empire*

**Control Data Corporation**
8100 34th Ave. S., Box O
Minneapolis, MN 55440
Lawrence Perlman, President and CEO
*Computer manufacturer*

**Converse Inc.**
One Fordham Rd.
North Reading, MA 01864
Richard B. Loynd, Chairman
*Sneaker company*

**Conway, Tim**
P.O. Box 17047
Encino, CA 91416
*Comedian*

**Cookson, Catherine (Ann McMullen)**
Bristol Lodge
Langley on Tyne
Hexham, Northumberland
NE47 5LA England
*Author*

**Cooper Industries, Inc.**
P.O. Box 4446, First City Tower
1001 Fannin St., Suite 4000
Houston, TX 77002
Robert Cizik, Chairman,
President and CEO
*Tool and equipment manufacturer*

**Coopers & Lybrand**
1251 Ave. of the Americas
New York, NY 10020
Peter R. Scanlon, Chairman and CEO
*Fifth largest U.S. accounting firm*

**Coors (Adolph) Co.**
Golden, CO 80401
William K. Coors, Chairman and President
*Beer company*

**Copperfield, David**
9107 Wilshire Blvd., #500
Beverly Hills, CA 90210
*Magician*

**Coptic Orthodox Church**
427 W. Side Ave.
Jersey City, NJ 07304
Father Gabriel Abdelsayed,
Archpriest
*Religious group*

**Corbin, Barry**
9301 Wilshire Blvd., #312
Beverly Hills, CA 90210
*Actor*

**Corbin, Kathy**
1309 E. Northern, #308
Phoenix, AZ 85020
*Golf teacher for the physically challenged*

**Corbin, Tyrone**
c/o Minnesota Timberwolves
600 First Ave. N.
Minneapolis, MN 55403
*Professional basketball player*

**Corcoran Gallery of Art, The**
17th St. and New York Ave., NW
Washington, DC 20006
David W. Scott, Acting Director

**Corman, Roger**
11600 San Vicente Blvd.
Los Angeles, CA 90049
*Film producer*

**Cornelius, Don**
9255 Sunset Blvd., #420
Los Angeles, CA 90039
*Host of "Soul Train"*

**Corning Inc.**
Houghton Park
Corning, NY 14831
James R. Houghton, Chairman
   and CEO
*Glass company that pioneered
   optical fiber*

**Cosby, Bill**
P.O. Box 808
Greenfield, MA 01301
*Actor/comedian*

**Cossiga, Francesco**
Palazzo del Quirinale
00187 Rome, Italy
*Premier of Italy*

**Costco Wholesale
   Corporation**
10809 120th Ave. NE
Kirkland, WA 98033
Jeffrey H. Brotman, Chairman
*Membership wholesale club*

**Costner, Kevin**
151 El Camino
Beverly Hills, CA 90212
*Actor, director, producer*

**Cotti, Flavio**
Office of the President
Bundeshaus West
Bundesgassse, 3003 Berne,
   Switzerland
*President of Switzerland*

**Couch Potatoes**
P.O. Box 249
Dixon, CA 95620
Robert Armstrong, Elder #2
*TV addict support group*

**Council for Exceptional
   Children**
1920 Association Dr.
Reston, VA 22091
Jeptha V. Greer, Executive
   Director

**Council of Better Business
   Bureaus**
4200 Wilson Blvd., #800
Arlington, VA 22203
James H. McIlhenny, President

**Country Doctor Museum,
   The**
515 Vance St.
Bailey, NC 27807
Rose Pully, M.D., President

**Coupon Exchange Club**
P.O. Box 13708
Wauwatosa, WI 53213
Becky Thompson, Membership
   Director
*Group of grocery store coupon
   clippers*

**Couric, Katherine**
**(Katie)**
30 Rockefeller Plaza
New York, NY 10020
*"Today Show" host*

**Courier, Jim**
International Management
  Group
One Erieview Plaza, #1300
Cleveland, OH 44114
*Professional tennis player*

**Cousteau Society, Inc., The**
930 W. 21st St.
Norfolk, VA 23517
Jacques-Yves Cousteau,
  President and Chairman of
  the Board

**Cox, Courteney**
9830 Wilshire Blvd.
Beverly Hills, CA 90212
*Actress*

**Cox Enterprises, Inc.**
1400 Lake Hearn Dr.
Atlanta, GA 30319
James C. Kennedy, Chairman
  and CEO
*Publishing and broadcasting
  conglomerate*

**CPC International Inc.**
International Plaza
P.O. Box 8000
Englewood Cliffs, NJ 07632
Charles R. Shoemate,
  Chairman, President and
  CEO
*Produces Skippy, Best Foods
  Mayonnaise, Mazola, etc.*

**Cracked**
Globe Communications
535 5th Ave.
New York, NY 10017
Robert C. Sproul, Publisher
*Satirical magazine*

**Craig, Larry E.**
302 Senate Hart Office Bldg.
Washington, DC 20510
*Senator from Idaho*

**Craig, Yvonne**
6255 Sunset Blvd., #627
Los Angeles, CA 90028
*Actress, TV Batgirl*

**Cranston, Alan**
112 Senate Hart Office Bldg.
Washington, DC 20510
*Senator from California*

**Craven, Wes**
c/o Henri Bollinger
9200 Sunset Blvd., #418
Los Angeles, CA 90048
*Horror film director*

**Crawford, Christina**
3630 Pine Valley Dr.
Sarasota, FL 34239
*Author*

**Crawford, Cindy**
9115 Cordell Dr.
Los Angeles, CA 90069
*Model, MTV host*

**Cray Research, Inc.**
655-A Lone Oak Dr.
Eagan, MN 55121
John A. Rollwagen, Chairman
  and CEO
*Supercomputer manufacturer*

**Creedon, Michael A.**
3530 Pine Valley Dr.
Sarasota, FL 34239
*Expert on aging*

**Crist, Judith Klein**
180 Riverside Dr.
New York, NY 10024
*Film critic*

**Cristiani, Alfredo**
Oficina del Presidente
San Salvador, El Salvador
*President of El Salvador*

**Croft, Mary Jane**
Box 416
Gleneden Beach, OR 97388
*Former "Lucy" co-star*

**Crosby, Mary**
9000 Sunset Blvd., #1200
Los Angeles, CA 90069
*Actress*

**Crosby, Stills & Nash**
1588 Crossroads of the World
Los Angeles, CA 90028
*Musicians*

**Crossfield, Albert Scott**
2321 Rayburn House Office
    Building
Washington, DC 20515
*Aeronautical science consultant,*
    *pilot*

**Crown International**
    **Pictures, Inc.**
8701 Wilshire Blvd.
Beverly Hills, CA 90211
Mark Tenser, President/CEO
*Movie production company*

**Cruise, Tom**
**(Thomas Cruise Mapother IV)**
9830 Wilshire Blvd.
Beverly Hills, CA 90212
*Actor*

**Cryer, Jon**
10000 West Washington Blvd.,
    #3018
Culver City, CA 90232
*Actor*

**Crystal, Billy**
c/o Rollins
801 Westmount Dr.
Los Angeles, CA 90069
*Comedic actor*

**CSX Corporation**
One James Center
901 E. Cary St.
Richmond, VA 23219
John W. Snow, Chairman,
    President and CEO
*Transportation services*

**Culkin, Macaulay**
8899 Beverly Blvd.
Los Angeles, CA 90048
*Actor*

**Culture Club**
34 Green Lane
Northwood, Middlesex,
    England
*Pop group*

**Cummins Engine Company,**
    **Inc.**
500 Jackson St.
Columbus, IN 47202
Henry B. Schacht, Chairman
    and CEO
*World's largest diesel engine maker*

**Cumpsty, Michael**
606 N. Larchmont Blvd., #309
Los Angeles, CA 90004
*Actor*

**Cuomo, Mario M.**
State Capitol
Albany, NY 12224
*Governor of New York*

**Curb Records**
3907 Alameda Ave., 2nd Fl.
Burbank, CA 91505
Mike Curb, Chairman/President
*Recording company*

**Curry, Adam**
c/o MTV
1515 Broadway, 23rd Fl.
New York, NY 10036
*MTV video countdown veejay*

**Curtis, Jamie Lee**
8899 Beverly Blvd.
Los Angeles, CA 90048
*Actress*

**Cycles Peugeot, USA, Inc.**
Subsidiary of Cycles Peugeot
555 Gotham Pkwy.
Carlstadt, NJ 07072
Alexander Sacerdoti, Executive
  Vice-President
*Bicycle manufacturer*

**Cyprus Minerals Company**
9100 E. Mineral Circle
Englewood, CO 80112
Calvin A. Campbell, Jr.,
  Chairman
*Mining company*

D

A letter is a conversation you can hold.

**D'Agostino, Ralph Benedict**
Boston University
Department of Mathematics
11 Cummington St.
Boston, MA 02215
*Mathematician, statistician*

**D'Angelo, Beverly**
9830 Wilshire Blvd.
Beverly Hills, CA 90212
*Actress*

**D.A.R.E.**
**(Drug Abuse Resistance**
**Education)**
150 North Los Angeles St.,
#439
Los Angeles, CA 90012
*Anti-drug clubs sponsored by local
police enforcement organizations*

**D'Aviano, Grand Duke Jean**
**Benoit Guillaume Marie**
**Robert Louis Antoine**
**Adolphe Marc**
Grand Ducal Palace
2013 Luxembourg
*Ruler of Luxembourg*

**Dailey, Janet**
P.O. Box 2197
Branson, MO 65616
*Author*

**Daily Variety**
5700 Wilshire Blvd., #120
Los Angeles, CA 90036
Michael Silverman, Publisher
*Entertainment trade paper*

**Dairy Queen**
P.O. Box 35286
Minneapolis, MN 55435
Michael P. Sullivan, CEO
*Fast food chain*

**D.J. Jazzy Jeff**
**(Jeff Townes)**
1133 Ave. of the Americas
New York, NY 10036
*Singer*

**Dakin Inc.**
P.O. Box 7746
San Francisco, CA 94120
Harold A. Nizamian, President
*Stuffed animal manufacturer*

**Dalai Lama, The**
Thekchen Choling
McLeaod Gunji
Kangra, Himachal, India

**Dallas Cowboys**
One Cowboys Pkwy.
Irving, TX 75063
Jerry Jones, President
*Professional football team*

**Dallas Mavericks**
Reunion Arena
777 Sports St.
Dallas, TX 75207
Norm Sonju, General Manager/
  CEO
*Professional basketball team*

**Dalton, Timothy**
c/o James Sharkey
15 Golden Sq.
London W1 England
*Actor, current James Bond*

**Daly, Tyne**
822 S. Robertson Blvd., #200
Los Angeles, CA 90035
*Actress*

**D'Amato, Alfonse M.**
520 Senate Hart Office Bldg.
Washington, DC 20510
*Senator from New York*

**Damone, Vic**
P.O. Box 2999
Beverly Hills, CA 90013
*Singer*

**Dana, Frank Mitchell**
221 W. 82nd St.
New York, NY 10024
*Theatrical lighting designer*

**Dana Corporation**
4500 Dorr St.
Toledo, OH 43697
Southwood J. Morcott,
  Chairman, CEO, President
  and COO
*Manufactures vehicle components*

**Dance Magazine**
33 W. 60th St.
New York, NY 10023
Richard Philp, editor-in-chief

**Danforth, John**
249 Senate Russell Office Bldg.
Washington, DC 20510
*Senator from Missouri*

**Daniels, Charlie**
17060 Central Pike
Lebanon, TN 37087
*Musician, songwriter*

**Danson, Ted**
9830 Wilshire Blvd.
Beverly Hills, CA 90212
*Actor*

**Dante, Joe**
232 N. Canon Dr.
Beverly Hills, CA 90210
*Director*

**Danza, Tony**
8899 Beverly Blvd.
Los Angeles, CA 90048
*Actor*

**Daroff, Robert B., Dr.**
University Hospitals of
  Cleveland
Cleveland, OH 44106
*Neurologist, neuro-ophthalmologist*

**Darren, James**
P.O. Box 1088
Beverly Hills, CA 90213
*Singer, actor, food entrepreneur*

**Daschk, Thomas A.**
317 Senate Hart Office Bldg.
Washington, DC 20510
*Senator from South Dakota*

**Data General Corporation**
4400 Computer Dr.
Westboro, MA 01580
Ronald L. Skates, President and
  CEO
*Minicomputer manufacturer*

**Daughters and Sons United**
840 Guadalupe Parkway
San Jose, CA 95110
Dr. Henry Giarretto, Executive
  Director
*Support for abused children*

**Daughters of the Republic of
  Texas**
5758 Balcones Dr., #201
Austin, TX 78731
Carolyn Weed, CRT Director

**Davis, Geena**
9830 Wilshire Blvd.
Beverly Hills, CA 90212
*Actress*

**Davis, Jim
(James Robert)**
c/o United Features Syndicate
200 Park Ave.
New York, NY 10016
*Cartoonist, creator of "Garfield"*

**Davis, Judy**
8899 Beverly Blvd.
Los Angeles, CA 90048
*Actress*

**Davison, Beverly C.**
American Baptist Churches in
  the U.S.A.
P.O. Box 851
Valley Forge, PA 19482
*Religious group president*

**Dawber, Pam**
8899 Beverly Blvd.
Los Angeles, CA 90048
*Actress*

**Dawson, Richard**
9903 Kip Dr.
Beverly Hills, CA 90210
*Replaced game show host*

**Dayton Hudson Corporation**
777 Nicollet Mall
Minneapolis, MN 55402
Kenneth A. Macke, Chairman
  and CEO
*Target, Mervyn's, Marshall Fields,
  Dayton's stores*

**de Klerk, Frederik Willem**
Tuynhuys
Cape Town 8000, South Africa
*President of South Africa*

**De Pasquale, Paul**
606 S. Olive St., 10th Fl.
Los Angeles, CA 90017
*Defense attorney in the Rodney
  King incident*

**Dean, Howard**
Pavilion Office Bldg.
Montpelier, VT 05602
*Governor of Vermont*

**DeBarge, El**
6255 Sunset Blvd., #624
Los Angeles, CA 90028
*Singer*

**Deby, Colonel Idriss**
Office of the President
N'Djamena, Chad
*President of Chad*

**Decker-Slaney, Mary Teresa**
2923 Flintlock St.
Eugene, OR 97401
*Athlete*

**DeConcini, Dennis**
328 Senate Hart Office Bldg.
Washington, DC 20510
*Senator from Arizona*

**Deep Purple**
P.O. Box 254
Sheffield S6 1DF England
*Rock group*

**Deere & Company**
John Deere Rd.
Moline, IL 61265
Hans W. Becherer, Chairman
and CEO
*Largest manufacturer of farm
equipment in the world*

**Def Leppard**
P.O. Box 670
Old Chelsea Station
New York, NY 10113
*Hard rock band*

**Defenders of Wildlife**
1244 19th St., NW
Washington, DC 20036
M. Rupert Cutler, President

**DeHartog, Jan**
c/o HarperCollins
10 E. 53rd St.
New York, NY 10022
*Author*

**Deighton, Len**
10 Iron Bride House
Bridge Approach
London NW1 8BD England
*Author*

**Delany, Dana**
10100 Santa Monica Blvd., 16th
Fl.
Los Angeles, CA 90067
*Actress*

**Delaware Art Museum**
2301 Kentmere Pkwy.
Wilmington, DE 19806
Stephen T. Bruni, Executive
Director

**Dell Computer Corporation**
9505 Arboretum Blvd.
Austin, TX 78759
Michael S. Dell, Chairman and
CEO
*PC manufacturer*

**Deloitte and Touche**
10 Westport Rd., P.O. Box 820
Wilton, CT 06897
J. Michael Cook, Chairman and
CEO
*Accounting firm*

**Delta Airlines, Inc.**
Hartsfield Atlanta International
  Airport
Atlanta, GA 30320
Ronald W. Allen, Chairman and
  CEO
*Airline*

**DeLuise, Peter**
151 El Camino
Beverly Hills, CA 90212
*Actor*

**Deluxe Corporation**
1080 W. County Rd. F
St. Paul, MN 55126
Eugene R. Olson, Chairman
*Number-one check printer in the
  U.S.*

**Dement, William Charles**
Stanford Sleep Disorders Center
701 Welch Rd., #2226
Palo Alto, CA 94304
*Sleep researcher*

**Demme, Jonathan**
9830 Wilshire Blvd.
Beverly Hills, CA 90212
*Film director*

**Democratic Party**
430 S. Capitol St.
Washington, DC 20003
Ronald H. Brown, Chairman

**DeMornay, Rebecca**
8899 Beverly Blvd.
Los Angeles, CA 90048
*Actress*

**Dempsey, Patrick**
9830 Wilshire Blvd.
Beverly Hills, CA 90212
*Actor*

**Dennehy, Brian**
121 N. San Vicente Blvd.
Beverly Hills, CA 90211
*Actor*

**Densa**
P.O. Box 23584
Rochester, NY 14692
J. D. "Dull" Stewart, Chairman
  of the Board
*Bestows Golden Toad Award for
  public acts of denseness*

**Denver, John**
P.O. Box 1587
Aspen, CO 81612
*Singer, songwriter, activist*

**Denver Art Museum, The**
100 W. 14th Ave. Pkwy.
Denver, CO 80204
Lewis J. Sharp, Director

**Denver Broncos**
5700 Logan St.
Denver, CO 80216
John Beake, General Manager
*Professional football team*

**Denver Museum of Natural
  History**
City Park
Denver, CO 80205
John G. Welles, Executive
  Director and CEO

**Denver Nuggets**
P.O. Box 4658
Denver, CO 80204
Jon Spoelstra, President/General
  Manager
*Professional basketball team*

**DePalma, Brian Russell**
25 5th Ave., #4A
New York, NY 10003
*Film director*

**Department of Agriculture**
The Mall, 12th and 14th Streets
Washington, DC 20250
Edward Madigan, Secretary of
Agriculture

**Department of Commerce**
14th Street between
Constitution and E Streets,
NW
Washington, DC 20230
Robert Mosbacher, Secretary of
Commerce

**Department of Defense**
The Pentagon
Washington, DC 20301
Richard B. Cheney, Secretary of
Defense

**Department of Education**
400 Maryland Avenue, SW
Washington, DC 20202
Lamar Alexander, Secretary of
Education

**Department of Energy**
1000 Independence Avenue, SW
Washington, DC 20585
James D. Watkins, Secretary of
Energy

**Department of Health and
Human Services**
200 Independence Avenue, SW
Washington, DC 20201
Louis W. Sullivan, Secretary of
Health and Human Services

**Department of Housing and
Urban Development**
451 7th Street, SW
Washington, DC 20410
Jack Kemp, Secretary of
Housing and Urban
Development

**Department of Justice**
Constitution Avenue and 10th
Street, NW
Washington, DC 20530
William P. Barr, Attorney
General

**Department of Labor**
200 Constitution Avenue, NW
Washington, DC 20210
Lynn Martin, Secretary of
Labor

**Department of State**
2201 C Street, NW
Washington, DC 20520
Lawrence S. Eagleburger, Acting
Secretary of State

**Department of the Air Force**
The Pentagon
Washington, DC 20330
Donald B. Rice, Secretary of the
Air Force

**Department of the Army**
The Pentagon
Washington, DC 20310
Michael P. W. Stone, Secretary
of the Army

**Department of the Interior**
C Street between 18th and 19th
Streets, NW
Washington, DC 20240
Manuel Lujan, Secretary of the
Interior

**Department of the Navy**
The Pentagon
Washington, DC 20350
J. Daniel Howard, Acting
Secretary of the Navy

**Department of the Treasury**
1500 Pennsylvania Avenue, NW
Washington, DC 20220
Nicholas F. Brady, Secretary of
the Treasury

**Department of Transportation**
400 7th Street, SW
Washington, DC 20590
Samuel K. Skinner, Secretary of Transportation

**Department of Veterans Affairs**
810 Vermont Avenue, NW
Washington, DC 20420
Edward J. Derwinski, Secretary of Veterans Affairs

**De-Patie, David Hudson**
De-Patie Freleng Enterprises, Inc.
3425 Stiles Ave.
Camarillo, CA 93010
*Cartoon executive, vintner*

**Depp, Johnny**
1901 Ave. of the Stars, #840
Los Angeles, CA 90067
*Actor*

**Dern, Laura**
131 S. Rodeo Dr., #300
Beverly Hills, CA 90212
*Actress*

**Dershowitz, Alan**
Harvard University Law School
Cambridge, MA 02138
*Author, everybody who's anybody's lawyer*

**DesBarres, Michael**
P.O. Box 4160
Hollywood, CA 90078
*Singer, actor*

**Desert Botanical Garden**
1201 N. Galvin Pkwy.
Papago Park
Phoenix, AZ 86001
Robert G. Breunig, Director and CEO

**Desert Tortois Preserve Committee, Inc.**
P.O. Box 453
Ridgecrest, CA 93556
Jayne L. Chavez-Scales, President

**Detroit Lions**
Pontiac Silverdome
1200 Featherstone Road
P.O. Box 4200
Pontiac, MI 48057
Russell Thomas, Executive Vice-President/General Manager
*Professional football team*

**Detroit Pistons**
One Championship Dr.
Auburn Hills, MI 48057
Jack McCloskey, General Manager
*Professional basketball team*

**Detroit Red Wings**
Joe Louis Arena
600 Civic Center Dr.
Detroit, MI 48226
Jim Devellano, President/General Manager
*Professional hockey team*

**Detroit Tigers**
Tiger Stadium
Michigan and Trumbull Avenues
Detroit, MI 48216
Jim Campbell, President
*Professional baseball team*

**Deva, King Birendra Bir Bikram Shah**
Narayanhity Royal Palace
Kathmandu, Nepal
*Ruler of Nepal*

**Devereaux, Jude**
**(Jude Gilliam White)**
1937 Tijeras Rd.
Santa Fe, NM 87501
*Historical romance writer*

**DeVito, Danny**
9830 Wilshire Blvd.
Beverly Hills, CA 90212
*Actor/Director*

**Dey, Susan**
8899 Beverly Blvd.
Los Angeles, CA 90048
*Actress*

**Diadora America**
6529 S. 216th, Bldg. E
Kent, WA 98032
Galliano Mondin, Chief
   Operating Officer
*Tennis shoe manufacturer*

**Dial Corp., The**
Greyhound Tower
Phoenix, AZ 85077
John W. Teets, Chairman,
   President and CEO
*Greyhound buses and Dial soap*

**Diamond, Harvey**
3530 Pine Valley Dr.
Sarasota, FL 34239
*Nutrition expert*

**Diamond, Matthew Philip**
3508 Alana Dr.
Sherman Oaks, CA 91403
*TV director*

**Diamond, Neil Leslie**
8730 Sunset Blvd., Penthouse W
Los Angeles, CA 90069
*Singer, songwriter*

**Dickerson, Eric**
c/o Indianapolis Colts
P.O. Box 53500
Indianapolis, IN 46253
*Professional football player*

**Dickinson, Angie**
822 S. Robertson Blvd., #200
Los Angeles, CA 90035
*Actress*

**Diddley, Bo**
Box 474
Archer, FL 32618
*Musician*

**Diebold, John**
2 Depot Pl.
Bedford Hills, NY 10507
*Management consultant*

**Digital Equipment**
   **Corporation**
146 Main St.
Maynard, MA 01754
Kenneth H. Olsen, President
*Computer networks and workstation*
   *manufacturer*

**Dillard, Annie**
c/o Blanche Gregory
2 Tudor City Place
New York, NY 10017
*Author*

**Dillard Department Stores,**
   **Inc.**
1600 Cantrell Rd.
Little Rock, AR 72201
William Dillard, Chairman and
   CEO
*Department store chain*

**Dinkins, David N.**
City Hall
New York, NY 10007
*Mayor of New York*

**Diocese of the Armenian Church of America**
630 Second Ave.
New York, NY 10016
Archbishop Vatche Housepian, Primate
*Religious group*

**Diouf, Abdou**
Office of the President
Avenue Roume
BP 168, Dakar, Senegal
*President of Senegal*

**Dire Straits**
10 Southwick Mews
London W2 England
*Rock group*

**Dirt Band, The**
Box 1915
Aspen, CO 81611
*Musical group*

**Discovery Channel, The**
7700 Wisconsin Avenue
Bethesda, MD 20814
Ruth Ott, President
*Cable channel*

**Disney Channel, The**
3800 West Alameda Ave.
Burbank, CA 91505
John F. Cooke, President
*Mouse-owned cable channel*

**Dittrick Museum of Medical History**
11000 Euclid Ave.
Cleveland, OH 44106
*Patsy A. Gerstner, Chief Curator*

**Divac, Vlade**
c/o Los Angeles Lakers
P.O. Box 10
Inglewood, CA 90306
*Professional basketball player*

**Divorce Anonymous**
P.O. Box 5313
Chicago, IL 60680
Melody Broadwell, President
*Support group*

**Dixon, Alan J.**
331 Senate Hart Office Bldg.
Washington, DC 20510
*Senator from Illinois*

**Dixon, Donna**
151 El Camino
Beverly Hills, CA 90212
*Actress*

**Dixon, Sharon Pratt**
Office of the Mayor, DC Bldg.
Washington, DC 20004
*Mayor of the District of Columbia*

**Djohar, Said Mohammed**
Office of the President
Moroni, Comoros
*President of Comoros*

**Dobson, Kevin**
9744 Wilshire Blvd., #308
Beverly Hills, CA 90212
*Actor*

**Dodd, Christopher J.**
444 Senate Russell Office Bldg.
Washington, DC 20510
*Senator from Connecticut*

**Dodson, Daryl Theodore**
1650 Broadway, #800
New York, NY 10019
*Ballet administrator*

**Doherty, Shannen**
2525 Sunset Blvd., 6th Fl.
Los Angeles, CA 90028
*Actress*

**Dolan, Ken and Daria**
3530 Pine Valley Dr.
Sarasota, FL 34239
*Husband and wife financial experts*

**Dole, Robert J.**
141 Senate Hart Bldg.
Washington, DC 20510
*Senator from Kansas*

**Dole Food Company, Inc.**
10900 Wilshire Blvd.
Los Angeles, CA 90024
David H. Murdock, Chairman
and CEO
*World's largest producer of fresh
fruits and vegetables*

**Domenici, Pete V.**
434 Senate Dirksen Office Bldg.
Washington, DC 20510
*Senator from New Mexico*

**Domingo, Placido**
10601 Wilshire Blvd., #1502
Los Angeles, CA 90024
*Opera star*

**Domino, Fats**
**(Antoine)**
9229 Sunset Blvd., 4th Fl.
Los Angeles, CA 90069
*Pianist, singer, songwriter*

**Domino's Pizza Inc.**
P.O. Box 997
Ann Arbor, MI 48106
Tom Monaghan, President
*Fast food chain*

**Donahue, Phil**
51 W. 52nd St.
New York, NY 10019
*Talk show host*

**Donaldson, Sam**
1717 DeSales St.
Washington, DC 20036
*Television journalist*

**Donati, Enrico**
222 Central Park S.
New York, NY 10019
*Painter*

**Donen, Stanley**
151 El Camino
Beverly Hills, CA 90212
*Film director*

**Donleavy, James Patrick**
Levington Park
Mulingar County, Westmeath,
Ireland
*Writer*

**Donnelley, R. R., & Sons
Company**
2223 Martin Luther King Dr.
Chicago, IL 60616
John R. Walter, Chairman and
CEO
*World's largest printer*

**Donner, Richard**
9830 Wilshire Blvd.
Beverly Hills, CA 90212
*Film director.*

**Donohoe, Amanda**
10100 Santa Monica Blvd.,
#700
Beverly Hills, CA 90067
*Actress*

**Donovan**
Box 472
London SW7 2QB England
*Singer*

**Doobie Brothers**
15140 Sonoma Hwy.
Glen Ellen, CA 95442
*Pop group*

**Doohan, James**
3800 Barham Blvd.
Los Angeles, CA 90068
*Actor, original cast member "Star
Trek"*

**Doris Day Collectors**
1534 Cambria
East Lansing, MI 48823
Michael V. Doyle, President

**Dorsett, Tony**
**(Anthony Drew)**
5700 Logan St.
Denver, CO 80216
*Football player*

**dos Santos, Jose Eduardo**
Gabinete de Presidente
Luanda, Angola
*President of Angola*

**Dougherty, Brad**
c/o Cleveland Cavaliers
2923 Statesboro Rd.
Richfield, OH 44286
*Professional basketball player*

**Douglas, Michael**
P.O. Box 49054
Los Angeles, CA 90049
*Actor, director, producer*

**Douglas, Sherman**
c/o Miami Heat
Miami Arena
Miami, FL 33136
*Professional basketball player*

**Dow Chemical Company, The**
2030 Willard H. Dow Center
Midland, MI 48674
Paul F. Oreffice, Chairman
*America's second largest chemical*
  *company*

**Dow Jones & Company, Inc.**
World Financial Center
200 Liberty St.
New York, NY 10281
Peter R. Kann, Chairman and
  CEO
*Leading provider of business and*
  *financial news in the U.S.*

**Downey, Robert, Jr.**
9830 Wilshire Blvd.
Beverly Hills, CA 90212
*Actor*

**Downs, Hugh**
Box 1132
Carefree, AZ 85331
*"20/20" host*

**Doyle, John Lawrence**
P.O. Box 715
Burnsville, NC 28714
*Artist*

**Dr. John Harris Dental**
  **Museum**
1370 Dublin Rd.
Columbus, OH 43215
Dr. Jack Gottchalk, CEO

**Dr Pepper/Seven-Up**
  **Companies, Inc.**
P.O. Box 655986
Dallas, TX 75265
John Albers, President and CEO
*Soft drink manufacturer*

**Dramatists Play Service**
440 Park Ave. S.
New York, NY 10016
F. Andrew Leslie, President
*Theatrical script publisher*

**Dresser Industries, Inc.**
1600 Pacific Bldg.
Dallas, TX 75201
John J. Murphy, Chairman,
  President and CEO
*Industrial equipment manufacturer*

**Drew, Elizabeth**
1717 Massachusetts Ave., NW,
  Rm. LL220
Washington, DC 20036
*TV commentator, journalist*

**Drexler, Clyde**
c/o Portland Trail Blazers
700 NE Multnomah St.
Portland, OR 97232
*Professional basketball player*

**Dreyer's Grand Ice Cream Inc.**
5929 College Ave.
Oakland, CA 94618
T. Gary Rogers, CEO/Chairman
of the Board
*Ice cream manufacturer*

**Dreyfuss, Richard**
8899 Beverly Blvd.
Los Angeles, CA 90048
*Actor*

**Drifters, The**
10 Chelsea Court
Neptune City, NJ 07753
*Musicians*

**Drucker, Mort**
c/o *Mad* Magazine
485 Madison Ave.
New York, NY 10022
*Cartoonist*

**Drugs Anonymous**
P.O. Box 473
Ansonia Station
New York, NY 10023
Mary Lou Phippen, Secretary

**Ducks Unlimited, Inc.**
One Waterfowl Way
Long Grove, IL 60047
John E. Walker, President
*Duck preservation*

**Duckworth, Kevin**
c/o Portland Trailblazers
700 NE Multnomah St.
Portland, OR 97232
*Professional basketball player*

**Dudrick, Stanley John**
Hermann Hospital
6411 Fannin
Houston, TX 77030
*Surgeon, educator*

**Duff, John Ewing**
7 Doyers St.
New York, NY 10013
*Sculptor*

**Duffy, Julia**
10100 Santa Monica Blvd.,
#700
Los Angeles, CA 90067
*Actress*

**Duffy, Patrick**
P.O. Box "D"
Tarzana, CA 91356
*Actor*

**Dukakis, Olympia**
888 Seventh Ave.
New York, NY 10106
*Actress*

**Duke, David**
500 N. Arnoult
Metairie, LA 70001
*Politician*

**Duke Power Company**
422 S. Church St.
Charlotte, NC 28242
William S. Lee, Chairman and
President
*Electric company*

**Dulles, Avery**
Fordham University
Jesuit Community
Bronx, NY 10158
*Priest, theologian*

**Dumars, Joe**
c/o Detroit Pistons
One Championship Dr.
Auburn Hills, MI 48057
*Professional basketball player*

**Dummar, Melvin**
Dummar's Restaurant
Gabbs, NV 89409
*Howard Hughes's purported legatee*

**Dun & Bradstreet
  Corporation, The**
299 Park Ave.
New York, NY 10171
Charles W. Moritz, Chairman
  and CEO
*Marketing and business
  information supplier*

**Dunaway, Faye**
9830 Wilshire Blvd.
Beverly Hills, CA 90212
*Actress*

**Dungeon Master**
Desmodus Inc.
Box 11314
San Francisco, CA 94101
T. A. Feldwebel, Editor
*Quarterly magazine of gay male
  erotic s/m*

**Dunne, Philip**
24708 Pacific Coast Hwy.
Malibu, CA 90265
*Screenwriter, director*

**Du Pont De Nemours, E. I.,
  and Company**
1007 Market St.
Wilmington, DE 19898
Edgar S. Woolard, Jr.,
  Chairman and CEO
*Largest chemical producer in the
  U.S.*

**Duran, Roberto**
Box 157
Arena Colon
Panama City, Panama
*Boxer*

**Duran Duran**
Box 600
London NW18 1EN England
*Rock group*

**Durenberger, Dave**
154 Senate Russell Office Bldg.
Washington, DC 20510
*Senator from Minnesota*

**Durslag, Melvin**
Times Mirror Square
Los Angeles, CA 90053
*Columnist, author*

**Dwoiyogo, Bernard**
c/o Parliament House
Nauru, Central Pacific
*President of Nauru*

**Dylan, Bob**
Box 264
Coopers Station
New York, NY 10003
*Singer*

**Dysart, Richard**
11726 San Vicente Blvd., #300
Los Angeles, CA 90049
*Actor*

A letter is the mind alone without corporeal friend.

—EMILY DICKINSON

**E, Sheila**
9830 Wilshire Blvd.
Beverly Hills, CA 90212
*Musician*

**E! Entertainment Television, Inc.**
5670 Wilshire Blvd., 2nd Fl.
Los Angeles, CA 90036
Lee Masters, President/CEO
*Cable network*

**Earnhardt, R. Dale**
Rte. 8, Box 463
Mooresville, NC 28115
*Race car driver*

**Earthwatch**
680 Mount Auburn St.
Box 403N
Watertown, MA 02272
Brian A. Rosborough, President
*Environmental group*

**East Coast Rocker**
7 Oak Place
P.O. Box 137
Montclair, NJ 07042
James Rensenbrink, Editor and Publisher
*Music publication*

**East End Lights**
**The Quarterly Magazine for Elton John Fans**
Voice Communications Corp.
P.O. Box 760
31950 23 Mile Road
New Baltimore, MI 48047
Tom Stanton, Editor

**Eastman Kodak Company**
343 State St.
Rochester, NY 14650
Kay R. Whitmore, Chairman, President and CEO
*Film and camera company*

**Easton, Robert**
9169 Sunset Blvd.
Los Angeles, CA 90069
*"Henry Higgins of Hollywood"*

**Easton, Sheena**
151 El Camino
Beverly Hills, CA 90212
*Singer, actress*

**Eastwood, Clint**
Box 4366
Carmel, CA 93921
*Actor, director, politician*

**Eating Well
The Magazine of Food and
Health**
Telemedia Communications,
Inc.
Ferry Rd.
Charlotte, VT 05445
Barry Estabrook, Editor

**Eaton Corporation**
Eaton Center
Cleveland, OH 44114
James R. Stover, Chairman
*Manufacturer of automobile and
truck components*

**Eberley, Helen-Kay**
EB-SRO Productions
1726 Sherman Ave.
Evanston, IL 60201
*Opera singer*

**Eberstadt, Nicholas**
3530 Pine Valley Dr.
Sarasota, FL 34239
*Third-world economic expert*

**Ebony Magazine**
820 S. Michigan Ave.
Chicago, IL 60605
John H. Johnson, Editor

**Ebsen, Buddy**
8150 Beverly Blvd., #303
Los Angeles, CA 90048
*Actor*

**Eckert, Allan W.**
71 W. 23rd St., #1600
New York, NY 10010
*Author*

**Economaki, Chris**
79 Chestnut St., Box 608
Ridgewood, NJ 07454
*Racing commentator, publisher,
editor*

**Edberg, Stefan**
c/o Proserv
1101 Wilson Blvd., #1800
Arlington, VA 22209
*Professional tennis player*

**Eden, Barbara**
10100 Santa Monica Blvd.,
16th Fl.
Los Angeles, CA 90067
*Actress*

**Edgar, James**
State Capitol
Springfield, IL 62706
*Governor of Illinois*

**Edgar Allan Poe National
Historic Site**
313 Walnut St.
Philadelphia, PA 19106
Charles L. Andes, Chairman

**Edison Brothers**
501 N. Broadway
St. Louis, MO 63102
Andrew E. Newman, Chairman
*Shoe and apparel retailer*

**Edmonton Oilers**
Northlands Coliseum
7424 118th Ave.
Edmonton, Alberta T5B 4M9
Canada
Glen Sather, President/General
Manager
*Professional hockey team*

**Edward J. DeBartolo
Corporation**
7620 Market St., P.O. Box 3287
Youngstown, OH 44513
Edward J. DeBartolo, Chairman
and CEO
*Builder and operator of enclosed
shopping malls*

**Edward-Dean Museum of Decorative Arts**
Riverside County Museum Department
9401 Oak Glen Rd.
Cherry Valley, CA 92223
Jan Holmlund, Director

**Edwards, Blake**
P.O. Box 666
Beverly Hills, CA 90213
*Director, producer*

**Edwards, Edwin**
State Capitol
Baton Rouge, LA 70904
*Governor of Louisiana*

**Edwards Theatres Circuit, Inc.**
300 Newport Center Dr.
Newport Beach, CA 92660
James Edwards, Sr., Chairman
*Movie theater chain*

**EG & G, Inc.**
45 William St.
Wellesley, MA 02181
John M. Kucharski, Chairman and CEO
*Aerospace, nuclear weapons testing, energy research, etc.*

**Eggert, Nicole**
c/o William Carroll Agency
120 South Victory Blvd., Suite 502
Burbank, CA 91502
*Actress*

**Eikenberry, Jill**
10100 Santa Monica Blvd., 16th Fl.
Los Angeles, CA 90067
*Actress*

**Elder, Eldon**
27 W. 67th St.
New York, NY 10023
*Stage designer, theater consultant*

**Electronic Arts**
2755 Campus Drive
San Mateo, CA 94403
Larry Probst, President/CEO
*Video software manufacturer*

**Electronic Gaming Monthly**
Sendai Publishing Group, Inc.
1920 Highland Ave.
Lombard, IL 60148
Steve Harris, Publisher/Editor-in-Chief
*Buyer's guide for electronic games*

**Elektra Entertainment**
a division of Warner Communications
345 N. Maple Dr., #123
Beverly Hills, CA 90210
Bob Krasnow, Chairman
*Record label*

**Eli Lilly and Co.**
Lilly Corporate Center
Indianapolis, IN 46285
Vaughn D. Bryson, Chairman, President and CEO
*Drug company*

**Elias, Joge Serrano**
Oficina del Presidente
Guatemala City, Guatemala
*President of Guatemala*

**Elizabeth Sage Historic Costume Collection**
Wylie Hall 203
Indiana University
Bloomington, IN 47405
Neld, M. Crist, Executive Director

**Elizondo, Hector**
151 El Camino
Beverly Hills, CA 90212
*Actor*

**Ellis Island Immigration Museum**
Ellis Island
New York, NY 10004
Kevin C. Buckley,
Superintendent

**Ellison, Harlan Jay**
3484 Coy Dr.
Sherman Oaks, CA 91423
*Author*

**Elsa Wild Animal Appeal**
P.O. Box 4572
N. Hollywood, CA 91617
Joy Adamson, Founder

**Elvira**
**(Cassandra Peterson)**
Box 38246
Los Angeles, CA 90212
*Mistress of the Dark*

**Elway, John**
c/o Denver Broncos
13655 E. Dove Valley Pkwy.
Englewood, CO 80112
*Professional football player*

**Embery, Joan**
San Diego Zoo
Park Blvd.
San Diego, CA 92104
*Talk show zookeeper*

**Emerson Electric Co.**
8000 W. Florissant Ave., P.O.
Box 4100
St. Louis, MO 63136
Charles F. Knight, Chairman
and CEO
*Maker of electrical and electronic products*

**EMF**
**(Mark Decloedt, James Atkin, Zac Foley, Ian Dench, Derry Brownson)**
810 Seventh Ave.
New York, NY 10022
*Punk rock group*

**EMI**
a division of Capitol-EMI Music,
Inc.
1800 North Vine St.
Hollywood, CA 90028
*Record label*

**Emmy Magazine**
Academy of Television Arts &
Sciences
3500 W. Olive, Suite 700
Burbank, CA 91505
Hank Rieger, Editor

**Emotions Anonymous**
P.O. Box 4245
St. Paul, MN 55104
William Roath, Coordinator
*Self-help group*

**En Vogue**
75 Rockefeller Plaza, 4th Fl.
New York, NY 10019
*Singing group*

**Encyclopaedia Britannica Educational Corporation**
425 North Michigan Ave.
Chicago, IL 60611
Ralph C. Wagner, President
*Encyclopedia publisher*

**End Hunger Project**
222 N. Beverly Dr.
Beverly Hills, CA 90210
Jerry Michaud, Executive
Director

**End-O-Line Railroad Park
and Museum**
440 N. Mill St.
Currie, MN 56123
Louise Gervais, Director
*Railroad museum complete with
turntable*

**Enforcers, The
(Arn Anderson and Larry
Zbyszko)**
P.O. Box 105366
Atlanta, GA 30348
*Professional "tag team" wrestlers*

**Engleiter, Susan Shannon**
Small Business Administration
1441 L St., NW
Washington, DC 20416
*Director*

**Engler, John**
State Capitol
Lansing, MI 48909
*Governor of Michigan*

**Englund, Robert**
9200 Sunset Blvd., #625
Los Angeles, CA 90069
*Freddy Krueger actor*

**Enigma Records**
136 West 18th St., 2nd Fl.
New York, NY 10011
William Hein, President
*Recording company*

**Enoch, Jay Martin**
University of California School
of Optometry
Berkeley, CA 94720
*Vision scientist*

**Enron Corp.**
1400 Smith St.
Houston, TX 77002
Kenneth L. Lay, Chairman and
CEO
*Natural gas company*

**Entergy Corporation**
225 Baronne St.
New Orleans, LA 70112
Edwin Lupberger, Chairman
and CEO
*Electric company*

**Environmental Defense
Fund, Inc.**
257 Park Ave. S.
New York, NY 10010
Frank E. Loy, Chairman

**Ephron, Nora**
40 W. 57th St.
New York, NY 10019
*Author, director*

**Epic Records**
1801 Century Park W.
Los Angeles, CA 90067
Glen Brunman, V.P. Media and
Artist Development
*Record label*

**Episcopal Church, The**
815 Second Ave.
New York, NY 10017
Most Rev. Edmond L. Browning,
Presiding Bishop
*Religious group*

**Epps, Roselyn Elizabeth
Payne**
9000 Rockville Pike, EPN 241
Bethesda, MD 20892
*Pediatrician, educator*

**Equitable, The**
**The Equitable Life Assurance**
**Society of the United States**
787 Seventh Ave.
New York, NY 10019
Richard H. Jenrette, Chairman
and CEO
*Life insurance and investment
company*

**Erla, Karen**
Old Orchard St., N
White Plains, NY 10604
*Artist, painter, collagist*

**Erlichman, John**
Box 5559
Santa Fe, NM 87502
*Former government official*

**Ernst & Young**
277 Park Ave., 32nd Fl.
New York, NY 10127
William L. Gladstone, Co-CEO
Ray J. Groves, Co-CEO
*Accounting firm*

**Erving, Julius**
P.O. Box 25040
Southpark Station
Philadelphia, PA 19147
*Basketball player*

**Esiason, Boomer**
**(Norman)**
c/o Cincinnati Bengals
200 Riverfront Stadium
Cincinnati, OH 45202
*Professional football player*

**Esperian, Kallen Rose**
119 W. 57th St.
New York, NY 10019
*Soprano*

**ESPN, Inc.**
ESPN Plaza
Bristol, CT 06010
Steven Bornstein, President
*Cable sports channel*

**Espy, Willard Richard**
529 W. 42nd St.
New York, NY 10036
*"Word" author*

**Esquire**
1790 Broadway
New York, NY 10019
Lee Eisenger, Editor-in-Chief
*Magazine*

**Estée Lauder, Inc.**
767 Fifth Ave.
New York, NY 10153
Estée Lauder, Chairman
*Cosmetic company*

**Eu, March Xong Fong**
Secretary of State
State of California
1230 J St.
Sacramento, CA 95814
*California Secretary of State since
1975*

**Eurythmics**
**(Annie Lennox/Dave**
**Stewart)**
P.O. Box 245
London N8 90G England
*Rock musicians*

**Evangelical Covenant Church**
5101 N. Francisco Ave.
Chicago, IL 60625
Dr. Paul E. Larsen, President
*Religious group*

**Evans, Linda**
8899 Beverly Blvd.
Los Angeles, CA 90048
*Actress*

**Evans, Rowland, Jr.**
1750 Pennsylvania Ave., NW,
#1312
Washington, DC 20006
*Columnist*

**Everlast Sporting Goods
Manufacturing Company**
750 E. 132nd St.
Bronx, NY 10454
Ben Nadorf, President
*Sporting goods company*

**Evert, Chris**
One Erieview Plaza, #1300
Cleveland, OH 44114
*Retired tennis player*

**Evigan, Greg**
151 El Camino
Beverly Hills, CA 90212
*Actor*

**Ewing, Maria Louise**
c/o Harold Holt
31 Sinclair Rd.
London W14 ONS England
*Soprano*

**Ewing, Patrick**
c/o New York Knickerbockers
4 Pennsylvania Plaza
New York, NY 10001
*Basketball player*

**Exon, J. James**
528 Senate Hart Office Bldg.
Washington, DC 20510
*Senator from Nebraska*

**Exxon Corporation**
225 E. John W. Carpenter
Freeway
Irving, TX 75062
Lawrence G. Rawl, Chairman
and CEO
*Oil and gas company*

**Eyadema, General
Gnassingbe**
Présidence de la République
Lome, Togo
*President of Togo*

F

A letter is a cozy quilt, hand-stitched with the thread of friendship.

**Fabares, Shelley**
10100 Santa Monica Blvd.,
    16th Fl.
Los Angeles, CA 90067
*Actress*

**Faber, Adele**
351 I U Willetts Rd.
Roslyn Heights, NY 11577
*Kid communication author*

**Fairbanks, Douglas Elton, Jr.**
Inverness Corp.
545 Madison Ave.
New York, NY 10022
*Actor, writer*

**Falk, Peter**
10100 Santa Monica Blvd.,
    16th Fl.
Los Angeles, CA 90067
*Actor*

**Families Anonymous**
P.O. Box 528
Van Nuys, CA 91408
*Help for drug-abusing teens and
    their families*

**Family Channel, The**
1000 Centerville Turnpike
Virginia Beach, VA 23463
Tim Robertson, President/CEO
*Cable channel*

**Family Service America**
11700 W. Lake Park Dr.
Milwaukee, WI 53224
Geneva B. Johnson, CEO/
    President
*Family stress support group*

**FamilyNet**
P.O. Box 196
Forest, VA 24551
David Lewis, Marketing
    Manager
*Family programming network*

**Fan Club Directory**
2730 Baltimore Ave.
Pueblo, CO 81003

**Fanatic Limited**
Robin Hill Corporate Park
Rte. 22
Patterson, NY 12563
Peter Juen, President
*Sailboard company*

**Fancher, Michael Reilly**
*Seattle Times*
P.O. Box 70
Seattle, WA 98111
*Newspaper editor, publishing
   executive*

**F.A.O. Schwarz**
767 Fifth Ave.
New York, NY 10153
*Great toy store*

**Farley, Inc.**
233 S. Wacker Dr.
5000 Sears Tower
Chicago, IL 60606
William F. Farley, Chairman and
   CEO
*Fruit of the Loom, J. P. Stevens &
   Co., etc.*

**Farmer's Museum, The**
P.O. Box 800
Cooperstown, NY 13326
Alan McEwan, President
*Village of restored buildings with
   resident craftsmen*

**Farrell, Mike**
P.O. Box 5961
Sherman Oaks, CA 91413
*Actor, director*

**Farrell, Suzanne**
NYC Ballet, Inc.
State Theater, Lincoln Center
   Plaza
New York, NY 10023
*Ballerina, author*

**Farrow, Mia**
135 Central Park W.
New York, NY 10018
*Actress*

**Fat Boys, The**
250 W. 57th St., #1723
New York, NY 10107
*Rap group*

**Faurer, Louis**
463 West St., Studio 520
New York, NY 10014
*Photographer*

**Fawcett, Farah**
9830 Wilshire Blvd.
Beverly Hills, CA 90212
*Actress*

**Federal Aviation
   Administration
(FAA)**
400 Seventh Street, SW
Washington, DC 20590
James Busey, Chairman

**Federal Bureau of
   Investigation
(FBI)**
Ninth St. and Pennsylvania Ave.
Washington, DC 20535
William Steele Sessions, Director

**Federal Communications
   Commission
(FCC)**
1919 M St., N
Washington, DC 20554
Al Sikes, Director

**Federal Express Corporation**
2990 Airway
Memphis, TN 38194
Frederick W. Smith, Chairman,
   President and CEO
*World's largest expedited delivery
   service*

**Federal National Mortgage Association**
3900 Wisconsin Ave., NW
Washington, DC 20016
James A. Johnson, Chairman
and CEO
*Fannie Mae, a source of credit for
low- and moderate-income home
buyers*

**Federal Trade Commission
(FTC)**
Pennsylvania Ave. at 6th St., NW
Washington, DC 20580
Daniel Oliver, Chairman

**Feininger, Andreas Bernhard
Lyonel**
5 E. 22nd St.
New York, NY 10010
*Photographer*

**Feldman, Corey**
9000 Sunset Blvd., #1200
Los Angeles, CA 90069
*Actor*

**Feldman, Eliane Bossak**
Medical College, Georgia School
of Medicine
1120 15th St., Rm. BG 230
Augusta, GA 30912
*Medical nutritionist*

**Feliciano, Jose**
c/o Thomas Cassidy
417 Marawood Dr.
Woodstock, IL 60098
*Entertainer*

**Fellowship of Reconciliation**
P.O. Box 271
Nyack, NY 10960
Jo Becker, Coordinator, Youth
Activities
*Promotes nonviolent responses to
conflict*

**Fenn, Sherilyn**
151 El Camino
Beverly Hills, CA 90212
*Actress*

**Fenton, Mike**
Mike Fenton and Associates
100 Universal City Plaza
Bungalow 477
Universal City, CA 91608
*Film casting director*

**Ferguson, Maynard**
Box 716
Ojai, CA 93023
*Musician*

**Ferguson, Sarah Margaret
(Windsor)**
Buckingham Palace
London SW1 England
*"Fergie"*

**Ferrante & Teicher**
Box 12403, NS Station
Atlanta, GA 30355
*Musicians*

**Ferrare, Cristina**
15301 Ventura Blvd., #345
Sherman Oaks, CA 91403
*Talk show hostess, actress*

**Field Museum of Natural
History**
Roosevelt Rd. and Lake Shore Dr.
Chicago, IL 60605
Willard L. Boyd, CEO and
President

**Fieldcrest Cannon, Inc.**
725 N. Regional Rd.
Greensboro, NC 27409
James M. Fitzgibbons, Chairman
and CEO
*Sixth largest textile manufacturer in
the U.S.*

**Film Quarterly**
University of California Press
Berkeley, CA 94720
Ernest Callenbach, Editor
*Film magazine*

**Fine Young Cannibals**
1680 N. Vine St., #1101
Hollywood, CA 90028
*Rock group*

**Finnbogadottir, Mrs. Vigdis**
Office of the President
Reykjavik, Iceland
*President of Iceland*

**Finney, Albert**
8899 Beverly Blvd.
Los Angeles, CA 90048
*Actor*

**Finney, Joan**
State House
Topeka, KS 66612
*Governor of Kansas*

**Fiorentino, Linda**
9200 Sunset Blvd., PH 25
Los Angeles, CA 90069
*Actress*

**First Chicago Corporation**
One First National Plaza
Chicago, IL 60670
Barry F. Sullivan, Chairman
*Bank holding company*

**First Executive Corporation**
11444 W. Olympic Blvd.
Los Angeles, CA 90064
Fred Carr, Chariman and CEO
*Bankrupt insurance company,
largest buyer of Drexel Burnham
junk bonds*

**First Fidelity Bancorporation**
1009 Lenox Dr.
Lawrenceville, NJ 08648
Anthony P. Terracciano,
Chairman, President and
CEO
*Operates 550 banking offices in
New Jersey and Pennsylvania*

**First Interstate Bancorp**
633 W. Fifth St.
Los Angeles, CA 90071
Edward M. Carson, Chairman
and CEO
*Banks in 14 states*

**Fisher, Carrie**
9830 Wilshire Blvd.
Beverly Hills, CA 90212
*Actress, author*

**Fisher-Price**
636 Girard Ave.
East Aurora, NY 14052
Ronald Jackson, Chairman/CEO
*Toy manufacturer*

**Fishman, Joshua Aaron**
Einstein College
1300 Morris Park Ave.
Bronx, NY 10461
*Sociolinguist*

**Fitzallen, James**
Prime Minister's Office
Kingstown, St. Vincent
*Prime Minister of St. Vincent and
the Grenadines*

**Flanders, Ed**
P.O. Box 210
Willow Creek, CA 95573
*Actor*

**Flash**
DC Comics, Inc.
355 Lexington Ave.
New York, NY 10017
Julius Schwartz, Editor
*Superhero comic book*

**Flash Gordon**
King Features Syndicate
235 E. 45th St.
New York, NY 10017
William Harris, Editor
*Comic book*

**Fleet/Norstar Financial Group, Inc.**
50 Kennedy Plaza
Providence, RI 02903
J. Terrence Murray, Chairman, President and CEO
*Large New England banking organization*

**Fleetwood Enterprises, Inc.**
3125 Myers St.
Riverside, CA 92503
John C. Crean, Chairman and CEO
*Largest producer of motor homes and travel trailers in the U.S.*

**Fleetwood Mac**
29169 W. Heathercliff, #574
Malibu, CA 90265
*Rock group*

**Fleisher, Charles**
c/o Walt Disney Pictures
500 South Buena Vista St.
Burbank, CA 91521
*Actor, comedian, voice of Roger Rabbit*

**Fleming Companies, Inc.**
P.O. Box 26647, 6301 Waterford Blvd.
Oklahoma City, OK 73126
E. Dean Werries, Chairman and CEO
*Wholesale food distributor*

**Flintstones, The (Fred, Wilma, Pebbles, Dino)**
3400 Cahuenga Blvd., W.
Hollywood, CA 90068
*Cartoon family*

**Florida Museum of Natural History**
University of Florida
Gainesville, FL 32611
Dr. Thomas Peter Bennett, CEO and Director

**Florio, James J.**
State House, Office of the Governor, CN-001
Trenton, NJ 08625
*Governor of New Jersey*

**Fluor Corporation**
3333 Michelson Dr.
Irvine, CA 92730
Leslie G. McCraw, Chairman and CEO
*World's largest engineering and construction firm*

**FMC Corporation**
200 E. Randolph Dr.
Chicago, IL 60601
Robert N. Burt, Chairman, President and CEO
*Produces chemicals, machinery and defense systems*

**Foch, Nina**
P.O. Box 1884
Beverly Hills, CA 90213
*Acting teacher, actress*

**Folger Shakespeare Library**
201 E. Capitol St., SE
Washington, DC 20003
Dr. Werner Gundersheimer,
  CEO & Director

**Folkenberg, Robert S.**
Seventh-Day Adventists
12501 Old Columbia Pike
Silver Spring, MD 20904
*Religious group president*

**Follett, Ken
(Simon Myles)**
Box 708
London SW10 ODH England
*Author*

**Fonda, Jane**
c/o Fonda Films
P.O. Box 1198
Santa Monica, CA 90406
*Actress, exercise queen, mogul wife*

**Fonda, Peter**
RR #38
Livingston, MT 59047
*Actor*

**Fontaine, Joan**
P.O. Box 222600
Carmel, CA 93922
*Actress*

**Food & Drug Administration
(FDA)**
5600 Fishers Ln.
Rockville, MD 20857
Frank E. Young, Commissioner

**Food & Wine**
American Express Publishing
  Corp.
1120 Ave. of the Americas
New York, NY 10036
Mary Simon, Editor
*Magazine*

**Food Lion, Inc.**
P.O. Box 1330, 2110 Executive
  Dr.
Salisbury, NC 28145
Tom E. Smith, Chairman,
  President and CEO
*Supermarket chain*

**Ford, Chris**
c/o Boston Celtics
151 Merrimac St.
Boston, MA 02114
*Basketball coach*

**Ford, Faith**
151 El Camino
Beverly Hills, CA 90212
*Actress*

**Ford, Harrison**
P.O. Box 49344
Los Angeles, CA 90049
*Actor*

**Ford, Wendell H.**
173A Senate Russell Office
  Bldg.
Washington, DC 20510
*Senator from Kentucky*

**Ford Foundation, The**
320 E. 43rd St.
New York, NY 10017
Edson W. Spencer, Chairman
*Largest philanthropic foundation in
  the U.S.*

**Ford Motor Company**
The American Road
Dearborn, MI 48121
Harold A. Poling, Chairman
  and CEO
*Automobile manufacturer*

**Fordice, Kirk**
P.O. Box 139
Jackson, MS 39205
*Governor of Mississippi*

**Foreigner**
1790 Broadway, PH
New York, NY 10019
*Musicians*

**Forest Lawn Museum**
1712 S. Glendale Ave.
Glendale, CA 91205
Margaret Burton, Director
*Cemetery museum*

**Forman, Howard Irving**
Albidale-Winmill Circle
P.O. Box 66
Huntingdon Valley, PA 19006
*Lawyer, international patents
   specialist*

**Foster, Jodie**
**(Alicia Christian)**
8899 Beverly Blvd.
Los Angeles, CA 90048
*Actress, director*

**Foster, Meg**
822 S. Robertson Blvd., #200
Los Angeles, CA 90035
*Actress*

**Foster Grant Corp.**
Foster Grant Plaza
Leominster, MA 01453
Richard Wright, President
*Sunglass manufacturer*

**Fosterfields Living Historical
   Farm**
P.O. Box 1295
Morristown, NJ 07962
Quentin C. Schlieder, Jr.,
   Director
*Agriculture museum*

**Four Freshman**
P.O. Box 70404
Las Vegas, NV 89160
*Nostalgia harmony group*

**Four Seasons**
Box 262
Carteret, NJ 07008
*Singing group*

**Four Wheeler Magazine**
6728 Eton Ave.
Canoga Park, CA 91303
John Stewart, Editor
*Recreational vehicle magazine*

**4-H Youth Development**
Cooperative Extension Service,
   U.S. Department of
   Agriculture
Washington, DC 20250
Dr. Leah Hoopfer, Deputy
   Administrator
*Kids' club*

**Fournier, Rafael Angel
   Calderon**
Casa Presidencial
Apdo 520 Zapote
San Jose, Costa Rica
*President of Costa Rica*

**Fowler, Wyche Jr.**
204 Senate Russell Office Bldg.
Washington, DC 20510
*Senator from Georgia*

**Fox, Michael J.**
9560 Wilshire Blvd., Suite 500
Beverly Hills, CA 90212
*Actor*

**Fox Broadcasting Company**
a division of Fox Inc.
10201 West Pico Blvd.
Los Angeles, CA 90035
Jamie Kellner, President
*Small television network*

**FPL Group, Inc.**
700 Universe Blvd.
Juno Beach, FL 33408
James L. Broadhead, Chairman,
President and CEO
*Electric company*

**Frakes, Jonathan**
10100 Santa Monica Blvd.,
#700
Los Angeles, CA 90067
*Actor*

**Francis, Dick**
Blewbury, Didcot
Oxfordshire OX11 9NH
England
*Jockey turned author*

**Franklin, Aretha**
P.O. Box 12137
Birmingham, MI 48012
*The "Respect" lady*

**Franklin Institute**
Science Museum and
Planetarium
20th and The Benjamin
Franklin Pkwy.
Philadelphia, PA 19103
Charles L. Andes, Chairman

**Frasier, Debra**
c/o Harcourt, Brace, Jovanovich
Children's Book Division
1250 Sixth Ave.
San Diego, CA 92101
*Author*

**Fratcher, William Franklin**
University of Missouri School of
Law
Columbia, MO 65211
*Lawyer*

**Fred Meyer, Inc.**
P.O. Box 42121, 3800 SE 22nd
Ave.
Portland, OR 97202
Robert G. Miller, Chairman and
CEO
*Retail store chain*

**Free Methodist Church of
North America**
P.O. Box 535002
Winona Lake, IN 46590
R. F. Andrews, Bishop
*Religious group*

**Freebies**
P.O. Box 20283
Santa Barbara, CA 93120
Abel Magana, Editor
*A magazine that lists free and low-
cost items*

**Fresh Prince
(Will Smith)**
1133 Ave. of the Americas
New York, NY 10036
*Singer, actor*

**Fresno Art Museum**
2233 N. First St.
Fresno, CA 93703
Robert Barrett, CEO and
Executive Director

**Fricke, Janie**
P.O. Box 680785
San Antonio, TX 78268
*Singer*

**Friedan, Betty**
University of Southern
California
Taper Hall #331M
Los Angeles, CA 90089
*Author, educator*

**Friedkin, William**
c/o Edgar Gross
9696 Culver Blvd.
Culver City, CA 90232
*Film director*

**Friends General Conference**
1502B Race St.
Philadelphia, PA 19102
Meredith Walton, General
    Secretary
*Religious group*

**Friends of the Earth**
Environmental Policy Institute,
    Oceanic Society
218 D St., SW
Washington, DC 20003
Michael S. Clark, President

**Friends of the River, Inc.**
Friends of the River Foundation
Bldg. C, Fort Mason Ctr.
San Francisco, CA 94123
Larry Orman, Chairman

**Frito-Lay**
7701 Legacy Drive
Plano, Texas 75024
Michael H. Jordan, President
*Junk food company*

**FRONTLASH**
815 16th Street NW
Washington, DC 20006
Joel Klaverkamp, Executive
    Director
*AFL-CIO support group*

**Frost, Lindsay**
9200 Sunset Blvd., #625
Los Angeles, CA 90069
*Actress*

**Frye, Soleil Moon**
1801 Ave. of the Stars, #1250
Los Angeles, CA 90067
*Actress*

**Fujimori, Alberto Kenyo**
Office of the President
Lima, Peru
*President of Peru*

**Fund for Animals, Inc., The**
200 W. 57th St.
New York, NY 10019
Cleveland Amory, President

**Furness, Betty**
NBC News
30 Rockefeller Plaza
New York, NY 10112
*Broadcast journalist, consumer
    adviser*

**Futter, Ellen V.**
Barnard College
New York, NY 10027
*College CEO*

**Future Farmers of America**
National FFA Center
5632 Mt. Vernon Highway, P.O.
    Box 15160
Alexandria, VA 22309
Larry D. Case, National Adviser

**Future Homemakers of
    America**
1910 Association Dr.
Reston, VA 22091
Alan T. Rains, Jr., Executive
    Director

G

A letter sings of love and hope, still warm from the hug of an envelope.

**Gabriel, Peter**
Probono
132 Liverpool Rd.
London N1 1B2 England
*Vocalist, composer*

**Gager, Diane**
8885 Rio San Diego Dr., #335
San Diego, CA 92108
*Public relations/marketing expert*

**Galarraga, Andre**
c/o St. Louis Cardinals
Busch Stadium
St. Louis, MO 63102
*Professional baseball player*

**Galati, Frank Joseph**
Northwestern University
  Theatre/Interpretation
  Center
Evanston, IL 60201
*Writer, actor, director and educator*

**Gale, Robert Peter**
UCLA School of Medicine
Los Angeles, CA 90024
*Physician, expert volunteer at
  Chernobyl*

**Galimany, Guillermo Endara**
Oficina del Presidente
Valija 50, Panama 1, Panama
*President of Panama*

**Gallagher, Peter**
151 El Camino
Beverly Hills, CA 90212
*Actor*

**Galligan, Zach**
c/o A. Thornton
5657 Wilshire Blvd., #290
Los Angeles, CA 90036
*Actor*

**Gallo Winery, E. & J.**
P.O. Box 1130
Modesto, CA 95353
Ernest Gallo, Chairman
Julio Gallo, President
*World's largest winemaker*

**Galway, James**
P.O. Box 1077
Bucks SL2 4DB England
*Flutist*

**Gamble, Kevin**
c/o Boston Celtics
151 Merrimac St.
Boston, MA 02114
*Professional basketball player*

**Gamblers Anonymous**
2703A W. 8th St.
Los Angeles, CA 90005
Karen H., International
 Executive Secretary

**Ganilau, Ratu Sir Penaia
 Kanatabatu**
Office of the President
Suva, Fiji
*President of Fiji*

**Gannett Co., Inc.**
1100 Wilson Blvd.
Arlington, VT 22234
John J. Curley, Chairman,
 President and CEO
*Publishes* USA Today *and over
 one hundred other newspapers*

**GAP Inc., The**
One Harrison
San Francisco, CA 94105
Donald G. Fisher, CEO
*Clothing store chain*

**Garden Club of America, The**
598 Madison Ave.
New York, NY 10022
Mrs. Edward A. Blackburn, Jr.,
 President

**Gardenia, Vincent**
c/o Jay Julien
1501 Broadway
New York, NY 10036
*Actor*

**Gardner, Booth**
State Capitol
Olympia, WA 98504
*Governor of Washington*

**Gardner, David Pierpont**
University of California, Office
 of the President
300 Lakeside Dr.
Oakland, CA 94612
*University president*

**Gardner, Richard Alan**
155 County Rd.
Cresskill, NY 07626
*Author,* Sex Abuse Hysteria,
 Salem Witch Trials Revisited

**Garn, Jake**
505 Senate Dirksen Office Bldg.
Washington, DC 20510
*Senator from Utah*

**Garner, James**
8899 Beverly Blvd.
Los Angeles, CA 90048
*Actor*

**Garrett, Leif**
9000 Sunset Blvd., #515
Los Angeles, CA 90069
*Actor, former teen idol*

**Garth, Jennie**
12725 Ventura Blvd., #E
Studio City, CA 91604
*Actress*

**Garvey, Steven Patrick**
Garvey Marketing Group
4320 La Jolla Village Dr.
San Diego, CA 92122
*Ex-baseball player*

**Gates, Daryl**
P.O. Box 30158
Los Angeles, CA 90030
*Embattled ex-L.A. police chief,
 author*

**Gayoom, Maumoon-Abdul**
Office of the President
Male, Maldives
*President of Maldives*

**Gazis, Denos C.**
3530 Pine Valley Dr.
Sarasota, FL 34239
*IBM spokesman*

**Geary, Anthony**
9000 Sunset Blvd., #1200
Los Angeles, CA 90069
*Actor*

**Geary, Cynthia**
232 N. Canon Dr.
Beverly Hills, CA 90212
*Actress*

**Geffen Records**
9130 Sunset Blvd.
Los Angeles, CA 90069
David Geffen, Chairman
*Record label*

**GEICO Corporation**
GEICO Plaza
Washington, DC 20076
William B. Snyder, Chairman
and CEO
*Holding company for insurance
companies*

**Geldof, Sir Bob**
Davington Priory
Faversham, Kent
England
*Singer, activist*

**Gene Autry Western Heritage
Museum**
4700 Zoo Dr.
Los Angeles, CA 90027
Gene Autry, Chairman

**Genentech, Inc.**
460 Point San Bruno Blvd.
South San Francisco, CA 94080
Robert A. Swanson, Chairman
*Biotechnology company*

**General Cinema Corporation**
27 Boylston St.
Chestnut Hill, MA 02167
Richard A. Smith, Chairman
and CEO
*Movie theater chain*

**General Conference of
Mennonite Brethren
Churches, The**
8000 W. 21st St.
Wichita, KS 67212
Edmund Janzen, Moderator
*Religious group*

**General Dynamics
Corporation**
Pierre Laclede Center
St. Louis, MO 63105
William A. Anders, Chairman
and CEO
*Second largest defense contractor in
the U.S.*

**General Electric Company**
3135 Easton Turnpike
Fairfield, CT 06431
John F. Welch, Jr., Chairman
and CEO
*Tenth largest company in the world*

**General Federation of
Women's Clubs**
1734 N St., NW
Washington, DC 20036
Alice C. Donahue, President

**General Mills**
9200 Wayzata Blvd.
Minneapolis, MN 55440
H. B. Atwater, Jr., Chief
Executive Officer
*Food manufacturer*

**General Motors Corporation**
3044 W. Grand Blvd.
Detroit, MI 48202
Robert C. Stempel, Chairman
and CEO
*Automobile manufacturer*

**General Re Corporation**
695 E. Main St.
Stamford, CT 06904
Ronald E. Ferguson, Chairman,
President and CEO
*Nation's largest reinsurer*

**General Signal Corporation**
1 High Ridge Park, P.O. Box
10010
Stamford, CT 06904
Edmund M. Carpenter,
Chairman and CEO
*Supplier of equipment for electrical,
semiconductor and process
control industries*

**Genesis**
81–83 Walton St.
London SW3 England
*Pop group*

**Gentleman's Quarterly**
Conde Nast
350 Madison Ave.
New York, NY 10017
Arthur Cooper, Editor-in-Chief
*Magazine*

**George, Thomas Frederick**
SUNY Buffalo
411 Capen Hall
Buffalo, NY 14260
*Chemistry professor*

**Georgia-Pacific Corporation**
133 Peachtree St. NE
Atlanta, GA 30303
T. Marshall Hahn, Jr.,
Chairman and CEO
*World's second largest forest
products company*

**Gerber Products Company**
445 State St.
Fremont, MI 49413
Alfred A. Piergalllini,
Chairman, President and
CEO
*World's leading producer of
processed baby foods*

**Gerry & The Pacemakers**
28A Manor Row
Brodford BDL 4QU England
*One of original British Invasion
groups*

**Gertz, Jamie**
8899 Beverly Blvd.
Los Angeles, CA 90048
*Actress*

**Getty, Estelle**
1999 Ave. of the Stars, #2850
Los Angeles, CA 90067
*Actress*

**Gettysburg National Military
Park**
Gettysburg, PA 17325
Jose Cisneros, Superintendent

**Geyer, Georgie Anne**
800 25th St., NW
Washington, DC 20037
*Syndicated columnist, author,
educator*

**Ggozo, Brigadier General
Oupa**
c/o Head of State
Zwelitsha, Ciskei, South Africa
*Head of State of Ciskei, South
Africa*

**Ghirardelli Chocolate
Company**
111 139th St.
San Leandro, CA 94578
Dennis DeDomenico, Chairman
*Candy company*

**Giant Food Inc.**
6300 Sheriff Rd.
Landover, MD 20785
Israel Cohen, Chairman,
    President and CEO
*Supermarket chain*

**Gibb, Cynthia**
151 El Camino
Beverly Hills, CA 90212
*Actress*

**Gibson, Debbie**
P.O. Box 489
Merrick, NY 11566
*Singer, songwriter*

**Gibson, Mel**
P.O. Box 2156
Santa Monica, CA 90406
*Actor*

**Gifford, Kathie Lee**
ABC Television Network
77 W. 66th St.
New York, NY 10023
*Talk show host*

**Gifted Child Society**
190 Rock Road
Glen Rock, NJ 07452
Gina Ginsberg Riggs, Executive
    Director

**Gilbert, Pia S.**
Juilliard School of Music
60 Lincoln Center Plaza
New York, NY 10023
*Schoenberg Award–winning
    composer*

**Gilbert, Sara**
10100 Santa Monica Blvd.,
    16th Fl.
Los Angeles, CA 90067
*Actress*

**Gilbert-Brinkman, Melissa**
151 El Camino
Beverly Hills, CA 90212
*Actress*

**Gilder, George**
150 E. 35th St.
New York, NY 10016
*Journalist, author*

**Gillette Company, The**
Prudential Tower Bldg.
Boston, MA 02199
Alfred M. Zeien, Chairman and
    CEO
*Razor and toiletries manufacturer*

**Gilliam, Terry**
The Old Hall, South Grove
Highgate, London N6 England
*Director*

**Gimbel, Norman**
P.O. Box 50013
Montecito, CA 93150
*Lyricist*

**Ginsberg, Allen**
Box 582
Stuyvesant Station
New York, NY 10009
*Author*

**Ginsburg, Daniel Evan**
142 E. Ontario St.
Chicago, IL 60611
*Founder of Society for American
    Baseball Research*

**Ginzburg, Ralph**
Better Living Avant-Garde
    Media Inc.
1780 Broadway, #811
New York, NY 10019
*Writer, editor*

**Giobbi, Edward Giacchino**
161 Croton Lake Rd.
Katonah, NY 10536
*Artist*

**Girl Scouts of the U.S.A.**
830 Third Ave.
New York, NY 10022
Frances Hesselbein, Executive
 Director

**Girls Clubs of America**
30 E. 33rd St.
New York, NY 10016
Margaret Gates, Executive
 Director

**Gish, Annabeth**
P.O. Box 5617
Beverly Hills, CA 90210
*Actress*

**Givens, Bill**
7510 Sunset Blvd., #551
Los Angeles, CA 90046
*Author of* Film Flubs

**Glamour Magazine**
350 Madison Ave.
New York, NY 10015
Ruth Whitney, Editor

**Glenn, John**
503 Senate Hart Office Bldg.
Washington, DC 20510
*Senator from Ohio*

**Glenn Miller Society**
18 Crendon St.
High Wycombe, Bucks,
 England

**Gless, Sharon**
9830 Wilshire Blvd.
Beverly Hills, CA 90212
*Actress*

**Global Tomorrow Coalition,
 Inc.**
1325 G. St., NW, #915
Washington, DC 20005
Donald R. Lesh, President

**Global Wrestling Federation**
1692 Sprinter St., NW
Atlanta, GA 30318
Joe Pedicino, President
*Professional wrestling association*

**Gloria Estefan and the Miami
 Sound Machine**
8390 SW Fourth St.
Miami, FL 33144
*Pop group*

**Glover, Danny**
P.O. Box 1648
San Francisco, CA 94101
*Actor*

**Go Go's**
345 N. Maple Dr., #325
Beverly Hills, CA 90210
*Pop/rock group*

**Godden, Rumer
(Margaret)**
Ardnacloich, Moniaive,
 Thornhill
Dumfriesshire D63 4HZ
 Scotland
*Author*

**Godunov, Alexander**
1999 Ave. of the Stars, #2850
Los Angeles, CA 90067
*Actor, retired ballet dancer*

**Godwin, Gail Kathleen**
P.O. Box 946
Woodstock, NY 12498
*Author*

**Golan, Menahem**
8200 Wilshire Blvd.
Beverly Hills, CA 90211
*Film producer, director*

**Gold, Tracey**
3500 W. Olive, #1400
Burbank, CA 91505
*Actress*

**Goldberg, Gary David**
Box 84168
Los Angeles, CA 90077
*TV producer, writer*

**Goldberg, Whoopi
(Caryn Johnson)**
9830 Wilshire Blvd.
Beverly Hills, CA 90212
*Actress, comedienne*

**Goldblum, Jeff**
8899 Beverly Blvd.
Los Angeles, CA 90048
*Actor*

**Golden Gloves Association of
America, Inc.**
1503 Linda Ln.
Hutchinson, KS 67502
Jim Beasley, Secretary/Treasurer
*Boxing competition for teenagers*

**Golden Spike National
Historic Site**
P.O. Box W
Brigham City, UT 84302
Bill Herr, Superintendent
*Commemorates completion of
transcontinental railroad*

**Golden State Warriors**
The Oakland Coliseum Arena
Nimitz Freeway and
Hegenberger Rd.
Oakland, CA 94621
Daniel F. Finnane, President
*Professional basketball team*

**Goldman, William**
50 E. 77th St.
New York, NY 10021
*Screenwriter, author*

**Goldman Sachs Group, LP,
The**
85 Broad St.
New York, NY 10004
Stephen Friedman, Senior
Partner and Co-Chairman
Robert E. Rubin, Senior Partner
and Co-Chairman
*Financial services company*

**Goldsmith, Jerry**
2049 Century Park E., #3700
Los Angeles, CA 90067
*Composer*

**Golub, Leon Albert**
530 LaGuardia Pl.
New York, NY 10012
*Artist*

**Goncz, Arpad**
Office of the President
1055 Budapest
Kossuth Lajos ter 1
Hungary
*President of Hungary*

**Good, Robert Alan**
All Children's Hospital
801 Sixth St. S.
St. Petersburg, FL 33701
*Physician, educator*

**Good Housekeeping**
Hearst Corp.
959 Eighth Ave.
New York, NY 10019
John Mack Carter, Editor-in-
Chief
*Magazine*

**Goodall, Jane**
P.O. Box 41720
Tucson, AZ 85717
*Chimp expert*

**Goodman, John**
P.O. Box 5617
Beverly Hills, CA 90210
*Actor*

**Goodyear Tire & Rubber Company, The**
1144 E. Market St.
Akron, OH 44316
Stanley C. Gault, Chairman and CEO
*Largest rubber producer in the world*

**Gopher Tortoise Council**
Florida Museum of Natural History
University of Florida
Gainesville, FL 32611
George Heinrich, Jennifer D. McMurtray, Co-Chair
*Turtle preservation*

**Gorbachev, Mikhail Sergeyevich**
Leningradsky Prospekt 49
Moscow, Russia
*Former president of the U.S.S.R.*

**Gorbunovos, Anatolijs**
Presidium of Latvian Supreme Soviet
Riga, Latvia
*President of Latvia*

**Gordon, Irvin**
2B Summit St.
East Patchogue, NY 11772
*Owner of the world's longest-running Volvo*

**Gore, Albert, Jr.**
393 Senate Russell Office Bldg.
Washington, DC 20501
*Senator from Tennessee*

**Gores, Joseph Nicholas**
P.O. Box 446
Fairfax, CA 94978
*Novelist, scriptwriter*

**Gortari, Carlos Salinas del**
Palacio de Gobierno
Mexico, D.F., Mexico
*President of Mexico*

**Gorton, Slade**
730 Senate Hart Office Bldg.
Washington, DC 20501
*Senator from Washington*

**Gosselaar, Mark Paul**
261 S. Robertson Blvd.
Beverly Hills, CA 90211
*Actor*

**Gossett, Louis, Jr.**
P.O. Box 6187
Malibu, CA 90264
*Actor*

**Gottfried, Gilbert**
c/o "USA Up All Night"
1230 Ave. of the Americas
New York, NY 10020
*Late night host, comedian*

**Gotti, John**
#18261-053
Route 5, P.O. Box 2000
Marion, IL 62959
*Convicted mobster*

**Grace, J. Peter**
CCAGW
1301 Connecticut Ave., NW, #400
Washington, DC 20036
*Business leader*

**Grace, W. R., & Company**
One Town Center
Boca Raton, FL 33486
J. Peter Grace, Chairman and CEO
*Baker & Taylor Books, Grace Cocoa, textiles, chemicals, etc.*

**Grace Contrino Abrams
Peace Education
Foundation**
3550 Biscayne Blvd., #400
Miami, FL 33137
Warren S. Hoskins, Executive
   Director
*Teaches kids to "fight fair"*

**Gracy, David Bergen**
University of Texas Graduate
   School Library
Information Sciences
Austin, TX 78712
*Archivist*

**Graf, Steffi
(Stephanie Maria)**
Luftschiffring 8
D-6835 Bruhl, Germany
*Tennis player*

**Graham, Bob**
241 Senate Dirksen Office Bldg.
Washington, DC 20510
*Senator from Florida*

**Gramm, Phil**
370 Senate Russell Office Bldg.
Washington, DC 20501
*Senator from Texas*

**Grammer, Kelsey**
10000 Santa Monica Blvd.,
   #305
Los Angeles, CA 90067
*Actor*

**Grand Ole Opry**
2804 Opryland Dr.
Nashville, TN 37214

**Grandparents Anonymous**
1924 Beverly
Sylvan Lake, MI 48053
Shella M. Davison, Founder

**Grandy, Fred**
418 Connon House Office Bldg.
Washington, DC 20515
*Actor turned pro-ethics
   congressman*

**Grant, Amy**
P.O. Box 50701
Nashville, TN 37205
*Singer*

**Grant, Horace**
c/o Chicago Bulls
980 N. Michigan Ave.
Chicago, IL 60611
*Professional basketball player*

**Grant, Lee**
8899 Beverly Blvd.
Los Angeles, CA 90048
*Actress, director*

**Grant, Virginia Annette**
*The New York Times*
229 W. 43rd St.
New York, NY 10036
*Newspaper editor, journalist*

**Grassley, Charles E.**
135 Senate Hart Office Bldg.
Washington, DC 20510
*Senator from Idaho*

**Grateful Dead, The**
P.O. Box 1566, Main Office
   Street
Montclair, NJ 07043
*Cult rock band*

**Graves, Earl Gilbert**
*Black Enterprise*
130 Fifth Ave.
New York, NY 10011
*Publisher*

**Graves, Michael**
341 Nassau St.
Princeton, NJ 08540
*Architect*

**Gray, George**
47 Fifth Ave.
New York, NY 10003
*Mural painter*

**Gray, Linda**
P.O. Box 1370
Canyon Country, CA 91351
*Actress*

**Graybeal, Sidney Norman**
Scientific Applications
   International Corp.
1710 Goodridge Dr.
McLean, VA 22101
*National security executive*

**Great Atlantic & Pacific Tea
   Company, The (A & P)**
2 Paragon Dr.
Montvale, NJ 07645
James Wood, Chairman,
   President and CEO
*Grocery store chain*

**Great Bear Foundation**
P.O. Box 2699
Missoula, MT 59806
Lance Olsen, President
*Bear conservation*

**Great Jones**
a subsidiary of Island Records
14 E. Fourth St.
New York, NY 10012
Mike Bone, President
*Record label*

**Great Western Financial
   Corporation**
8484 Wilshire Blvd.
Beverly Hills, CA 90211
James F. Montgomery, Chairman
   and CEO
*Holding company for second largest
   U.S. thrift institution*

**Great White**
P.O. Box 67487
Los Angeles, CA 90067
*Rock band*

**Greater Yellowstone
   Coalition**
P.O. Box 1874
13 South Wilson
Bozeman, MT 59771
John Winsor, President
*Park support group*

**Greek Orthodox Archdiocese
   of North and South
   America**
8–10 E. 79th St.
New York, NY 10021
Archbishop Iakovos, President
*Religious group*

**Greeley, Andrew Moran**
c/o G.P. Putnam's Sons
200 Madison Ave.
New York, NY 10016
*Sociologist, author*

**Green Bay Packers**
1265 Lombardi Ave.
Green Bay, WI 54303
Robert E. Harlan, President/
   CEO
*Professional football team*

**Green, A. C.**
c/o L.A. Lakers
P.O. Box 10
Inglewood, CA 90306
*Basketball player*

**Green, Adolph**
211 Central Park W.
New York, NY 10024
*Playwright, lyricist*

**Green, Brian Austin**
7813 Sunset Blvd.
Los Angeles, CA 90046
*Actor*

**Green, Shirley Moore**
400 Maryland Ave., SW
Washington, DC 20546
*Presidential assistant*

**Greene, A. C.
(Alvin Carl)**
c/o Jonathan Matson
276 Fifth Ave.
New York, NY 10001
*Commentator, author*

**Greene, Graham**
121 N. San Vicente Blvd.
Beverly Hills, CA 90211
*Actor*

**Greenpeace USA, Inc.**
1436 U St., NW
Washington, DC 20009
Peter Bahouth, Executive
 Director
*Environmental group*

**Greenwood, Bruce**
9200 Sunset Blvd., #1200
Los Angeles, CA 90069
*Actor*

**Gregg, Judd**
State House, Room 208
Concord, NH 03301
*Governor of New Hampshire*

**Gregory, Dick**
Box 3266
Tower Hill Farm
Plymouth, MA 02361
*Comedian, activist*

**Gretzky, Wayne**
c/o Los Angeles Kings
P.O. Box 17013
Inglewood, CA 90308
*Hockey player*

**Grey, Jennifer**
9830 Wilshire Blvd.
Beverly Hills, CA 90212
*Actress*

**Grieco, Richard**
9830 Wilshire Blvd.
Beverly Hills, CA 90212
*Actor*

**Grief Education Institute**
1780 South Bellaire St., #132
Denver, CO 80222
Tom Lose, Director

**Griffin, Merv**
9860 Wilshire Blvd.
Beverly Hills, CA 90210
*Singer, entrepreneur*

**Griffith, Andy**
151 El Camino
Beverly Hills, CA 90212
*Actor*

**Griffith, Melanie**
8899 Beverly Blvd.
Los Angeles, CA 90048
*Actress*

**Griffith Observatory**
2800 E. Observatory Rd.
Los Angeles, CA 90027
Dr. Edwin C. Krupp, Director
*Famous "Rebel Without a Cause"
 location*

**Grillo, Joann Danielle**
240 Central Park S., #3N
New York, NY 10019
*Mezzo-soprano*

**Groening, Matt**
10201 West Pico Blvd.
Los Angeles, CA 90035
*"Simpsons" cartoonist*

**Gross, Michael**
151 El Camino
Beverly Hills, CA 90212
*Actor*

**Group Project for Holocaust Survivors and Their Children**
60 Riverside Dr., #11G
New York, NY 10024
Eva Fogelman, Executive Officer

**Grumman Corporation**
1111 Stewart Ave.
Bethpage, NY 11714
Renso L. Caporali, Chairman and CEO
*Aerospace manufacturer*

**GTE Corporation**
One Stamford Forum
Stamford, CT 06904
James L. Johnson, Chairman and CEO
*Largest U.S.-based local telephone company*

**Guardian Angels**
982 E. 89th St.
Brooklyn, NY 11236
Curtis Sliwa, Founder

**Guare, John**
c/o R. A. Boose
1 Dag Hammarskjold Plaza
New York, NY 10017
*Playwright*

**Guerrero, Pedro**
c/o St. Louis Cardinals
Busch Stadium
St. Louis, MO 63102
*Professional baseball player*

**Guess Inc.**
1444 S. Alameda St.
Los Angeles, CA 90021
Maurice Marziano, President
*Clothing manufacturer*

**Guideposts Magazine**
747 Third Ave.
New York, NY 10017
Van Varner, Editor

**Guinness, Sir Alec**
Kettle Brook Meadows
Petersfield, Hampshire, England
*Actor*

**Guisewite, Cathy Lee**
c/o Universal Press Syndicate
4900 Main St.
Kansas City, MO 64112
*"Cathy" cartoonist*

**Gumbel, Bryant**
30 Rockefeller Plaza
New York, NY 10020
*"Today Show" host*

**Guns N' Roses**
9130 Sunset Blvd.
Los Angeles, CA 90069
*Rock group*

**Guthrie, Arlo**
The Farm
Washington, MA 01223
*Singer, songwriter*

**Guttenberg, Steve**
9830 Wilshire Blvd.
Beverly Hills, CA 90212
*Actor*

**Guy, Jasmine**
14755 Ventura Blvd., #1-710
Sherman Oaks, CA 91403
*Actress, singer, dancer*

News from home is best carried in a letter, and so much can be written on a little piece of paper. Inside the envelope can be sunshine or dark dismal days.

—HANS CHRISTIAN ANDERSEN

**H & R Block, Inc.**
4410 Main St.
Kansas City, MO 64111
Henry W. Bloch, Chairman and
    CEO
*America's largest tax preparer*

**H. F. Ahmanson & Co.**
660 S. Figueroa St.
Los Angeles, CA 90017
Richard H. Deihl, Chairman
    and CEO
*Largest savings and loan
    organization*

**H. J. Heinz Company**
600 Grant St.
Pittsburgh, PA 15219
Anthony J. F. O'Reilly,
    Chairman, President and
    CEO
*One of the world's leading food
    processing companies*

**Häagen-Dazs Company Inc.**
Glen Pointe
Teaneck, NJ 07666
Michael L. Bailey, President
*Ice cream manufacturer*

**Habyarimana, Major General
    Juvenal**
Président de la République
Kigali, Rwanda
*President of Rwanda*

**Hackford, Taylor**
9830 Wilshire Blvd.
Beverly Hills, CA 90212
*Film director*

**Haggard, Merle**
P.O. Box 536
Palo Cedro, CA 96073
*Singer*

**Hagley Museum & Library,
    The**
P.O. Box 3630
Wilmington, DE 19807
Glenn Porter, CEO
*Textile, patent and business
    technology museum*

**Hailey, Arthur**
1st Canada Pl., Box 130, #3400
Toronto, Ontario M5X1A4
    Canada
*Author*

**Haim, Corey**
9000 Sunset Blvd., #1200
Los Angeles, CA 90069
*Actor*

**Haje, Khrystyne**
P.O. Box 8750
Universal City, CA 91608
*Actress*

**HAL, Inc.**
1164 Bishop St., P.O. Box 30008
Honolulu, HI 96820
John A. Ueberroth, Chairman
and CEO
*Parent company of Hawaiian
Airlines and the West Maui
Airport*

**Halberstam, David**
c/o William Morrow & Co.
105 Madison Ave.
New York, NY 10016
*Journalist, author*

**Hale, Barbara**
P.O. Box 1980
N. Hollywood, CA 91604
*Actress, Perry Mason's loyal
secretary*

**Haley, Jack, Jr.**
8255 Beverly Blvd.
Los Angeles, CA 90048
*Director, producer, writer*

**Hall, Arsenio**
c/o Paramount Television
5555 Melrose Avenue
Hollywood, CA 90038
*Talk show host*

**Hall, Deirdre**
9000 Sunset Blvd., #1200
Los Angeles, CA 90069
*Soap opera queen*

**Hall, Sir Peter Reginald
Frederick**
18 Exeter St.
London WC2E 7DU England
*Theater, opera and film director*

**Hall & Oates**
130 W. 57th St., #2A
New York, NY 10019
*Singing duo*

**Hall of History**
Boys Town, NE 68010
Joan L. Flinspach, Director
*Father Flanagan's history*

**Halliburton Company**
3600 Lincoln Plaza
Dallas, TX 75201
Thomas H. Cruikshank,
Chairman and CEO
*One of the world's leading oil field
engineering and construction
services*

**Hallmark Cards**
2501 McGee Trafficway,
#419580
Kansas City, MO 64141
Irvine O. Hockaday, Jr., Chief
Executive Officer
*Greeting card company*

**Halprin, Anna Schuman**
810 Cole Ave., #10
Kentfield, CA 94904
*Dancer, choreographer*

**Hamaker, Ronald C.**
1633 N. Capitol Ave., #780
Indianapolis, IN 46202
*Surgeon specializing in voice
restoration for larynx cancer
patients*

**Hamill, Dorothy**
8730 Sunset Blvd., 6th Fl.
Los Angeles, CA 90069
*Ice skater, actress*

**Hamill, Mark**
P.O. Box 124
Malibu, CA 90265
*Actor*

**Hamilton, Donald Bengtsson**
P.O. Box 1045
Santa Fe, NM 87504
*Author*

**Hamilton, Linda**
10100 Santa Monica Blvd.,
  16th Fl.
Los Angeles, CA 90067
*Actress*

**Hamilton, Scott Scovell**
c/o M. Sterling
455 Westmount Dr.
Los Angeles, CA 90048
*Professional figure skater, Olympic
  medalist*

**Hamlin, Harry**
P.O. Box 25578
Los Angeles, CA 90025
*Actor*

**Hammer
(formerly M.C.)**
1750 N. Vine St.
Hollywood, CA 90028
*Rapper*

**Hammer, The
(Greg Valentine)**
P.O. Box 3857
Stamford, CT 06905
*Professional wrestler*

**Hammons, Roger**
Primitive Advent Christian
  Church
395 Frame Rd.
Elkview, WV 25071
*Religious group president*

**Hampden-Booth Theatre
  Library at the Players**
16 Gramercy Park S.
New York, NY 10003
Wilfred J. Halpern, CEO
*Theater museum and library*

**Hampton, Rev. Ralph**
Free Will Baptists
P.O. Box 1088
Nashville, TN 27202
*Religious leader*

**Handford, Martin**
c/o Little, Brown and Company
1271 Ave. of the Americas
New York, NY 10019
Where's Waldo *author*

**Hanks, Tom**
P.O. Box 1276
Los Angeles, CA 90049
*Actor*

**Harewood, Dorian**
9169 Sunset Blvd.
Los Angeles, CA 90069
*Actor*

**Harkin, Tom**
531 Senate Hart Office Bldg.
Washington, DC 20510
*Senator from Iowa*

**Harlem Globetrotters**
6121 Sunset Blvd.
Los Angeles, CA 90038
*Comedy basketball team*

**Harley-Davidson Inc.**
3700 W. Juneau Ave.
Milwaukee, WI 53208
Vaughn Le Roy Beals, Jr.,
   President
*Last American motorcycle company*


**Harman, Willard Nelson**
RD #2, Box 1066
Cooperstown, NY 13326
*Malacologist*


**Harp, Rufus William**
915 N. Citrus Ave.
Hollywood, CA 90038
*Set decorator*


**Harper, Derek**
c/o Dallas Mavericks
777 Sports St.
Dallas, TX 75207
*Professional basketball player*


**Harper, Ron**
c/o Los Angeles Clippers
3939 S. Figueroa
Los Angeles, CA 90037
*Professional basketball player*


**Harper, Valerie**
P.O. Box 7187
Beverly Hills, CA 90212
*Actress*


**Harrelson, Woody**
9830 Wilshire Blvd.
Beverly Hills, CA 90212
*Actor*


**Harris, Emmylou**
P.O. Box 1384
Brentwood, TN 37027
*Singer*


**Harris, Mel**
232 N. Canon Dr.
Beverly Hills, CA 90210
*Actress*


**Harris, Mrs. Jean**
Bedford Hills Correctional
   Facility
Bedford Hills, NY 10507
*Scarsdale diet murderess*


**Harris, Neil Patrick**
11350 Ventura Blvd., #206
Studio City, CA 91604
*Actor*


**Harris Corporation**
1025 W. NASA Blvd.
Melbourne, FL 32919
John T. Hartley, Chairman,
   President and CEO
*Printing, electronics,
   semiconductors, etc.*


**Harrison, George**
Friar Park Road
Henly-On-Thames, England
*Singer, musician*


**Hart, Cecil William Joseph**
707 N. Fairbanks Ct.
Chicago, IL 60611
*Otolaryngologist*


**Hart, John Richard**
World Monitor
175 Huntington Ave., C21
Boston, MA 02115
*Journalist, TV news correspondent*


**Hart, Mary**
c/o "Entertainment Tonight"
5555 Melrose Ave.
Hollywood, CA 90038
*Host of entertainment news
   magazine show*

**Hartford Whalers**
242 Trumbull St., 8th Fl.
Hartford, CT 06103
Eddie Johnston, Vice-President/
    General Manager
*Professional hockey team*

**Harth, Robert**
Music Associates of Aspen
P.O. Box AA
Aspen, CO 81612
*President and CEO*

**Harth, Sidney**
c/o Sheldon Souffer Mgmt.
130 W. 56th St.
New York, NY 10019
*Violinist, conductor, educator*

**Hartman, Lisa**
15301 Ventura Blvd., #345
Sherman Oaks, CA 91403
*Actress, singer*

**Hartmarx Corporation**
101 N. Wacker Dr.
Chicago, IL 60606
Harvey A. Weinberg, Chairman
    and CEO
*Manufactures and retails clothing*

**Hartsfield, Henry Warren, Jr.**
NASA Flight Crew Operations,
    Code CA
Lyndon B. Johnson Space
    Center
Houston, TX 77058
*Astronaut*

**Harvard University**
1350 Massachusetts Ave.
Cambridge, MA 02138
Neil L. Rudenstine, President

**Harvey, Paul**
333 N. Michigan Ave.
Chicago, IL 60601
*News commentator, author,
    columnist*

**Hasbro Inc.**
1027 Newport Avenue
Pawtucket, RI 02862
Alan G. Hassenfeld, Chairman,
    President and CEO
*Toy and game manufacturer*

**Haskins, George Lee**
University of Pennsylvania Law
    School
3400 Chestnut St.
Philadelphia, PA 19104
*Lawyer, educator*

**Hassanali, Noor Mohammed**
President's House
St. Ann's, Trinidad and Tobago
*President of Trinidad and Tobago*

**Hatch, Orrin G.**
135 Senate Russell Office Bldg.
Washington, DC 20501
*Senator from Utah*

**Hatfield, Mark O.**
711 Senate Hart Office Bldg.
Washington, DC 20501
*Senator from Oregon*

**Haughey, Charles J.**
Abbeville, Kinsealy
County Dublin, Ireland
*Taoiseach (Prime Minister) of
    Ireland*

**Havel, Vaclav**
Kancelar prezidenta republiky
11908 Praha-Hradcany
Prague, Czechoslovakia
*Former president of Czechoslovakia*

**Havers, Nigel**
9320 Wilshire Blvd., 3rd Fl.
Beverly Hills, CA 90212
*Actor, King of Masterpiece Theatre
mini-series*

**Hawke, Robert J. L.**
Parliament House
Canberra, A.C.T., Australia
*Prime Minister of Australia*

**Hawkins, Joseph Elmer**
University of Michigan Medical
School
Kresge Hearing Research
Institute
Ann Arbor, MI 48109
*Acoustic physiologist*

**Hawkins, Sophie B.**
51 W. 52nd St.
New York, NY 10019
*Singer*

**Hayes, Susan Seaforth**
9113 Sunset Blvd.
Los Angeles, CA 90069
*Actress*

**Hays, David Arthur**
National Theatre of the Deaf
Hazel E. Stark Center
Chester, CT 06412
*Theater producer, stage designer*

**Headline News**
(a division of CNN)
One CNN Center, P.O. Box
105366
Atlanta, GA 30348-5366
W. Thomas Johnson, President
*Syndicated world and national
news briefs*

**Headly, Glenne**
8899 Beverly Blvd.
Los Angeles, CA 90048
*Actress*

**Heard Museum, The**
22 E. Monte Vista Rd.
Phoenix, AZ 85004
Martin Sullivan, Director

**Hearns, Thomas**
c/o E. Steward
19600 W. McNichol St.
Detroit, MI 48219
*Boxer*

**Hearst Corporation, The**
959 Eighth Ave.
New York, NY 10019
Randolph A. Hearst, Chairman
*A privately owned diversified media
company*

**Hearst San Simeon State
Historical Monument**
750 Hearst Castle Rd.
San Simeon, CA 93452
Deborah A. Weldon, CEO
*American castle*

**Heckerling, Amy**
232 N. Canon Dr.
Beverly Hills, CA 90210
*Film director*

**Heflin, Howell**
728 Senate Hart Office Bldg.
Washington, DC 20510
*Senator from Alabama*

**Hefner, Hugh**
10236 Charing Cross Rd.
Los Angeles, CA 90024
*Playboy mogul*

**Helgenberger, Marg**
232 N. Canon Dr.
Beverly Hills, CA 90210
*Actress*

**Heller, Joseph**
c/o Simon & Schuster
1230 Ave. of the Americas
New York, NY 10020
*Writer*

**Helmond, Katherine**
151 El Camino
Beverly Hills, CA 90212
*Actress*

**Helms, Jesse A.**
403 Senate Dirksen Office Bldg.
Washington, DC 20510
*Senator from North Carolina*

**Helmsley, Leona**
c/o Harry Helmsley
36 Central Park S.
New York, NY 10019
*Queen of Mean, currently in prison in Connecticut*

**Helmsley Enterprises Inc.**
60 E. 42nd St.
New York, NY 10165
Harry Helmsley, President
*Real estate, hotel, and shipping holding company*

**Heloise**
P.O. Box 795000
San Antonio, TX 78279
*Columnist, lecturer, author*

**Helwig, Elson Bowman**
Armed Forces Institute of Pathology
Washington, DC 20305
*Pathologist*

**Hemingway, Mariel**
8899 Beverly Blvd.
Los Angeles, CA 90048
*Actress*

**Henderson, Florence**
9000 Sunset Blvd., #1200
Los Angeles, CA 90069
*Actress, singer, Brady Bunch mom*

**Henderson, Rickey**
c/o Oakland Athletics
Oakland-Alameda County Stadium
Oakland, CA 94621
*Professional baseball player*

**Henley, Don**
9130 Sunset Blvd.
Los Angeles, CA 90069
*Singer/songwriter*

**Henley Group, Inc., The**
Liberty Ln.
Hampton, NH 03842
Michael D. Dingman, Chairman and CEO
*Fisher Scientific, Pneumo Abex, etc.*

**Henning, Doug**
11940 San Vicente Blvd., #49032
Los Angeles, CA 90049
*Magician*

**Henry, Marguerite**
c/o Macmillan Publishing Co.
866 Third Ave.
New York, NY 10022
*Author*

**Henry Ford Museum & Greenfield Village**
P.O. Box 1970
Dearborn, MI 48121
Harold K. Skranstad, Jr., President and CEO

**Henshel, Harry Bulova**
1 Bulova Ave.
Woodside, NY 11377
*Watch manufacturer*

**Herbert Hoover Presidential
Library—Museum**
P.O. Box 488
West Branch, IA 52358
Richard Norton Smith, Director

**Hercules Inc.**
Hercules Plaza
1313 N. Market St.
Wilmington, DE 19894
Thomas L. Gossage, Chairman
  and CEO
*Chemicals, aerospace, etc.*

**Herman, Pee-Wee
(Paul Reubens)**
P.O. Box 48243
Los Angeles, CA 90048
*Comic actor*

**Herrmann, Lacy Bunnell**
200 Park Ave.
New York, NY 10017
*Venture capitalist*

**Hershey, Barbara**
9830 Wilshire Blvd.
Beverly Hills, CA 90212
*Actress*

**Hershey Foods Corporation**
100 Mansion Road E.
Hershey, PA 17033
R. A. Zimmerman, Chairman
  and CEO
*Chocolate manufacturers*

**Hertz Corporation, The**
225 Brae Blvd.
Park Ridge, NJ 07656
Frank A. Olson, Chairman,
  CEO and COO
*The first car rental company*

**Hervey, Jason**
9200 Sunset Blvd., #625
Los Angeles, CA 90069
*Actor*

**Hewes, Henry**
1326 Madison Ave.
New York, NY 10028
*Drama critic*

**Hewitt, Don S.**
CBS News
524 W. 57th St.
New York, NY 10019
*"60 Minutes" producer*

**Hewitt, Love**
1901 Ave. of the Stars, 16th Fl.
Los Angeles, CA 90067
*Singer, actress*

**Hewlett-Packard Company**
3000 Hanover St.
Palo Alto, CA 94304
David Packard, Chairman
*Manufactures computers and
  electronic components*

**Heyerdahl, Thor**
Hullen Meadows
Ketchum, ID 83340
*Author, explorer*

**Hickel, Walter J.**
P.O. Box A
Juneau, AK 99811
*Governor of Alaska*

**Hickman, John Hampton III**
Mount Morris Rd.
Geneseo, NY 14454
*Entrepreneurial industrialist*

**Higgins, Jack**
Septembertide
Mont De Rocque
Jersey, Channel Islands, United
  Kingdom
*Author*

**Highlights for Children**
803 Church St.
Honedale, PA 18431
Kent L. Brown, Jr., Editor
*Waiting room magazine*

**Highwater, Jamake**
Native Lands Foundation
Rte. 97
Hampton, CT 06247
*Author, lecturer*

**Hill, Anita**
University of Oklahoma
School of Law
Norman, OK 73069
*Clarence Thomas accuser*

**Hill, Draper**
Detroit News
615 W. Lafayette Blvd.
Detroit, MI 48231
*Editorial cartoonist*

**Hill, Walter**
8899 Beverly Blvd.
Los Angeles, CA 90048
*Film director*

**Hilleman, Maurice Ralph**
Merck, Sharp & Dohme
   Research Labs
West Point, PA 19486
*Virus research scientist*

**Hills, Beverlee**
P.O. Box 24465
San Diego, CA 92124
*Stripper*

**Hilton Hotels Corporation**
9336 Civic Center Dr.
Beverly Hills, CA 90209
Barron Hilton, Chairman,
   President and CEO

**Himmell, Richard**
1729 Merchandise Mart
Chicago, IL 60654
*Interior designer, writer*

**Hines, Gregory**
9830 Wilshire Blvd.
Beverly Hills, CA 90212
*Dancer, actor*

**Hintikka, Jaako**
Institute of Philosophy
Unioninkatu 40B
SF 100170 Helsinki, Finland
*Philosopher, educator*

**Hinton, Bruce C.**
MCA Records
1514 South St.
Nashville, TN 37212
*Record company executive*

**Hinton, S. E.
(Susan Eloise)**
8955 Beverly Blvd.
Los Angeles, CA 90048
*Author*

**Hirsch, Judd**
P.O. Box 25909
Los Angeles, CA 90025
*Actor*

**Hirshenson, Janet**
The Casting Company
8925 Venice Blvd.
Los Angeles, CA 90034
*Film casting director*

**Historic Annapolis
   Foundation**
194 Prince George St.
Annapolis, MD 21401
Joseph M. Coale III, President
*Naval Academy Museum*

**Historic New Orleans Collection, The**
533 Royal St.
New Orleans, LA 70130
Dode Platou, Director

**Hit Man, The
(Brett Hart)**
P.O. Box 3857
Stamford, CT 06905
*Professional wrestler*

**Ho, Don
(Donald Tai Loy)**
Hilton Hawaiian Village
2005 Kalia Rd.
Honolulu, HI 96815
*Singer*

**Hochstadt, Joy**
Princeton Polymer Labs
501 Plainsboro Rd.
Plainsboro, NJ 08036
*Biomedical research scientist*

**Hoffman, Dustin**
9830 Wilshire Blvd.
Beverly Hills, CA 90212
*Actor*

**Hoffmann, Cecil**
9200 Sunset Blvd., #625
Los Angeles, CA 90069
*Actress*

**Hogan, Hulk
(Terry Gene Bollea)**
P.O. Box 3859
Stamford, CT 06905
*Professional wrestling champion*

**Hogestyn, Drake**
9255 Sunset Blvd., #315
Los Angeles, CA 90069
*Actor*

**Holbrook, Hal**
244 W. 54th St., #707
New York, NY 10019
*Actor*

**Hollings, Ernest F.**
125 Senate Russell Office Bldg.
Washington, DC 20510
*Senator from South Carolina*

**Holloway, Sterling Price**
P.O. Box 38001
Los Angeles, CA 90038
*Actor, recording artist*

**Hollywood Pictures**
500 S. Buena Vista St.
Burbank, CA 91521
Richard Mestres, President
*Movie production company*

**Hollywood Reporter, The**
6715 Sunset Blvd., #612
Hollywood, CA 90028
Tichi Wilkerson Kassel,
   Publisher
*Daily "trade" publication*

**Hollywood Studio Museum**
2100 N. Highland Ave.
Hollywood, CA 90069
Richard A. Adkins, Executive
   Director
*Film museum*

**Holt, Victoria
(Eleanor Alice Burford
   Hibbert)**
c/o A. M. Heath
40 Williams IV Street
London WC2N 4DD England
*Romance novelist*

**Holzer, Hans**
140 Riverside Dr.
New York, NY 10024
*Parapsychologist, author*

**Home Box Office, Inc.
(HBO)**
1100 Ave. of the Americas
New York, NY 10036
Michael Fuchs, Chairman/CEO
*Premium cable movie channel*

**Home Depot, Inc., The**
2727 Paces Ferry Rd.
Atlanta, GA 30339
Bernard Marcus, Chairman,
    CEO and Secretary
*Home improvement supply stores*

**Honeywell Inc.**
Honeywell Plaza
Minneapolis, MN 55408
James J. Renier, Chairman and
    CEO
*World's leading producer of
    industrial control systems*

**Honig, Edwin**
Brown University
Box 1852
Providence, RI 02912
*Comparative literature educator,
    poet*

**Hooks, Jan**
10100 Santa Monica Blvd.,
    16th Fl.
Los Angeles, CA 90067
*Actress*

**Hooks, Valerie Brisco**
P.O. Box 21053
Long Beach, CA 90801
*Athlete*

**Hope, Bob**
3808 Riverside Dr.
Burbank, CA 91505
*Comedian*

**Hopkins, Anthony Philip**
c/o Jeremy Conway
Eagle House
109 Jermyn St.
London SW1 6HB England
*Actor*

**Hopper, Dennis**
9830 Wilshire Blvd.
Beverly Hills, CA 90212
*Actor, director*

**Horatio Alger Society**
4907 Allison Dr.
Lansing, MI 48910
Carl T. Hartmann, Secretary
*Rags to riches society*

**Horowitz, David**
P.O. Box 49915
Los Angeles, CA 90049
*"Fight Back" consumer activist*

**Horowitz, Lewis Jay**
New York Futures Exchange
20 Broad St., 10th Fl.
New York, NY 10005
*Stock exchange executive*

**Horsford, Anna Maria**
P.O. Box 29765
Los Angeles, CA 90029
*Actress*

**Horsley, Lee**
1999 Ave. of the Stars, #2850
Los Angeles, CA 90067
*Actor*

**Hoskins, Bob**
9830 Wilshire Blvd.
Beverly Hills, CA 90212
*Actor*

**Hospital Corporation of America**
One Park Plaza
Nashville, TN 37203
Thomas F. Frist, Jr., Chairman, President and CEO
*Operates 75 medical/surgical and 53 psychiatric hospitals*

**Hotchner, Aaron Edward**
14 Hillandale Rd.
Westport, CT 06880
*Author, Hemingway expert*

**Houphouet-Boigny, Felix**
Présidence de la République
Abidjan, Côte d'Ivoire
*President of Côte d'Ivoire*

**Household International, Inc.**
2700 Sanders Rd.
Prospect Heights, IL 60070
Donald C. Clark, Chairman and CEO
*A financial services company*

**Houston, Whitney**
410 E. 50th St.
New York, NY 10022
*Singer*

**Houston Astros**
P.O. Box 288
Houston, TX 77001
Bill Wood, General Manager
*Professional baseball team*

**Houston Oilers**
6910 Fannin St.
Houston, TX 77030
Mike Holovak, General Manager
*Professional football team*

**Houston Rockets**
The Summit
Houston, TX 77046
Ray Patterson, President
*Professional basketball team*

**Howard, Desmond**
c/o Michigan State University Athletic Department
East Lansing, MI 48824
*1991 Heisman Trophy winner, received more votes than any other recipient*

**Howard, Ron**
9830 Wilshire Blvd.
Beverly Hills, CA 90212
*Director, actor*

**Howell, C. Thomas**
9830 Wilshire Blvd.
Beverly Hills, CA 90212
*Actor*

**Hoyt, Herbert Austin Aikins**
WGBH
125 Western Ave.
Boston, MA 02134
*PBS TV producer*

**Hoyt, William F., Dr.**
University of California, San Francisco
San Francisco, CA 94143
*"Dean" of American neuro-ophthalmology*

**Hrawi, Elias**
Office of the President
Beirut, Lebanon
*President of Lebanon*

**Hsu, Chen Chao**
U.S. Army Chemical Research,
Development & Engineering
Ctr.
Aberdeen Proving Ground, MD
21001
*Chemist*

**Hudson, Eleanor**
c/o Random House Children's
Books
201 E. 50th St.
New York, NY 10022
*Author*

**Hudson Soft**
400 Oyster Point Blvd., #515
S. San Francisco, CA 94080
*Electronic game software
manufacturer*

**Huffy Corp.**
P.O. Box 1204
Miamisburg, OH 45401
Harry A. Shaw III, President
*Bicycle manufacturer*

**Hug-A-Tree and Survive**
6465 Lance Way
San Diego, CA 92120
Jacquie Beveridge,
Administrator
*Survival techniques for kids*

**Hughes, John**
100 Universal City Plaza, #507
Universal City, CA 91608
*Film writer, producer, director*

**Humana Inc.**
P.O. Box 1438, 500 W. Main St.
Louisville, KY 40202
David A. Jones, Chairman and
CEO
*Largest U.S. hospital chain*

**Hunger Project, The**
One Madison Ave., #8A
New York, NY 10010
Joan Holmes, Executive Director

**Hungerford, David S.**
Good Samaritan Hospital
Professional Office Bldg., G1
5601 Lock Raven Blvd.
Baltimore, MD 21239
*Orthopedic surgeon*

**Hunt, Guy**
State Capitol
Montgomery, AL 36130
*Governor of Alabama*

**Hunt, Helen**
9830 Wilshire Blvd.
Beverly Hills, CA 90212
*Actress*

**Hunter, Tab**
Box 1048, La Tierra Nueva
Santa Fe, NM 87501
*50's/60's heartthrob*

**Huntington Library**
Art Collections and Botanical
Gardens
1151 Oxford Rd.
San Marino, CA 91108
R. Stanton Avery, Chairman,
Board of Trustees

**Huntsville Museum of Art**
700 Monroe St., SW
Huntsville, AL 35301
David M. Robb, Jr., Director and
CEO

**Hurt, William**
RD 1, Box 251A
Palisades, NY 10964
*Actor*

**Husa, Karel Jaroslav**
Cornell University Department
  of Music
Ithaca, NY 14853
*Composer, conductor, educator*

**Hussein, Saddam**
Revolutionary Command
  Council
Baghdad, Iraq
*President of Iraq*

**Hussein I, King**
Royal Palace
Amman, Jordan
*Ruler of Jordan*

**Huston, Anjelica**
151 El Camino
Beverly Hills, CA 90212
*Actress*

**Hutton, Lauren**
9830 Wilshire Blvd.
Beverly Hills, CA 90212
*Actress, model*

**Hutton, Timothy**
10100 Santa Monica Blvd.,
  #1600
Los Angeles, CA 90067
*Actor*

**Hyams, Joe**
c/o St. Martin's Press
175 Fifth Ave.
New York, NY 10010
*Writer*

**Hyatt, Missy**
P.O. Box 105366
Atlanta, GA 30348
*Professional wrestler*

**Hyatt Corporation**
200 W. Madison
Chicago, IL 60606
Jay Pritzker, Chairman and
  CEO
*Hotel chain*

# I

Persons do not become a society by living in physical proximity, any more than a man ceases to be socially influenced by being so many feet or miles removed from others. A letter may institute a more intimate association between human beings separated thousands of miles from each other than exists between dwellers under the same roof.

—JOHN DEWEY

**Ice Skating Institute of America**
1000 Skokie Blvd.
Wilmette, IL 60091
Justine Townsend Smith, Executive Director

**Ice-T**
c/o Sire Records
75 Rockefeller Plaza
New York, NY 10019
*Rap singer*

**Idaho State Historical Museum**
610 N. Julia Davis Dr.
Boise, ID 83702
Kenneth J. Swanson, Administrator

**Iliescu, Ion**
Office of the President
Bucharest, Romania
*President of Romania*

**Imagine Films Entertainment, Inc.**
1925 Century Park E., #2300
Los Angeles, CA 90067
Brian Grazer, Ron Howard, Co-Chairman
*Film production company*

**Iman**
11726 San Vicente Blvd., #201
Los Angeles, CA 90049
*Model, actress*

**Incest Survivors Anonymous**
P.O. Box 5613
Long Beach, CA 90805

**Independent Fundamental Churches of America**
2684 Meadow Ridge Dr.
Bryon Center, MI 49315
Dr. Richard Gregory, National Executive Director
*Religious group*

**Indian Museum of North America**
Avenue of the Chiefs, Black Hills
Crazy Horse, SD 57730
Anne Ziolkowski Davidson, Executive Director

**Indian State Museum**
202 N. Albama St.
Indianapolis, IN 46204
Lee Scott Theisen, Ph.D., CEO

**Indiana Pacers**
Market Square Arena
300 East Market St.
Indianapolis, IN 46204
Donnie Walsh, President
*Professional basketball team*

**Indianapolis Colts**
7001 W. 56th St.
P.O. Box 535000
Indianapolis, IN 46254
James Irsay, Vice-President/
General Manager
*Professional football team*

**Ingersoll-Rand Company**
200 Chestnut Ridge Rd.
Woodcliff Lake, NJ 07675
Theodore H. Black, Chairman,
President and CEO
*Major international producer of
industrial machinery and
equipment*

**Ink Spots, The**
1385 York Ave., #15H
New York, NY 10021
*Singing group*

**Inland Steel Industries, Inc.**
30 W. Monroe St.
Chicago, IL 60603
Frank W. Luerssen, Chairman
and CEO
*Produces high strength, low alloy
steel*

**Inouye, Daniel K.**
722 Senate Hart Office Bldg.
Washington, DC 20510
*Senator from Hawaii*

**Institute of Meteoritics**
Meteorite Museum
University of New Mexico
Albuquerque, NM 87131
Dr. James J. Papike, Director

**Institute of Totally Useless
Skills**
20 Richmond St.
Dover, NH 03820
Rick Davis, Master of
Uselessness

**Intel Corporation**
3065 Bowers Ave.
Santa Clara, CA 95052
Andrew S. Grove, President and
CEO
*Third largest U.S. semiconductor
manufacturer*

**Interco Inc.**
101 S. Hanley Rd.
St. Louis, MO 63105
Richard B. Loynd, Chairman,
President and CEO
*Broyhill Lane, Converse and
Florsheim; in Chapter 11*

**Intergraph Corporation**
Huntsville, AL 35894
James W. Meadlock, Chairman
and CEO
*Produces computer peripherals and
software*

**International Airline
Passengers Association**
4341 Lindburg Dr.
Dallas, TX 75244
James E. Dunne II, Chairman

**International Anti-
Counterfeiting Coalition**
818 Connecticut Ave., NW,
12th Fl.
Washington, DC 20006
*Group against counterfeited
machinery and parts*

**International Association of Professional Bureaucrats**
National Press Bldg.
Washington, DC 20045
Dr. James H. Boren, President
*Motto: "When in doubt, mumble."*

**International Association of Psychosocial Rehabilitation Services**
P.O. Box 278
McLean, VA 22101
Robert C. Vandiver, Executive Director

**International Business Machines Corporation**
Old Orchard Rd.
Armonk, NY 10504
John F. Akers, Chairman
*Largest computer maker in the world*

**International Center of Photography**
1130 Fifth Ave.
New York, NY 10128
Cornell Capa, Director

**International Cheerleading Foundation**
10660 Barkley
Shawnee Mission, KS 66212
Randolph L. Neil, President

**International Chili Society**
P.O. Box 2966
Newport Beach, CA 92663
Jim West, Executive Director
*Sponsors cook-offs*

**International Churchill Society**
P.O. Box 385A
Hopkinton, NH 03229
*Preserving Sir Winston's memory and teaching the next generation*

**International Concerns Committee for Children**
911 Cypress Drive
Boulder, CO 80303
AnnaMarie Merrill, Treasurer
*International adoptions*

**International Flavors & Fragrances Inc.**
521 W. 57th St.
New York, NY 10019
Eugene P. Grisanti, Chairman and President
*World's leading independent producer of synthetic tastes and smells*

**International Friendship League**
55 Mount Vernon Street
Boston, MA 02108
Margaret MacDonough, Executive Director
*Pen pal organization*

**International Gymnastic Hall of Fame**
227 Brooks Street
Oceanside, CA 92054
Glenn M. Sundby, Director

**International Hockey Hall of Fame and Museum**
York and Alfred Sts.
Box 82
Kingston, Ontario K7L 4V6
Canada
Doug Nichols, Executive Director

**International Organization of Nerds**
P.O. Box 118555
Cincinnati, OH 45211
Bruce L. Chapman, Supreme Archnerd

**International Paper Company**
Two Manhattanville Rd.
Purchase, NY 10577
John A. Georges, Chairman and CEO
*World's leading integrated paper manufacturer*

**International Professional Hunters' Association**
P.O. Box 17444
San Antonio, TX 78217
Donald Lindsay, President

**International Snow Leopard Trust**
4649 Sunnyside Ave., N
Seattle, WA 98103
Helen Freeman, President

**International Soap Box Derby**
789 Derby Downs Dr.
Akron, OH 44306
Jeff Iula, General Manager

**International Society for the Prevention of Child Abuse and Neglect**
1205 Oneida St.
Denver, CO 80220
Kim Oates, President

**International Sport Karate Association**
Box 44095
Denver, CO 80201
Karyn Turner, Commissioner
*Kickboxing association*

**International Surfing Hall of Fame**
5580 La Jolla Blvd., #373
La Jolla, CA 92037
Lois Ronaldson, President

**International Swimming Hall of Fame**
One Hall of Fame Drive
Ft. Lauderdale, FL 33316
Dr. Sam Frees, Executive Director

**International Tennis Hall of Fame and Tennis Museum**
194 Bellevue Ave.
Newport, RI 02840
William McChesney Martin, Honorary Chairman

**International Thespian Society**
3368 Central Pkwy.
Cincinnati, OH 45225
Ronald L. Longstreth, Executive Director

**International Union for Conservation of Nature and Natural Resources (IUCN), World Conservation Union**
Avenue du Mont-Blanc
CH-1196 Gland, Switzerland
Monkombu S. Swaminathan, President

**International Wizard of Oz Club, Inc.**
220 North 11th St.
Escanaba, MI 49829
Fred Meyer, Secretary

**Iron Maiden**
P.O. Box 391
London W41LZ England
*Rock group*

**Ironside, Michael**
10100 Santa Monica Blvd., #1600
Los Angeles, CA 90067
*Actor*

**I.R.S.**
**International Record
    Syndicate, Inc.**
3939 Lakershim Blvd.
Universal City, CA 91604
Miles Copeland, Chairman
*Recording company*

**Irvin, Robert Joseph**
P.O. Box 3410
Estes Park, CO 80517
*Rancher*

**Irvine, Reed**
Accuracy in Media, Inc.
1275 K Street, NW, #1150
Washington, DC 20005
*Media watchdog*

**Issel, Dan**
c/o Denver Nuggets
1635 Clay St.
Denver, CO 80204
*Basketball coach*

**ITT Corporation**
1330 Ave. of the Americas
New York, NY 10019
Rand V. Araskog, Chairman,
    President and CEO
*Broadly diversified conglomerate*

**Izaak Walton League of
    America, Inc., The**
1401 Wilson Blvd., Level B
Arlington, VA 22209
Donald L. Ferris, Chairman
*Conservation group*

**J**

Whatever happens to us in our lives, we find questions recurring that we would gladly discuss with some friend. Yet it is hard to find just the friend we should talk to. Often it is easier to *write* to someone whom we do not expect to ever see.

—Eleanor Roosevelt

**J. C. Penney Company, Inc.**
14841 N. Dallas Pkwy.
Dallas, TX 75240
William R. Howell, Chairman
   and CEO
*Largest clothing retailer in the U.S.*

**J. P. Morgan & Co. Inc.**
60 Wall St.
New York, NY 10260
Dennis Weatherstone, Chairman
   and CEO
*Arranges large-scale financing to
   governments and corporations*

**J. Paul Getty Museum, The**
17985 Pacific Coast Hwy.
Malibu, CA 90265
John Walsh, Director
*Art museum*

**Jack Eckerd Corporation**
8333 Bryan Dairy Rd.
Largo, FL 34618
Stewart Turley, Chairman,
   President and CEO
*Third largest drugstore chain in the
   U.S.*

**Jackée**
9320 Wilshire Blvd., 3rd Fl.
Beverly Hills, CA 90212
*Actress*

**Jack-in-the-Box Restaurants**
9330 Balboa Ave.
San Diego, CA 92112
Jack W. Goodall, Jr., Chairman
*Fast food chain*

**Jackson, Bo
(Vincent)**
P.O. Box 2517
Auburn, AL 36831
*Athlete*

**Jackson, Janet**
1416 N. LaBrea Ave.
Hollywood, CA 90028
*Singer*

**Jackson, Jesse Louis,
   Reverend**
930 E. 50th St.
Chicago, IL 60615
*Politician, civil rights leader*

**Jackson, Kate**
8899 Beverly Blvd.
Los Angeles, CA 90048
*Actress*

**Jackson, Michael**
KABC Radio
3321 S. La Cienega
Los Angeles, CA 90016
*Radio talk show host*

**Jackson, Michael**
1801 Century Park W.
Los Angeles, CA 90067
*Singer*

**Jackson Hole Museum**
P.O. Box 1005
Jackson, WY 83001
Robert C. Rudd, Director
*Plains Indians archives*

**Jagan, Cheddi**
Office of the President
New Garden St.
Georgetown, Guyana
*President of Guyana*

**Jakes, John**
Box 3248, Harbour Town
Station
Hilton Head Island, SC 29928
*Author*

**James Dean Memory Club**
10426 110th St.
Jamaica, NY 11416
Marie Giusti, President

**James River Corporation**
120 Tredegar St.
Richmond, VA 23219
Brenton S. Halsey, Chairman
*Produces paper towel and tissue
products (Brawny, Northern and
Gala)*

**Jarreau, Al**
c/o Patrick Rains
9034 Sunset Blvd., #250
Los Angeles, CA 90069
*Musician*

**Jawara, Sir Dawda K.**
Office of the President
Banjul, The Gambia
*President of The Gambia*

**Jeffers, Susan**
c/o Dial Books for Young
Readers
375 Hudson St.
New York, NY 10014
*Illustrator*

**Jeffords, James M.**
530 Senate Dirksen Office Bldg.
Washington, DC 20501
*Senator from Vermont*

**Jehovah's Witnesses**
25 Columbia Heights
Brooklyn, NY 11201
Frederick W. Franz, President
*Religious group*

**Jemison, Dr. T. J.**
National Baptist Convention,
U.S.A.
52 S. Sixth Ave.
Mt. Vernon, NY 10550
*President, religious organization*

**Jenkins, Jane**
The Casting Company
8925 Venice Blvd.
Los Angeles, CA 90034
*Film casting director*

**Jenner, Bruce**
P.O. Box 655
Malibu, CA 90265
*Athlete, sportscaster, sometime actor*

**Jennings, Stanford**
c/o Cincinnati Bengals
200 Riverfront Stadium
Cincinnati, OH 45202
*Professional football player*

**Jethro Tull**
12 Stratford Pl.
London W1N 9AF England
*Rock group*

**Jetsons, The**
**(George, Jane, Judy, Elroy and**
  **Astro)**
3400 Cahuenga Blvd.
West Hollywood, CA 90069
*Space-age cartoon family*

**Jillian, Ann**
151 El Camino
Beverly Hills, CA 90212
*Actress, singer, cancer spokesperson*

**Joe Public**
51 W. 52nd St.
New York, NY 10019
*Musicians*

**Joel, Billy**
**(William Martin)**
Maritime Music Inc.
200 W. 57th St.
New York, NY 10019
*Singer, songwriter*

**John, Elton**
**(Reginald Kenneth Dwight)**
c/o John Reid
32 Galena Rd.
London W6 0LT England
*Singer, songwriter*

**John Day Fossil Beds**
  **National Monument**
420 W. Main St.
John Day, OR 97845
B. Ladd, Superintendent

**John E. Allen, Inc.**
**Motion Picture Archives**
116 North Ave.
Park Ridge, NJ 07656
John E. Allen, Archivist
*Archive of films and memorabilia*
  *1896–1955*

**John F. Kennedy Presidential**
  **Library—Museum**
Columbia Point
Boston, MA 02125
Charles U. Daly, Director

**John Hancock Mutual Life**
  **Insurance Co.**
P.O. Box 111
Boston, MA 02117
E. James Morton, Chairman and
  CEO
*Life insurance company*

**John Nicholas Brown Center**
  **for the Study of American**
  **Civilization, The**
357 Benefit St.
Providence, RI 02903
Robert P. Emlen, Executive
  Director

**Johnson, Anne-Marie**
12700 Ventura Blvd., #350
Studio City, CA 91604
*Actress*

**Johnson, Betsey Lee**
209 W. 38th St.
New York, NY 10018
*Fashion designer*

**Johnson, Earvin "Magic"**
c/o First Team Marketing
1801 Ave. of the Stars
Los Angeles, CA 90067
*Lakers basketball star, fund-raiser*
  *for various charities and HIV*
  *spokesperson*

**Johnson, Georgann**
232 N. Canon Dr.
Beverly Hills, CA 90210
*Actress*

**Johnson, Kevin**
c/o Phoenix Suns
P.O. Box 1369
Phoenix, AZ 85001
*Professional basketball player*

**Johnson, Lady Bird**
LBJ Library
2313 Red River
Austin, TX 78705
*Former First Lady*

**Johnson, Rev. Ora J.**
General Association of General
    Baptists
100 Stinson Dr.
Poplar Bluff, MO 63901
*Religious leader*

**Johnson & Johnson**
One Johnson & Johnson Plaza
New Brunswick, NJ 08933
Ralph S. Larsen, Chairman and
    CEO
*Consumer products,
    pharmaceuticals, etc.*

**Johnson & Son, Inc., S. C.**
1525 Howe St.
Racine, WI 53403
Samuel C. Johnson, Chairman
*Raid, Off! and Pledge*

**Johnson Controls, Inc.**
5757 N. Green Bay Ave.,
    P.O. Box 591
Milwaukee, WI 53201
James H. Keyes, President and
    CEO
*Thermostat makers*

**Johnson Publishing
    Company, Inc.**
820 S. Michigan Ave.
Chicago, IL 60605
John H. Johnson, Chairman
    and CEO
Linda Johnson Rice, President
    and CEO
*Publishes* Ebony *and* Jet *and also
    makes Duke and Raveen hair
    care products*

**Johnson-Masters, Virginia E.**
24 S. Kings Highway
St. Louis, MO 63108
*Sexual psychologist*

**Johnston, J. Bennett**
136 Senate Hart Office Bldg.
Washington, DC 20510
*Senator from Louisiana*

**Jones, Brereton**
State Capitol
Frankfort, KY 40601
*Governor of Kentucky*

**Jones, Charlie**
8080 E. Paseo Grande
La Jolla, CA 92037
*Sportscaster for Super Bowl I.*

**Jones, Chuck**
P.O. Box 2319
Costa Mesa, CA 92628
*Cartoonist*

**Jones, Jack**
8019½ Melrose Ave., Suite 3
Los Angeles, CA 90046
*Singer*

**Jones, James Earl**
P.O. Box 55337
Sherman Oaks, CA 91413
*Actor*

**Jones, Quincy**
P.O. Box 48249
Los Angeles, CA 90048
*Composer, producer*

**Jones, Richard Wallace**
220 Central Park S.
New York, NY 10019
*Interior designer*

**Jones, Shirley**
c/o Roy Gerber
500 Vernon Ave.
Venice, CA 90291
*Actress, singer*

**Jones, Tommy Lee**
Box 966
San Saba, TX 76877
*Actor*

**Jones, William Bowdoin**
4807 17th St., NW
Washington, DC 20011
*Political scientist, retired diplomat*

**Jordan, Brian**
c/o St. Louis Cardinals
Busch Stadium
St. Louis, MO 63102
*Professional baseball player*

**Jordan, Michael**
c/o Chicago Bulls
980 North Michigan Ave.,
#1600
Chicago, IL 60611
*Professional basketball player*

**Jose, Felix**
c/o St. Louis Cardinals
Busch Stadium
St. Louis, MO 63102
*Professional baseball player*

**Journey**
P.O. Box 404
San Francisco, CA 94101
*Musicians*

**Judah L. Magnes Memorial Museum**
2911 Russell St.
Berkeley, CA 94705
Seymour Fromer, Director
*Museum of western Jewish history*

**Judds, The**
P.O. Box 17087
Nashville, TN 37217
*Country duo no longer singing together*

**Judy Garland Fan Club**
153 Fifth St.
Lock Haven, PA 17745

**Juggler's World**
International Jugglers
Association
Box 443
Davidson, NC 28036
Bill Giduz, Editor
*Magazine*

**Jugnauth, Aneerood**
Government House
Port Louis, Mauritius
*Prime Minister of Mauritius*

**Just Say No Clubs**
"Just Say No" Foundation
1777 N. California Blvd., #210
Walnut Creek, CA 94596
Ivy Cohen, Executive Director
*Anti-drug organization*

**Justice, Sid**
P.O. Box 3857
Stamford, CT 06905
*Professional wrestler*

**JWP Inc.**
2975 Westchester Ave.
Purchase, NY 10577
Andrew T. Dwyer, Chairman
and President
*Self-styled world's premier technical services company*

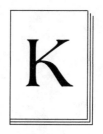

As long as there are postmen, life will have zest.

—WILLIAM JAMES

**Kachru, Braj Behari and
    Yamuna**
University of Illinois
    Department of Linguistics
Urbana, IL 61801
*Husband and wife linguists*

**Kaiser, Robert Greeley**
Washington Post Company
1150 15th St., NW
Washington, DC 20071
*Author, newspaper editor*

**Kalember, Patricia**
P.O. Box 5617
Beverly Hills, CA 90210
*Actress*

**Kalton, Robert Rankin**
Box 65, RR 2
Webster City, IA 50595
*Crop scientist*

**Kamen, Michael**
Cornell University Department
    of History
McGraw Hall
Ithaca, NY 14853
*Educator, historian*

**Kaminsky, Stuart**
Northwestern University
School of Speech
Evanston, IL 60201
*Film professor, writer and mystery
    novelist*

**Kane, Margaret Brassler**
30 Strickland Rd.
Cos Cob, CT 06807
*Sculptor*

**Kansas City Chiefs**
One Arrowhead Dr.
Kansas City, MO 64129
Carl Peterson, President/
    General Manager
*Professional football team*

**Kansas City Royals**
P.O. Box 419969
Kansas City, MO 64141
John Schuerholz, Executive
    Vice-President/General
    Manager
*Professional baseball team*

**Kanter, Hal**
Harper Associates
13063 Ventura Blvd.
Studio City, CA 91604
*Writer, producer, director*

**Kapture, Mitzi**
15301 Ventura Blvd., #345
Sherman Oaks, CA 91403
*Actress*

**Karamanlis, Konstantinos G.**
Office of the President
Odos Zalokosta 10
Athens, Greece
*President of Greece*

**Karnow, Stanley**
10850 Springknoll Dr.
Potomac, MD 20854
*Journalist, writer*

**Karoly, Bela**
c/o Karoly's Gymnastics
17203 Bamwood
Houston, TX 77090
*Gymnastic coach*

**Kassebaum, Nancy L.**
302 Senate Russell Office Bldg.
Washington, DC 20510
*Senator from Kansas*

**Kasten, Robert W., Jr.**
110 Senate Hart Office Bldg.
Washington, DC 20510
*Senator from Wisconsin*

**Katz, Hilda**
915 West End Ave., #5D
New York, NY 10025
*Artist*

**Katz, Omri**
12725 Ventura Blvd., Suite E
Studio City, CA 91604
*Actor*

**Kauffman, Mark D.**
11726 San Vicente Blvd., #300
Los Angeles, CA 90049
*Playwright*

**Kaunda, Kenneth David**
State House
P.O. Box 135
Lusaka, Zambia
*President of Zambia*

**Keating, Charles**
#H32037
California Men's Colony
P.O. Box 8101
San Luis Obispo, CA 93409
*Convicted of State Securities Fraud
over savings and loan crisis*

**Keaton, Diane**
151 El Camino
Beverly Hills, CA 90212
*Actress, director*

**Keebler Company**
1 Hollow Tree Lane
Elmhurst, IL 60126
Thomas M. Garvin, CEO/
President
*Sells cookies and crackers baked by
elves*

**Keep America Beautiful, Inc.**
9 West Brad St.
Stamford, CT 06902
Roger W. Powers, President

**Keepin' Track of Vettes**
P.O. Box 48
Spring Valley, NY 10977
Shelli Finkel, Editor
*Corvette magazine*

**Keeshan, Bob**
40 W. 5th St.
New York, NY 10019
*Captain Kangaroo*

**Keillor, Garrison Edward**
80 Eighth Ave., #1216
New York, NY 10011
*Writer, radio announcer*

**Keitel, Harvey**
Box 49
Palisades, NY 10964
*Actor*

**Keller, Mary Page**
10100 Santa Monica Blvd.,
   16th Fl.
Los Angeles, CA 90067
*Actress*

**Kelley, DeForest**
822 S. Robertson Blvd., #200
Los Angeles, CA 90035
*Actor, original "Star Trek" cast
   member*

**Kellogg, William Welch**
Naval Center Atmospheric
   Research
Boulder, CO 80307
*Meteorologist*

**Kellogg Company**
One Kellogg Square
Battle Creek, MI 49016
William E. LaMothe, Chairman
   and CEO
*Number-one producer of ready-to-
   eat cereals*

**Kelly, Jim**
c/o Buffalo Bills
1 Bills Dr.
Orchard Park, NY 14127
*Professional football player*

**Kelly, Lucie Stirm Young**
Nursing Outlook
555 W. 57th St.
New York, NY 10019
*Nursing educator*

**Kemp, Shawn**
c/o Seattle Supersonics
C-Box 900911
Seattle, WA 98109
*Professional basketball player*

**Kemper Corporation**
Long Grove, IL 60049
Joseph E. Luecke, Chairman
   and CEO
*Financial services holding company*

**Kendall, Peter Landis**
CNN
820 1st St., NE
Washington, DC 20002
*TV news executive*

**Kennedy, Anthony M.**
U.S. Supreme Court Building
One First Street, NE
Washington, DC 20543
*Associate Justice of the Supreme
   Court*

**Kennedy, Edward M.
(Ted)**
315 Senate Russell Office Bldg.
Washington, DC 20510
*Senator from Massachusetts*

**Kennedy, John F., Jr.**
1040 Fifth Ave.
New York, NY 10028

**Kennedy, Mimi**
10100 Santa Monica Blvd.,
   #1600
Los Angeles, CA 90067
*Actress*

**Kenner Products**
1014 Vine St.
Cincinnati, OH 45202
David Mauer, President
*Toy and game manufacturer*

**Kenny G**
**(Gorelick)**
648 N. Robertson Blvd.
Los Angeles, CA 90048
*Saxophonist*

**Kensit, Patsy**
151 El Camino
Beverly Hills, CA 90212
*Actress*

**Kentucky Fried Chicken**
P.O. Box 32070
Louisville, KY 40232
Richard P. Mayer, Chairman
*Fast food company*

**Kerbis, Gertrude Lempp**
Lempp Kerbis Assoc.
172 W. Burton Pl.
Chicago, IL 60610
*Architect*

**Kercheval, Ken**
P.O. Box 1350
Los Angeles, CA 90078
*Actor*

**Kern County Museum**
3801 Chester Ave.
Bakersfield, CA 93301
Carla Ruper Enriquez, Director
*Indian and pioneer history museum*

**Kerns, Joanna**
P.O. Box 49216
Los Angeles, CA 90049
*Actress*

**Kerrey, Bob**
316 Senate Hart Office Bldg.
Washington, DC 20510
*Senator from Nebraska, sometime
    presidential candidate*

**Kerry, John F.**
421 Senate Russell Office Bldg.
Washington, DC 20510
*Senator from Massachusetts*

**Kessler, A. D.**
Box 1144
Rancho Santa Fe, CA 92067
*Business, financial and real estate
    adviser*

**Khan, Ghulam Ishag**
Office of the President
Constitution Avenue
Islamabad, Pakistan
*President of Pakistan*

**Kidman, Nicole**
9830 Wilshire Blvd.
Beverly Hills, CA 90212
*Actress*

**Kiley, Daniel Urban**
Castle Forest
Charlotte, VT 05445
*Landscape architect, planner*

**Kilmer, Val**
P.O. Box 362
Tesuque, NM 87574
*Actor*

**Kimball, Robert Eric**
180 W. 58th St.
New York, NY 10019
*Author, music historian*

**Kimberly-Clark Corporation**
P.O. Box 619100, DFW Airport
    Station
Dallas, TX 75261
Darwin E. Smith, Chairman
    and CEO
*Kleenex*

**Kimbrough, Charles**
9200 Sunset Blvd., #710
Los Angeles, CA 90069
*Actor*

**King, B.B.**
P.O. Box 4396
Las Vegas, NV 89107
*Musician*

**King, Bruce**
State Capitol
Santa Fe, NM 87503
*Governor of New Mexico*

**King, Carole**
P.O. Box 7308
Carmel, CA 93921
*Singer, songwriter*

**King, Don**
32 E. 69th St.
New York, NY 10021
*Boxing promoter*

**King, Larry**
CNN
6430 Sunset Blvd.
Los Angeles, CA 90028
*Cable TV host*

**King, Rodney**
c/o Steven Lerman
9100 Wilshire Blvd., #250
Beverly Hills, CA 90212
*Controversial beaten, videotaped
   motorist*

**King, Stephen**
c/o Viking
375 Hudson St.
New York, NY 10014
*Horror author*

**King Harald V**
Royal Palace
Oslo, Norway
*Sovereign of Norway*

**King Hassan II**
Royal Palace
Rabat, Morocco
*Ruler of Morocco*

**King Juan Carlos I**
Palacio de la Zarzuela
Madrid, Spain
*Ruler of Spain*

**King Mswati III**
Royal Palace
Mbabane, Swaziland
*Ruler of Swaziland*

**King Ranch, Inc.**
Two Greenspoint Plaza
16825 Northchase, Suite 1450
Houston, TX 77060
Leroy G. Denman, Jr.,
   Chairman
*Ranch that inspired "Giant"*

**Kingston Trio, The**
107 Degas Road
Portola Valley, CA 94025
*Folk rock group*

**Kinsella, W. P. (William
   Patrick)**
Box 400
White Rock, British Columbia
   V4B 5G3 Canada
*Author*

**Kinsley, Michael**
1220 19th St., NW
Washington, DC 20036
*Editor, journalist*

**Kiplinger, Austin Huntington**
1729 H St.
Washington, DC 20006
*Editor, publisher*

**Kirby, Bruno**
9320 Wilshire Blvd., 3rd Fl.
Beverly Hills, CA 90212
*Actor*

**Kirk, Lynda Pounds**
Austin Biofeedback Center
4207 James Casey, #301
Austin, TX 78745
*Stress therapist*

**Kirkland, Gelsey**
c/o Zackin Mgmt.
67 Riverside Dr., #3 B/C
New York, NY 10024
*Dancer, author*

**Kirkland, Sally**
151 El Camino
Beverly Hills, CA 90212
*Actress*

**Kirkpatrick, Jeane**
American Enterprise Inst.
1150 17th St., NW
Washington, DC 20036
*Foreign affairs expert*

**KISS**
6363 Sunset Blvd., #417
Los Angeles, CA 90028
*Flamboyant rock group*

**Kissinger, Henry**
1800 K St., NW, #400
Washington, DC 20006
*International affairs expert*

**Kmart Corporation**
3100 W. Big Beaver Rd.
Troy, MI 48084
Joseph E. Antonini, Chairman,
    President and CEO
*Discount and specialty department
    stores*

**Knight, Christopher**
280 S. Beverly Dr., #400
Beverly Hills, CA 90212
*Actor, original Brady Bunch kid*

**Knight, Gladys**
Box 82, #342A
Great Neck, NY 11022
*Singer*

**Knight-Ridder, Inc.**
One Herald Plaza
Miami, FL 33132
James K. Batten, Chairman and
    CEO
*International newspaper publisher*

**Koch, Edward I.**
1290 Ave. of the Americas
New York, NY 10104
*Former mayor of New York*

**Koch Industries, Inc.**
P.O. Box 2256
Wichita, KS 67201
Charles Koch, Chairman and
    CEO
*Oil and gas company*

**Kohl, Helmut**
Marbacher Strasse 11
6700 Ludwigshafen/Rhein
Federal Republic of Germany
*Chancellor of Germany*

**Kohl, Herb**
330 Senate Hart Office Bldg.
Washington, DC 20501
*Senator from Wisconsin*

**Kohlberg Kravis Roberts & Co.**
9 W. 57th St., Suite 4200
New York, NY 10019
Henry R. Kravis, Founding
    Partner
George R. Roberts, Founding
    Partner
*Leveraged buyout kings*

**Kolingba, General Andre**
Présidence de la République
Bangui, Central African
    Republic
*President of Central African
    Republic*

**Koon, Stacey**
c/o Police Protective League
600 E. Eighth St.
Los Angeles, CA 90014
*Officer involved in the Rodney King
    incident*

**Koontz, Dean R.**
P.O. Box 5686
Orange, CA 92613
*Author*

**Koop, Charles Everett**
Children's National Medical
    Center—Safe Kids
111 Michigan Ave., NW
Washington, DC 20010
*Former surgeon general, activist*

**Kosinski, Andrzej Wladyslaw**
University of Pennsylvania
    Department of Human
    Genetics
John Morgan Bldg.
Philadelphia, PA 19104
*Educator, biologist*

**Kostelantz, Richard**
P.O. Box 444, Prince St.
New York, NY 10012
*Writer, artist*

**Kotler, Robert**
436 N. Bedford Dr., #201
Beverly Hills, CA 90210
*Plastic surgeon*

**Kovel, Terry Horvitz**
P.O. Box 22200
Beachwood, OH 44122
*Antiques authority*

**Kovisto, Mauno Henrik**
Presidential Palace
Helsinki, Finland
*President of Finland*

**KPMG**
**Klynveld Peat Marwick
    Goerdeler**
P.O. Box 74111
1070 BC Amsterdam, The
    Netherlands
P. Jim Butler, Chairman
*World's largest accounting firm*

**Kraag, Johan**
Office of the President
Paramaribo, Suriname
*President of Suriname*

**Kranning, Terry**
Kranning Custom Knives
1900 W. Quinn, #153
Pocatello, ID 83202
*Manager, Miniature Knifemakers
    Society*

**Krantz, Judith**
c/o Warner Books
666 Fifth Ave.
New York, NY 10103
*Novelist*

**Kreskin**
P.O. Box 1383
West Caldwell, NJ 07006
*Mentalist, writer*

**Kris Kross**
51 W. 52nd St.
New York, NY 10019
*Rap group*

**Kroger Co., The**
1014 Vine St.
Cincinnati, OH 45202
Joseph A. Pichler, Chairman
  and CEO
*Second largest grocery chain in the
  U.S.*

**Kuralt, Charles Bishop**
CBS News
524 W. 57th St.
New York, NY 10019
*TV news correspondent*

**Kurosawa, Akira**
Seijo 2-21-6, Setagaja-ku
Tokyo 157 Japan
*Film director*

**Kurtz, Swoosie**
151 El Camino
Beverly Hills, CA 90212
*Actress*

**Kushner, Harold**
Temple Israel
145 Hartford
Natick, MA 01760
*Rabbi, author*

L

People in the flesh are a lot more complicated than they appear on paper, which is both one of the attractions and one of the shortcomings of carrying on a prolonged correspondence.

—SHANA ALEXANDER

**L.A. Gear, Inc.**
4221 Redwood Ave.
Los Angeles, CA 90066
Robert Y. Greenberg, Chairman
and CEO
*U.S.'s third largest producer of
athletic shoes*

**Lacalle, Luis Alberto**
Oficina del Presidente
Montevideo, Uruguay
*President of Uruguay*

**LaCroix, Christian Marie
Marc**
73 Faubourg St. Honoré
75008 Paris, France
*Fashion designer*

**Lacrosse Hall of Fame and
Museum**
Lacrosse Foundation, Inc.
Newton H. White Athletic
Center
Baltimore, MD 21218
James L. Potter, President

**Ladd, Diane**
151 El Camino
Beverly Hills, CA 90212
*Actress*

**Laffer, Arthur**
4275 Executive Square, #330
La Jolla, CA 92037
*Economist*

**Lahti, Christine**
9830 Wilshire Blvd.
Beverly Hills, CA 90212
*Actress*

**Lakey, Andy**
826 Orange Ave., #102
Coronado, CA 92118
*Modern artist for the sighted and
non-sighted*

**LaLanne, Jack**
P.O. Box 1249
Burbank, CA 91507
*Fitness fanatic*

**Lambeer, Bill**
c/o Detroit Pistons
One Championship Dr.
Auburn Hills, MI 48057
*Professional basketball player*

**Lance, Bert**
P.O. Box 637
Calhoun, GA 30701
*Ex-government official*

**Landers, Ann**
**(Esther P. Lederer)**
Chicago Tribune
435 N. Michigan Ave.
Chicago, IL 60611
*Columnist*

**Landsbergis, Vytautas**
Office of the President
Supreme Council of Lithuania
Vilnius, Lithuania
*President of Lithuania*

**Laneuville, Eric**
8383 Wilshire Blvd., #923
Beverly Hills, CA 90211
*Actor turned director*

**Lang, K. D.**
41 Britain St., Suite 200
Toronto, Ontario M5A 1R7
    Canada
*Singer*

**Lange, Jessica**
9830 Wilshire Blvd.
Beverly Hills, CA 90212
*Actress*

**Lansbury, Angela**
151 El Camino
Beverly Hills, CA 90212
*Actress*

**Lansing, Sherry**
5555 Melrose Ave.
Los Angeles, CA 90038
*Film producer, executive*

**Larkin, Barry**
c/o Cincinnati Reds
100 Riverfront Stadium
Cincinnati, OH 45202
*Professional baseball player*

**LaRouche, Lyndon**
2111 Center St., E
Rochester, MN 55904
*Controversial politician*

**Larroquette, John**
Box 6303
Malibu, CA 90264
*Actor*

**Larson, Gary**
Universal Press Syndicate
4900 Main St., 9th Fl.
Kansas City, MO 64112
*Cartoonist*

**La's**
**Lee Mavers, Neil Mavers,**
    **Cammy Power, John Power**
825 Eighth Ave.
New York, NY 10022
*Musical group from England*

**Lassie**
16133 Soledad Canyon Rd.
Canyon Country, CA 91351
*Famous dog*

**Lauper, Cyndi**
c/o Dave Wolff
853 Seventh Ave.
New York, NY 10019
*Singer*

**Lauren, Tammy**
151 El Camino
Beverly Hills, CA 90212
*Actress*

**Laurents, Arthur**
Box 582
Quogue, NY 11959
*Writer*

**Lautenberg, Frank R.**
506 Senate Hart Office Bldg.
Washington, DC 20510
*Senator from New Jersey*

**Lawrence, Joey**
9200 Sunset Blvd., #710
Los Angeles, CA 90069
*Actor*

**Leach, Robin**
875 Third Ave., #1800
New York, NY 10022
*"Lifestyles of the Rich and Famous"*
*host*

**League of American**
**Wheelmen**
6707 Whitestone Rd., #209
Baltimore, MD 21207
John Cornelison, Executive
Director
*Bicycle enthusiasts*

**League of Conservation**
**Voters**
1150 Connecticut Ave., NW,
#201
Washington, DC 20036
Jim Maddy, Executive Director

**League of Women Voters of**
**the U.S.**
1730 M St., NW
Washington, DC 20036
Susan S. Lederman, President

**Leahy, Patrick J.**
433 Senate Russell Office Bldg.
Washington, DC 20510
*Senator from Vermont*

**Lear's**
Lear Publishing Inc.
655 Madison Ave.
New York, NY 10021
Myra Appleton, Editor
*Magazine*

**Leary, Timothy**
P.O. Box 69886
Los Angeles, CA 90069
*Psychologist, author*

**Lee, Rev. Vernon R.**
Baptist Missionary Association
of America
P.O. Box 1203
Van, TX 75790
*Religious leader*

**Lee, Sheryl**
151 El Camino
Beverly Hills, CA 90212
*Actress*

**Lee, Spike**
40 Acres and a Mule Filmworks
124 DeKalb Ave.
Brooklyn, NY 11217
*Film director, actor*

**Lefrak, Samuel J.**
97–77 Queens Blvd.
Forest Hills, NY 11374
*Business expert*

**Lefthander Magazine**
Lefthander International
P.O. Box 8249
Topeka, KS 66608
Suzan Ireland, Managing Editor

**Legion of Doom**
P.O. Box 3857
Stamford, CT 06905
*Professional "tag team" wrestlers*

**Leifer, Carol**
151 El Camino
Beverly Hills, CA 90212
*Comedienne*

**Leigh, Jennifer Jason**
8899 Beverly Blvd.
Los Angeles, CA 90048
*Actress*

**Leisure, David**
1999 Ave. of the Stars, #2850
Los Angeles, CA 90067
*Actor*

**Lemmon, Jack**
9830 Wilshire Blvd.
Beverly Hills, CA 90212
*Actor*

**LeMond, Greg**
c/o ProServ
1101 Wilson Blvd., #1800
Arlington, VA 22209
*Champion bicyclist*

**Lendl, Ivan**
International Management
  Group
One Erieview Plaza, #1300
Cleveland, OH 44144
*Professional tennis player*

**Lennon Sisters, The**
944 Harding Ave.
Venice, CA 90291
*Singers*

**Lennox, Annie**
Box 245
London N89 QG England
*Singer*

**Leno, Jay**
3000 W. Alameda Ave.
Burbank, CA 91523
*"Tonight Show" host*

**Leonard, Elmore John**
c/o H. N. Swanson
8523 Sunset Blvd.
Los Angeles, CA 90069
*Author*

**Leopold, Irving Henry**
Allergan, Inc.
2525 DuPont Dr.
Irvine, CA 92715
*Physician, medical educator*

**Letter Exchange, The**
Box 6218
Albany, CA 94706
*A magazine for letter writers*

**Letterman, David**
30 Rockefeller Plaza, #1400
New York, NY 10020
*"Late Night" host*

**Levi Strauss Associates, Inc.**
1155 Battery St.
San Francisco, CA 94111
Robert D. Haas, Chairman and
  CEO
*Jeans manufacturers*

**Levin, Carl**
459 Senate Russell Office Bldg.
Washington, DC 20510
*Senator from Michigan*

**Levine, Michael**
8730 Sunset Blvd., 6th Fl.
Los Angeles, CA 90069
*Author,* The Address Book

**Levinson, Barry**
9830 Wilshire Blvd.
Beverly Hills, CA 90212
*Director, writer*

**Lewis, Huey**
P.O. Box 819
Mill Valley, CA 94942
*Singer*

**Lewis, Jerry**
151 El Camino
Beverly Hills, CA 90212
*Fundraiser, comedian*

**Lewis, Jerry Lee**
P.O. Box 3864
Memphis, TN 37173
*Perennial rocker*

**Lewis Galoob Toys Inc.**
500 Forbes Blvd.
South San Francisco, CA 94080
David Galoob, Chairman/
President/CEO
*Toy manufacturer*

**Liberace Museum**
1775 E. Tropicana
Las Vegas, NV 89119
Joel Strote, President
*Pianos and candelabra galore*

**Libin, Paul**
Jujamcyn Theatres
St. James Theatre
246 W. 44th St.
New York, NY 10036
*Theater executive, producer*

**Library of Congress**
10 First St., SE
Washington, DC 20540
James H. Billington, Librarian
of Congress

**Liddy, G. Gordon**
9113 Sunset Blvd.
Los Angeles, CA 90069
*Actor, Watergate participant*

**Lieberman, Joseph I.**
502 Senate Hart Office Bldg.
Washington, DC 20510
*Senator from Connecticut*

**Life**
Time & Life Bldg.
Rockefeller Center
New York, NY 10020
James R. Gaines, Managing
Editor
*THE picture magazine*

**Lifetime Television**
34–12 36th St.
Astoria, NY 11106
Thomas Burchill, President
*Cable network*

**Light, Christopher Upjohn**
Old Kent Bank Bldg.
136 E. Michigan Ave.
Kalamazoo, MI 49007
*Computer musician*

**Light, Judith**
8899 Beverly Blvd.
Los Angeles, CA 90048
*Actress*

**Lightner, Candy Lynne**
22653 Pacific Coast Hwy.,
#1-289
Malibu, CA 90265
*Advocate, author, founder of
MADD*

**Lilyquist, Christine**
Metropolitan Museum of Art
1000 Fifth Ave.
New York, NY 10028
*Egyptologist, museum curator*

**Limited Inc., The**
Two Limited Pkwy., P.O. Box
16000
Columbus, OH 43216
Leslie H. Wexner, Chairman
and President
*Women's clothing store chain*

**Liotta, Ray**
9830 Wilshire Blvd.
Beverly Hills, CA 90212
*Actor*

**Little League Baseball, Inc.**
P.O. Box 3485
Williamsport, PA 17701
Dr. Creighton J. Hale, President

**Little Mermaid, The**
c/o Disney Studios
500 South Buena Vista St.
Burbank, CA 91521
*Cartoon heroine*

**Little River Band**
87–91 Palmerstin Cres.
Albert Park
Melbourne, Victoria 3206
   Australia
*Musical group*

**Litton Industries, Inc.**
360 N. Crescent Dr.
Beverly Hills, CA 90210
Orion L. Hoch, Chairman and
   CEO
*Marine engineering, industrial
   automation, etc.*

**Liz Claiborne, Inc.**
1441 Broadway
New York, NY 10018
Jerome A. Chazen, Chairman
*Women's clothing manufacturer*

**LL Cool J
(Ladies Love Cool James)**
298 Elizabeth St.
New York, NY 10012
*Rap singer*

**Lloyd, Christopher**
222 N. Canon Dr., #202
Beverly Hills, CA 90210
*Actor*

**Lockheed Corporation**
4500 Park Granada Blvd.
Calabasas, CA 91399
Daniel M. Tellpe, Chairman
   and CEO
*Sixth largest defense contractor and
   largest defense R & D company
   in U.S.*

**Loews Corporation**
667 Madison Ave.
New York, NY 10021
Laurence A. Tisch, Chairman
   and Co-CEO
*Hotels, CNA Financial, Bulova*

**Lofton, Dr. Fred C.**
Progressive National Baptist
   Convention
601 50th St., NE
Washington, DC 20019
*Religious leader*

**Logsdon, Thomas S.**
3530 Pine Valley Dr.
Sarasota, FL 34239
*Robotics expert*

**Long, Shelley**
9830 Wilshire Blvd.
Beverly Hills, CA 90212
*Actress*

**Longs Drug Stores
   Corporation**
141 N. Civic Dr.
Walnut Creek, CA 94596
Robert M. Long, Chairman and
   CEO
*261 drugstores*

**Lord, M. G.**
NY Newsday Inc.
2 Park Ave.
New York, NY 10016
*Editorial cartoonist, columnist*

**Lorimar Television**
300 Lorimar Plaza
Burbank, CA 91505
David Salzman, President
*Television production company*

**Los Angeles Clippers**
L.A. Memorial Sports Arena
3939 South Figueroa Avenue
Los Angeles, CA 90037
Elgin Baylor, Executive Vice-
  President/General Manager
*Professional basketball team*

**Los Angeles County
  Department of Arboreta &
  Botanic Gardens**
301 N. Baldwin Ave.
Arcadia, CA 91006
Leon G. Arnold, Acting
  Director
*Location of Fantasy Island house*

**Los Angeles County Museum
  of Art**
5905 Wilshire Blvd.
Los Angeles, CA 90036
Dr. Earl A. Powell III, Director
Maurice Tuchman, 20th century
  art curator

**Los Angeles Dodgers**
1000 Elysian Park Ave.
Los Angeles, CA 90012
Peter O'Malley, President
*Professional baseball team*

**Los Angeles Heat**
220 South Pacific Coast
  Highway, #104
Redondo Beach, CA 90277
Dan Olsen, Chairman
*Soccer team*

**Los Angeles Kings**
The Forum
P.O. Box 17013
Inglewood, CA 90308
Rogie Vachon, General Manager
*Professional hockey team*

**Los Angeles Lakers**
P.O. Box 10
Inglewood, CA 90306
Jerry West, General Manager
*Professional basketball team*

**Los Angeles Raiders**
332 Center St.
El Segundo, CA 90245
Al Davis, Managing General
  Partner
*Professional football team*

**Los Angeles Rams**
2327 W. Lincoln Ave.
Anaheim, CA 92801
Georgia Frontiere, President
*Professional football team*

**Los Lobos**
P.O. Box 1304
Burbank, CA 91507
*Singing group*

**Lott, Trent**
487 Senate Russell Office Bldg.
Washington, DC 20510
*Senator from Mississippi*

**Lotus Development
  Corporation**
55 Cambridge Pkwy.
Cambridge, MA 02142
Jim P. Manzi, Chairman,
  President, and CEO
*Lotus 1-2-3, and other computer
  software*

**Louganis, Greg**
P.O. Box 4068
Malibu, CA 90265
*Olympic diver*

**Loughlin, Lori**
151 El Camino
Beverly Hills, CA 90212
*Actress*

**Louisa May Alcott Memorial
 Association Library**
Box 343
Concord, MA 01742
Jayne Gordon, Director
*Collection of the Alcott family photos
 and papers*

**Louis-Dreyfus, Julia**
131 S. Rodeo Dr., #300
Beverly Hills, CA 90212
*Actress*

**Lowe, Chad**
151 El Camino
Beverly Hills, CA 90212
*Actor*

**Lowe, Rob**
232 N. Canon Dr.
Beverly Hills, CA 90210
*Actor*

**Lowe's Companies, Inc.**
P.O. Box 1111
North Wilkesboro, NC 28565
Robert L. Strickland, Chairman
*Hardware, consumer electronics,
 building supplies*

**LTV Corporation, The**
P.O. Box 655003, 2001 Ross
 Ave.
Dallas, TX 75265
David H. Hoag, Chairman,
 President and CEO
*Debt-ridden aerospace/steel
 company*

**Lubbers, Ruud**
Office of the Prime Minister
The Hague, The Netherlands
*Premier of The Netherlands*

**Lucas, George**
Box 2009
San Rafael, CA 94912
*Director, innovator*

**Lucci, Susan**
40 W. 57th St.
New York, NY 10019
*Actress, perennial Emmy bridesmaid*

**Ludlum, Robert**
P.O. Box 235
Bedford Hills, NY 10507
*Suspense writer*

**Lugar, Richard G.**
306 Senate Hart Office Bldg.
Washington, DC 20510
*Senator from Indiana*

**Luger, Lex**
P.O. Box 105366
Atlanta, GA 30348
*Professional wrestler*

**Lum & Abner Museum
 & Jot 'Em Down Store**
P.O. Box 38
Pine Ridge, AR 71966
Noah Lon Stucker, Director
*1904 store used for radio program*

**Lumet, Sidney**
LAH Film Corp.
1775 Broadway
New York, NY 10019
*Film director*

**Lunden, Joan**
c/o ABC
853 Seventh Ave.
New York, NY 10023
*Early morning hostess*

**Lundgren, Dolph**
1875 Century Park E., #2200
Los Angeles, CA 90067
*Actor*

**LuPone, Patti**
232 N. Canon Dr.
Beverly Hills, CA 90212
*Actress*

**Luther Burbank Home and Gardens**
P.O. Box 1678
Santa Rosa, CA 95402
Kay Voliva, Board Chairman

**Lynch, David**
P.O. Box 93624
Los Angeles, CA 90093
*Director*

**Lynne, Gillian Barbara**
18 Rutland St.
Knightsbridge, London SW7
 1EF England
*Director, choreographer, dancer*

M

Excuse me for not answering your letter sooner, but I've been so busy not answering letters that I couldn't get around to yours in time.

—GROUCHO MARX

**Ma, Yo Yo**
40 W. 57th St.
New York, NY 10019
*Cellist*

**Maas, Peter**
c/o ICM
40 W. 57th St.
New York, NY 10019
*Writer*

**MacAndrews & Forbes Holdings Inc.**
36 E. 63rd St.
New York, NY 10021
Ronald O. Perelman, Chairman and CEO
*Cosmetics, comic books and candy*

**MacDowell, Andie**
8899 Beverly Blvd.
Los Angeles, CA 90048
*Actress, model*

**Macho Man (Randy Savage)**
P.O. Box 3857
Stamford, CT 06905
*Professional wrestler*

**MacInnes, Jeff**
3530 Pine Valley Dr.
Sarasota, FL 34239
*Arctic explorer*

**Mack, Connie**
517 Senate Hart Office Bldg.
Washington, DC 20510
*Senator from Florida*

**Mack, Kevin**
c/o Cleveland Browns
Cleveland Stadium
Cleveland, OH 44114
*Professional football player*

**MacLachlan, Kyle**
131 S. Rodeo Dr., #300
Beverly Hills, CA 90212
*Actor*

**MacLaine, Shirley**
8899 Beverly Blvd.
Los Angeles, CA 90048
*Actress, author*

**MacLeod, Charlotte**
c/o Jed Mattes Inc.
175 W. 73rd St., #8H
New York, NY 10023
*Slightly off-center mystery writer*

**MacLeod, Gavin**
15301 Ventura Blvd., Suite 345
Sherman Oaks, CA 91403
*Actor*

**MacLeod, John**
Notre Dame University Athletics
  Department
South Bend, IN 46556
*Basketball coach*

**MacNeil/Lehrer NewsHour**
3620 27th St. S.
Arlington, VA 22206
*PBS news program*

**Macy, R. H., & Co., Inc.**
151 W. 34th St.
New York, NY 10001
Edward S. Finkelstein,
  Chairman and CEO
*Bankrupt famous department store
  and parade organizer*

**Mad Magazine**
485 Madison Ave.
New York, NY 10022
Nick Meglin/John Ficarra,
  Editors
*Cartoon magazine*

**Mademoiselle Magazine**
350 Madison Ave.
New York, NY 10017
Amy Levin Cooper, Editor
*Beauty and fashion magazine*

**Madonna
(Madonna Louise Ciccone)**
75 Rockefeller Plaza
New York, NY 10019
*Singer, performance artist*

**Madruga, Lenor**
3530 Pine Valley Dr.
Sarasota, FL 34239
*Author of* One Step at a Time

**Madsen, Virginia**
131 S. Rodeo Dr., #300
Beverly Hills, CA 90212
*Actress*

**Magnolia Mound Plantation**
2161 Nicholson Dr.
Baton Rouge, LA 70802
Gwen A. Edwards, Director
*Civil War plantation*

**Magope, Kgosi Lucas**
Department of the Presidency
Private Bag X2005
Mafeking, Botswana, South
  Africa
*President of Botswana, South
  Africa*

**Mahony, Roger**
1531 W. 9th St.
Los Angeles, CA 90012
*Roman Catholic cardinal*

**Maine State Museum**
State House Complex
Augusta, ME 04333
Paul E. Rivard, Director

**Major, John**
10 Downing St.
London SW1 England
*Prime Minister of England*

**Majors, John Terrill**
P.O. Box 15162
Knoxville, TN 37901
*Football coach*

**Make Today Count**
101½ South Union St.
Alexandria, VA 22314
Sandra Butler Whyte, Executive
  Officer
*Information for those with terminal
  illnesses*

**Malle, Louis**
8899 Beverly Blvd.
Los Angeles, CA 90048
*Director*

**Malone, Karl "The Mailman"**
c/o Utah Jazz
5 Triad Center
Salt Lake City, UT 84180
*Professional basketball player*

**Malone, Moses**
c/o Atlanta Hawks
1 CNN Center
Atlanta, GA 30303
*Professional basketball player*

**Maltby, Richard Eldridge, Jr.**
c/o F. Roberts
157 W. 57th St.
New York, NY 10019
*Director, lyricist*

**Mamaloni, Solomon**
Office of the Prime Minister
P.O. Box G01
Honiara, Guadalcanal
Solomon Islands
*Prime Minister of the Solomon Islands*

**Man Will Never Fly Memorial Society Internationale**
P.O. Box 1903
Kill Devil Hills, NC 27948
E. H. North, Jr., Thinker
*"Birds fly, men drink."*

**Manchester, William**
Wesleyan University
Middletown, CT 06459
*Writer*

**Mancini, Henry**
9200 Sunset Blvd., #823
Los Angeles, CA 90069
*Film music composer*

**Mandel, Howie**
9560 Wilshire Blvd., #500
Beverly Hills, CA 90212
*Comedian, actor*

**Mandela, Nelson and Winnie**
Orlando W. Soweto
Johannesburg, South Africa
*Controversial human rights activists*

**Mandrake the Magician**
King Features Syndicate
235 E. 45th St.
New York, NY 10017
Lee Falk, Creator
*Adventure and fantasy comic book*

**Manhattan Transfer, The**
3575 Cahuengua Blvd., W., #450
Los Angeles, CA 90068
*Harmonious singing group*

**Manilow, Barry**
6640 Sunset Blvd., #200
Los Angeles, CA 90028
*Singer, songwriter*

**Manley, Michael**
People's National Party
89 Old Hope Rd.
Kingston 6, Jamaica
*Prime Minister of Jamaica*

**Manning, Danny**
c/o Los Angeles Clippers
3939 S. Figueroa
Los Angeles, CA 90037
*Professional basketball player*

**Manning, Father Michael**
P.O. Box 8080
Riverside, CA 92515
*Catholic religious leader, author*

**Manoff, Dinah**
P.O. Box 5617
Beverly Hills, CA 90210
*Actress*

**Manson, Charles**
Corcoran Prison, 1002 Diary
Ave.
Corcoran, CA 93212
*Convicted murderous cult leader*

**Mantegna, Joe Anthony**
c/o P. Strain
1500 Broadway, #2001
New York, NY 10036
*Actor, playwright*

**Mantle, Mickey Charles**
Rahde & McLain
18080 Central, 9th Fl.
Dallas, TX 75206
*Former baseball player, marketing consultant*

**Manufacturers Hanover Corporation**
270 Park Ave.
New York, NY 10017
John F. McGillicuddy, Chairman and CEO
*Old established bank, merging with Chemical Bank*

**Manville Corporation**
717 17th St., P.O. Box 5108
Denver, CO 80217
W. Thomas Stephens,
Chairman, President and
CEO
*Forest product company whose controlling interest is held by a trust benefiting asbestos victims*

**Marilyn Forever, Marilyn Monroe International Fan Club**
P.O. Box 7544
Northridge, CA 91327
Wendy Beeby, President

**Marinaro, Ed**
151 El Camino
Beverly Hills, CA 90212
*Actor*

**Marky Mark
(Mark Wahlberg)**
10900 Wilshire Blvd.
Los Angeles, CA 90024
*Rap singer*

**Marriott Corporation**
10400 Fernwood Rd.
Bethesda, MD 20058
J. W. "Bill" Marriott, Jr.,
Chairman, President and
CEO
*Hotel chain*

**Mars, Inc.**
6885 Elm St.
McLean, VA 22101
Forrest E. Mars, Jr., Chairman,
CEO and Co-President
*Candy, ice cream and pet food*

**Marsh, Ozan James**
P.O. Box 64115
Tucson, AZ 85740
*Concert pianist*

**Marsh & McLennan Companies, Inc.**
1166 Ave. of the Americas
New York, NY 10036
Frank J. Tasco, Chairman and
CEO
*World's largest insurance broker*

**Marshall, Penny**
9830 Wilshire Blvd.
Beverly Hills, CA 90212
*Director, actress*

**Martens, Wilfried**
16 rue de la Loi
1000 Brussels, Belgium
*Prime Minister of Belgium*

**Martin, Ann M.**
c/o Scholastic, Inc.
730 Broadway
New York, NY 10003
*Author*

**Martin, James G., Jr.**
State Capitol
Raleigh, NC 27603
*Governor of North Carolina*

**Martin, Kellie**
6212 Banner Ave.
Hollywood, CA 90038
*Actress*

**Martin, Steve**
P.O. Box 929
Beverly Hills, CA 90213
*Actor, comedian*

**Martin Marietta Corporation**
6801 Rockledge Dr.
Bethesda, MD 20817
Norman R. Augustine,
    Chairman and CEO
*Aerospace, construction materials,*
    *etc.*

**Martinez, A**
151 El Camino
Beverly Hills, CA 90212
*Actor*

**Marvel Comics**
387 Park Ave. S.
New York, NY 10016
Tom DeFalco, Editor
*Comic book publisher*

**Marx, Richard**
1750 N. Vine St.
Hollywood, CA 90028
*Singer*

**Mary Pickford Foundation**
9171 Wilshire Blvd., #512
Beverly Hills, CA 90210

**Masco Corporation**
21001 Van Born Rd.
Taylor, MI 48180
Richard A. Manoogian,
    Chairman and CEO
*World's largest producer of faucets*

**Masire, Quett Ketumile Joni**
State House
Private Bag 001, Gaborone
Botswana
*President of Botswana*

**Mason, Bobbie Ann**
c/o A. Urban
40 W. 57th St.
New York, NY 10019
*Novelist, short story writer*

**Mason, Marsha**
40 W. 57th St.
New York, NY 10019
*Actress*

**Massachusetts Mutual Life**
    **Insurance**
1295 State St.
Springfield, MA 01111
Thomas B. Wheeler, President
    and CEO

**Matheson, Tim**
1642 Westwood Blvd., 3rd Fl.
Los Angeles, CA 90024
*Actor, entrepreneur*

**Matlin, Marlee**
8899 Beverly Blvd.
Los Angeles, CA 90048
*Actress*

**Mattel, Inc.**
5150 Rosecrans Ave.
Hawthorne, CA 90250
John W. Amerman, Chairman
and CEO
*Toy company*

**Mattingly, Don**
c/o New York Yankees
Yankee Stadium
Bronx, NY 10451
*Professional baseball player*

**Mattson, Francis O.**
New York Public Library
Fifth Ave. & 42nd St.
New York, NY 10018
*Rare books curator*

**Mattson, Robin**
9000 Sunset Blvd., #1200
Los Angeles, CA 90069
*Actress*

**Mature, Victor**
P.O. Box 706
Rancho Santa Fe, CA 92067
*Actor*

**Maung, General Saw**
Office of the Prime Minister
Yangon, Myanmar
*Head of State (Chairman) of
Myanmar*

**May Department Stores
Company, The**
611 Olive St.
St. Louis, MO 63101
David C. Farrell, Chairman and
CEO
*Largest "conventional" department
store operator*

**Mayflower Group, Inc.**
9998 N. Michigan Rd.
Carmel, IN 46032
John B. Smith, Chairman
*Moving company*

**Mayo Foundation**
Mayo Clinic
Rochester, MN 55905
Edson W. Spencer, Chairman,
Board of Trustees
*Governing body of largest private
medical center in the world*

**Maytag Corporation**
403 W. Fourth St., N.
Newton, IA 50208
Daniel J. Krumm, Chairman
and CEO
*Fourth largest appliance
manufacturer in the U.S.*

**Mbasogo, Colonel Teodro
Obiang Nguema**
Oficina del Presidente
Malabo, Equatorial Guinea
*President of Equatorial Guinea*

**MCA, Inc.**
100 Universal City Plaza
Universal City, CA 91608
Lew R. Wasserman, Chairman
of the Board/CEO
*Television and film production
company*

**MCA Records/MCA Music
Entertainment Group**
1755 Broadway, 8th Fl.
New York, NY 10019
Al Teller, Chairman
*Record label*

**McAnuff, Des**
La Jolla Playhouse
P.O. Box 12039
La Jolla, CA 92039
*Artistic director*

**McArthur, Alex**
8899 Beverly Blvd.
Los Angeles, CA 90048
*Actor*

**McBain, Ed
(Evan Hunter)**
c/o John Farquharson Ltd.
250 W. 57th St.
New York, NY 10017
*Police procedural writer*

**McCain, John**
111 Senate Russell Office Bldg.
Washington, DC 20510
*Senator from Arizona*

**McCartney, Paul**
Waterfall Estate Peamarsh
St. Leonard on the Sea
Sussex, England
*Singer, composer*

**McCaw Cellular
Communications, Inc.**
5400 Carillon Point
Kirkland, WA 98033
Craig O. McCaw, Chairman and
CEO
*Largest cellular telephone company
in the U.S.*

**McClanahan, Rue**
9000 Sunset Blvd., #1200
Los Angeles, CA 90069
*Actress*

**McClellan, Roger Orville**
Chemical Industry Institute of
Toxicology
P.O. Box 12137
Research Triangle Park, NC
27709
*Toxicologist*

**McClure, Jessica**
Box 3901
Midland, TX 79701
*Miracle rescue baby*

**McConnell, Mitch**
120 Senate Russell Office Bldg.
Washington, DC 20510
*Senator from Kentucky*

**McCormick, Maureen**
9744 Wilshire Blvd., #308
Beverly Hills, CA 90212
*Actress, original Brady Bunch kid*

**McCovey, Willie**
Box 620342
Woodside, CA 94062
*Former baseball great*

**McDermott International,
Inc.**
1010 Common St.
New Orleans, LA 70112
Robert E. Howson, Chairman
and CEO
*Power generation systems and
marine construction services*

**McDonald, Gregory
Christopher**
c/o A. Greene
101 Park Ave.
New York, NY 10178
*Author*

**McDonald's Corporation**
One McDonald Plaza
Oak Brook, IL 60521
Fred L. Turner, Senior
Chairman
*Fast food chain*

**McDonnell Douglas
Corporation**
P.O. Box 516
St. Louis, MO 63166
John F. McDonnell, Chairman
and CEO
*Largest U.S. defense contractor*

**McDowell, Jack**
c/o Chicago White Sox
324 W. 35th St.
Chicago, IL 60616
*Professional baseball player and
musician*

**McEntire, Reba**
1514 South St.
Nashville, TN 37212
*Singer*

**McGinley, Ted**
151 El Camino
Beverly Hills, CA 90211
*Actor*

**McGuire, Mark**
c/o Oakland Athletics
Oakland Coliseum
Oakland, CA 94621
*Professional baseball player*

**McGuire Sisters**
100 Rancho Circle
Las Vegas, NV 89119
*Perennial singing group*

**McHale, Kevin**
c/o Boston Celtics
150 Causeway St.
Boston, MA 02114
*Professional basketball player*

**MCI Communications
Corporation**
1133 Nineteenth St., NW
Washington, DC 20036
William G. McGowan,
Chairman and CEO
*The friends and family guys*

**McKellar, Danica**
6212 Banner Ave.
Hollywood, CA 90038
*Actress*

**McKeon, Nancy**
P.O. Box 6778
Burbank, CA 91510
*Actress*

**McKernan, John R., Jr.**
State House
Augusta, ME 04333
*Governor of Maine*

**McKesson Corporation**
McKesson Plaza
One Post St.
San Francisco, CA 94104
Alan Seelenfreund, Chairman
and CEO
*Largest distributor of drugs in the
U.S.*

**McKinsey & Co.**
55 E. 52nd St.
New York, NY 10022
Frederick W. Gluck, Managing
Director
*Oldest management consulting firm
in the U.S.*

**McKuen, Rod**
P.O. Box 2783
Hollywood, CA 90028
*Poet, composer, author*

**McLaughlin, John**
1211 Connecticut Ave., NW,
  #810
Washington, DC 20036
*Commentator*

**McMurtry, Larry**
Box 552
Archer City, TX 76351
*Western author*

**McNichol, Kristy**
P.O. Box 5813
Sherman Oaks, CA 91413
*Actress*

**McRaney, Gerald**
329 N. Wetherly Dr., #101
Beverly Hills, CA 90211
*Actor, producer*

**McWherter, Ned Ray**
State Capitol
Nashville, TN 37219
*Governor of Tennessee*

**Mead Corporation, The**
Mead World Headquarters
Courthouse Plaza NE
Dayton, OH 45463
Burnell R. Roberts, Chairman
  and CEO
*Fancy notebook manufacturers*

**Meadow, Lynne**
Manhattan Theatre Club
453 W. 16th St.
New York, NY 10011
*Theatrical director and producer*

**Meadows, Audrey**
1999 Ave. of the Stars, #2850
Los Angeles, CA 90067
*Actress, Honeymooner wife*

**Medoff, Mark Howard**
P.O. Box 3072
Las Cruces, NM 88003
*Playwright, screenwriter*

**Meese, Edwin III**
214 Massachusetts Ave., NE
Washington, DC 20002
*Former attorney general*

**Mehlhaff, Rev. Harvey**
North American Baptist
  Conference
1 S. 210 Summit Ave.
Oakbrook Terrace, IL 60181
*Religious leader*

**Mehta, Zubin**
240 E. 72nd St.
New York, NY 10021
*Conductor*

**Mellen, Brian**
c/o New York Rangers
Four Penn Plaza
New York, NY 10001
*Professional hockey player*

**Mellencamp, John
(formerly Cougar)**
Rte. #1, Box 361
Nashville, TN 47448
*Singer*

**Mellon Bank Corporation**
One Mellon Bank Center
Pittsburgh, PA 15258
Frank V. Cahouet, Chairman
  and CEO
*25th largest U.S. commercial
  banking organization*

**Melville Corporation**
One Theall Rd.
Rye, NY 10580
Stanley P. Golstein, Chairman,
    President and CEO
*Shoe stores, apparel stores, drug
    stores, etc.*

**Men at Work**
Box 289
Abbotsford, Victoria 3067
    Australia
*Singing group*

**Mended Hearts**
American Heart Association
7320 Greenville Ave.
Dallas, TX 75231
Joe Amato, President
*Heart surgery support group*

**Mennonite Church**
421 S. Second St., #600
Elkhart, IN 46516
David W. Mann, Contact
*Religious group*

**Men's Garden Clubs of
    America, Inc.**
5560 Merle Hay Rd.
Johnston, IA 50131
Robert L. Schwarz, President

**Mensa**
2626 E. 14th St.
Brooklyn, NY 11235
Margot Seitelman, Executive
    Director
*Members with IQs in the top 2% of
    the U.S. (based on in-house test)*

**Menuhin, Yehudi**
c/o H. Holt
122 Wigmore St.
London W1 England
*Violinist*

**Mercantile Stores Company,
    Inc.**
9450 Seard Rd.
Fairfield, OH 45014
David R. Huhn, Chairman and
    CEO
*Department store chain*

**Merck & Co., Inc.**
P.O. Box 2000
Rahway, NJ 07065
P. Roy Vagelos, Chairman,
    President and CEO
*World's largest pharmaceutical
    company*

**Meredith, Don**
P.O. Box 5426
Santa Fe, NM 87504
*Athlete, sportscaster and sometime
    actor*

**Meriwether, Lee**
P.O. Box 26042
Encino, CA 91326
*Actress, former Miss America*

**Merrill Lynch & Co., Inc.**
World Financial Center, North
    Tower
250 Vesey St.
New York, NY 10281
William A. Schreyer, Chairman
    and CEO
*Holding company for world's largest
    securities brokerage*

**Mesic, Stipe**
Federal Executive Council
11070 Belgrade, buli Lenjina 2
Yugoslavia
*President of Yugoslavia, prior to
    revolutions*

**Metallica**
75 Rockefeller Plaza
New York, NY 10019
*Rock group*

**Metcalf, Eric**
c/o Cleveland Browns
Cleveland Stadium
Cleveland, OH 45202
*Professional football player*

**Metheny, Patrick Bruce**
c/o T. Kurland
173 Brighton Ave.
Boston, MA 02134
*Musician*

**Metromedia Company**
1 Meadowlands Plaza
East Rutherford, NJ 07073
John W. Kluge, General Partner,
  Chairman, President and
  CEO
*Communications and steakhouses*

**Metropolitan Life Insurance
  Company**
One Madison Ave.
New York, NY 10010
Robert G. Schwartz, Chairman,
  President and CEO
*Number-two insurance company in
  the U.S.*

**Metropolitan Museum of Art,
  The**
1000 Fifth Ave.
New York, NY 10028
William H. Luers, President

**Metzenbaum, Howard M.**
140 Senate Russell Office Bldg.
Washington, DC 20501
*Senator from Ohio*

**Miami Dolphins**
2269 NW 199th St.
Miami, FL 33056
J. Michael Robbie, Executive
  Vice-President/General
  Manager
*Professional football team*

**Miami Heat**
Miami Arena
Miami, FL 33136-4102
Lewis Schaffel, Managing
  Partner
*Professional basketball team*

**Michael, George**
Ixworth Place, 1st Fl.
London SW1 England
*Singer*

**Michael, Judith
(Judith Barnard and Michael
  Fain)**
c/o Simon & Schuster
1230 Ave. of the Americas
New York, NY 10020
*Pseudonym for best-selling husband
  and wife authors*

**Michaels, Barbara
(Barbara Louise Gross Mertz)**
c/o D. Abel
498 West End Ave.
New York, NY 10024
*Mystery/romance writer*

**Michener, James A. (Albert)**
P.O. Box 125
Pipersville, PA 18947
*Author*

**Microsoft Corporation**
One Microsoft Way
Redmond, WA 98052
William H. Gates III, Chairman
  and CEO
*MS-DOS and other software*

**Midler, Bette**
500 S. Buena Vista, #1G2
Burbank, CA 91521
*Actress, singer*

**Midway Airlines, Inc.**
5959 S. Cicero Ave.
Chicago, IL 60638
David R. Hinson, Chairman
and CEO
*Bankrupt airline based at Chicago's
Midway Airport*

**Mikelson, George S.**
State Capitol
Pierre, SD 57501
*Governor of South Dakota*

**Mikulski, Barbara A.**
320 Senate Hart Office Bldg.
Washington, DC 20510
*Senator from Maryland*

**Milano, Alyssa**
P.O. Box 3684
Hollywood, CA 90078
*Actress*

**Miller, Arthur**
40 W. 57th St.
New York, NY 10019
*Playwright, author*

**Miller, Craig Johnson**
113 W. 69th St., #1A
New York, NY 10023
*Theatrical lighting designer*

**Miller, Dennis**
8730 Sunset Blvd., #480
Los Angeles, CA 90069
*Talk show host, comedian*

**Miller, Nolan**
241 S. Robertson
Beverly Hills, CA 90211
*Fashion designer*

**Miller, Reggie**
c/o Indiana Pacers
300 East Market Street
Indianapolis, IN 46204
*Professional basketball player and
teen talk show host*

**Miller, Robert**
State Capitol
Carson City, NV 89710
*Governor of Nevada*

**Miller, Zell**
State Capitol
Atlanta, GA 30334
*Governor of Georgia*

**Millett, Kate
(Katherine Murray)**
c/o G. Borchardt
136 E. 57th St.
New York, NY 10022
*Political activist, sculptor, writer*

**Milli Vanilli**
8730 Sunset Blvd., PH W
Los Angeles, CA 90069
*Singers??????*

**Milliken & Co., Inc.**
920 Milliken Rd.
Spartanburg, SC 29303
Roger Milliken, Chairman
*Number-one U.S. textile company*

**Mills, Donna**
822 S. Robertson Blvd., #200
Los Angeles, CA 90035
*Actress*

**Milsap, Ronnie**
12 Music Circle Sq.
Nashville, TN 37203
*Singer*

**Milton Bradley Company**
443 Shaker Road
East Longmeadow, MA 01028
George R. Ditamassi, President
*Game manufacturer*

**Milwaukee Brewers**
Milwaukee County Stadium
Milwaukee, WI 53214
Harry Dalton, Vice-President/
    General Manager
*Professional baseball team*

**Milwaukee Bucks**
1001 N. Fourth St.
Milwaukee, WI 53203
John Steinmiller, Vice-President
*Professional basketball team*

**Mindell, Earl**
10739 W. Pico Blvd.
Los Angeles, CA 90064
*Vitamin expert and author of* The
    Vitamin Bible

**Minkes, Linda**
4200 Biscayne Blvd.
Miami, FL 33137
*Talk show hostess, "Options,"
    produced by Hadassah*

**Minnesota Historical Society**
690 Cedar St.
St. Paul, MN 55101
Nina M. Archabel, CEO and
    Director

**Minnesota Mining and
    Manufacturing Co.**
3M Center
St. Paul, MN 55144
L. D. DeSimone, Chairman and
    CEO
*3M Company, inventors of the
    indispensable Post-its*

**Minnesota North Stars**
Met Center
7901 Cedar Ave., S.
Bloomington, MN 55425
Jack Fereirra, Vice-President/
    General Manager
*Professional hockey team*

**Minnesota Timberwolves**
500 City Pl.
730 Hennepin Ave., #500
Minneapolis, MN 55403
Bob Stein, President
*Professional basketball team*

**Minnesota Twins**
Hubert H. Humphrey
    Metrodome
501 Chicago Ave., S.
Minneapolis, MN 55415
Andy McPhail, Executive Vice-
    President/General Manager
*Professional baseball team*

**Minnesota Vikings**
9520 Viking Dr.
Eden Prairie, MN 55344
Mike Lynn, Executive Vice-
    President/General Manager
*Professional football team*

**Miss Manners**
1651 Harvard St., NW
Washington, DC 20009
*Etiquette for the new age*

**Mississippi Museum of Art**
201 Pascagoula St.
Jackson, MS 39201
Alexander Lee Nyerges,
    Director

**Mississippi Petrified Forest**
P.O. Box 37
Flora, MS 39071
R. J. Schabilion, Owner and
  Director

**Mitchelson, Marvin**
1801 Century Park E., #1900
Los Angeles, CA 90067
*Celebrity lawyer*

**Mitchum, Robert**
8899 Beverly Blvd.
Los Angeles, CA 90048
*Actor*

**Mitterrand, François Maurice
  Marie**
Palais de l'Elysée
55–57 rue du Faubourg Saint-
  Honoré
75008 Paris—France
*President of France*

**Miyazawa, Kilchi**
House of Representatives
Tokyo, Japan
*Prime Minister of Japan*

**Mobil Corporation**
3225 Gallows Rd.
Fairfax, VA 22037
Allen E. Murray, Chairman,
  President and CEO
*Fourth largest petroleum company
  in the U.S.*

**Moffett, D. W.**
151 El Camino
Beverly Hills, CA 90212
*Actor*

**Mohamed, D. S. Mahathir bin**
Office of the Prime Minister
Jalan Dato Onn
Kuala Lumpur, Malaysia
*Prime Minister of Malaysia*

**Mohammed, Ali Mahdi**
Office of the President
Mogadishu, Somalia
*President of Somalia*

**Moi, Daniel arap**
Office of the President
P.O. Box 30510
Nairobi, Kenya
*President of Kenya*

**Molly Brown House, The**
1340 Pennsylvania St.
Denver, CO 80203
Jennifer Moulton, Executive
  Director
*Former residence of the Unsinkable
  Molly Brown*

**Momoh, Major General
  Joseph Saidu**
Office of the President
Freetown, Sierra Leone
*President of Sierra Leone*

**Monday Night Football**
ABC Sports
47 W. 66th St.
New York, NY 10023
Jack O'Hara, Executive
  Producer

**Money World**
World Perspective
  Communications, Inc.
3443 Parkway Center Ct.
Orlando, FL 32808
G. Patrick Chauhas, Editor
*Magazine*

**Monitor**
1506 19th St., NW
Washington, DC 20036
Craig Van Note, Executive Vice-
  President
*Clearinghouse for info on
  endangered species*

**Monsanto Company**
800 N. Lindbergh Blvd.
St. Louis, MO 63167
Richard J. Mahoney, Chairman
and CEO
*Third largest U.S. chemical
company*

**Montana, Joe**
4949 Centennial Blvd.
Santa Clara, CA 95054
*Professional football player*

**Montana Historical Society**
225 N. Roberts
Helena, MT 59620
Lawrence J. Sommer, Director
and CEO

**Montgomery, Belinda**
15301 Ventura Blvd., #345
Sherman Oaks, CA 91403
*Actress*

**Montgomery, Elizabeth**
9830 Wilshire Blvd.
Beverly Hills, CA 90212
*Actress*

**Montgomery Museum of Fine
Arts**
One Museum Dr.
Montgomery, AL 36117
J. Brooks Joyner, Director

**Montgomery Ward Holding
Corp.**
One Montgomery Ward Plaza
Chicago, IL 60671
Bernard F. Brennan, Chairman,
President and CEO
*Retail store chain*

**Montreal Canadiens**
2513 Ste. Catherine W.
Montreal, Québec H3H 1N2
Canada
Fred Steer, Vice-President
*Professional hockey team*

**Montreal Expos**
P.O. Box 500, Station M
Montreal, Québec H1V 3P2
Canada
Bill Stoneman, Vice-President
*Professional baseball team*

**Monty Python Special
Interest Group**
2419 Greensburg Pike
Pittsburgh, PA 15221
*Henry Roll, Coordinator*

**Moody Blues**
11111 Santa Monica Blvd.,
20th Fl.
Los Angeles, CA 90023
*Rock group*

**Moon, Warren**
c/o Houston Oilers
6910 Fannin St.
Houston, TX 77030
*Professional football player*

**Moore, Demi**
9830 Wilshire Blvd.
Beverly Hills, CA 90212
*Actress*

**Moore, Roger**
822 S. Robertson Blvd., #200
Los Angeles, CA 90035
*Actor*

**Moran, Erin**
11075 Santa Monica Blvd.,
#150
Los Angeles, CA 90025
*Less than happy "Happy Days" star*

**Morgan Stanley Group Inc.**
1251 Ave. of the Americas
New York, NY 10020
Richard B. Fisher, Chairman
*International securities firm*


**Moriarty, Michael**
10351 Santa Monica Blvd.,
   #211
Los Angeles, CA 90025
*Actor*


**Morita, Pat (Noriyuki)**
P.O. Box 491278
Los Angeles, CA 90049
*Actor*


**Morris, Jack**
c/o Minnesota Twins
501 Chicago Ave., S.
Minneapolis, MN 55415
*Baseball pitcher, Most Valuable
   Player of the 1991 World Series*


**Morrow, Rob**
151 El Camino
Beverly Hills, CA 90212
*Actor*


**Morton International, Inc.**
110 N. Wacker Dr.
Chicago, IL 60606
Charles S. Locke, Chairman and
   CEO
*The salt company*


**Mother Jones Magazine**
The Foundation for National
   Progress
1663 Mission St., 2nd Fl.
San Francisco, CA 94103
Doug Foster, Editor


**Mothers Without Custody**
P.O. Box 56762
Houston, TX 77256
Janet Stockbridge, President
*Support group*


**Mötley Crüe**
345 North Maple Dr., #123
Beverly Hills, CA 90210
*Rock group*


**Motor Trend**
Petersen Publishing Co.
8490 Sunset Blvd.
Los Angeles, CA 90069
Jeff Karr, Editor
*Car magazine*


**Motorola, Inc.**
1303 E. Algonquin Rd.
Schaumburg, IL 60196
George M. C. Fisher, Chairman
   and CEO
*World's leading supplier of mobile
   radios, cellular telephone systems
   and pagers*


**Motown Record Company,
   L.P.**
729 Seventh Ave., 12th Fl.
New York, NY 10019
Jheryl Busby, President/CEO
*Recording company*


**Mount Vernon—Ladies'
   Association of the Union**
End of George Washington
   Pkwy., S.
Mt. Vernon, VA 22121
Neil W. Horstmann, CEO


**Mousekowitz, Fievel**
c/o Amblin Entertainment
100 Universal City Plaza
Universal City, CA 91609
*Cartoon mouse*

**Movie Channel, The**
c/o Showtime Networks, Inc.
1633 Broadway
New York, NY 10019
Winston H. Cox, Chairman/
   CEO
*Premium cable movie channel*

**Moynihan, Daniel P.**
464 Senate Russell Office Bldg.
Washington, DC 20510
*Senator from New York*

**Mr. Frick**
**(Werner Fritz Groebli)**
U.S. Figure Skating Association
20 First St.
Colorado Springs, CO 80906
*Professional ice skater*

**Mr. Rogers**
**(Fred)**
c/o Family Communications
4802 Fifth Ave.
Pittsburgh, PA 15213
*Kids' program host*

**Mr. Wizard**
**(Donald Jeffrey Herbert)**
P.O. Box 83
Canoga Park, CA 91305
*Television science teacher*

**Mrs. Fields Cookies**
P.O. Box 680370
Park City, UT 84068
Debbie Fields, Founder

**Ms. Elizabeth**
P.O. Box 3857
Stamford, CT 06905
*Professional wrestler*

**MTV Networks**
1515 Broadway
New York, NY 10019
Thomas E. Freston, Chairman/
   CEO
*Music television cable network*

**Mubarak, Hosni**
Presidential Palace
Abdeen, Cairo, Egypt
*President of Egypt*

**Mugabe, Robert**
Office of the President
Harare, Zimbabwe
*Executive President of Zimbabwe*

**Muldaur, Maria**
P.O. Box 5535
Mill Valley, CA 94942
*Singer*

**Mull, Martin**
9000 Santa Monica Blvd.,
   #1200
Los Angeles, CA 90069
*Comedian, actor*

**Mulligan, Gerry**
1416 N. LaBrea Ave.
Hollywood, CA 90028
*Jazz composer, arranger, musician,*
   *songwriter*

**Mulligan, Richard**
c/o Witt, Thomas, Harris
846 Cahuenga Blvd.
Hollywood, CA 90038
*Actor*

**Mullin, Chris**
c/o Golden State Warriors
Nimitz Freeway and
   Hegenberger Rd.
Oakland, CA 94621
*Professional basketball player*

**Mulroney, Brian**
Office of the Prime Minister
Langevin Block, 80 Wellington
    Street
Ottawa K1A 042 Canada
*Prime Minister of Canada*

**Munzer, Cynthia Brown**
165 W. 57th St.
New York, NY 10019
*Mezzo-soprano*

**Murkowski, Frank H.**
709 Senate Hart Office Bldg.
Washington, DC 20510
*Senator from Alaska*

**Murphy, Eddie**
5555 Melrose Ave.
Los Angeles, CA 90038
*Actor, comedian, producer*

**Murray, Bill**
RFD #1, Box 250A, Washington
    Springs
Palisades, NY 10964
*Actor*

**Murray-O'Hair, R.**
American Atheist Press
P.O. Box 140195
Austin, TX 78714
*Atheist*

**Muscle Mag International**
52 Bramsteele Rd., Unit 2
Brampton, Ontario L6W 3M5
    Canada
Robert Kennedy, Editor
*Bodybuilding magazine*

**Museum of Arts and Sciences**
1040 Museum Blvd.
Daytona Beach, FL 32114
Gary Russell Libby, CEO and
    Director

**Museum of Broadcasting,
    The**
25 W. 52nd St.
New York, NY 10019
Dr. Robert M. Batscha,
    President

**Museum of Church History
    and Art**
45 N. West Temple St.
Salt Lake City, UT 84150
Glen M. Leonard, Director

**Museum of Contemporary
    Art, The**
250 S. Grand Ave.
California Plaza
Los Angeles, CA 90012
Frederick M. Nicholas,
    Chairman Board of Trustees

**Museum of Migrating People**
Harry S. Truman High School
750 Baychester Ave.
Bronx, NY 10475
Peter Lerner, Curator

**Museum of Modern Art, The**
11 W. 53rd St.
New York, NY 10019
Richard E. Oldenburg, Director

**Museum of Neon Art**
704 Traction Ave.
Los Angeles, CA 90013
Lili Lakich, CEO and Director

**Museum of Northern Arizona**
Fort Valley Rd., Rt. 4, Box 720
Flagstaff, AZ 86001
Phillip M. Thompson, Director
    and CEO

**Museum of Robotics**
4026 Martin Luther King Jr.
 Way
Oakland, CA 94609
Richard L. Amoroso, Director
*Robot museum*

**Museveni, Yoweri Kaguta**
Office of the President
Kampala, Uganda
*President of Uganda*

**Mushing**
Stellar Communications, Inc.
P.O. Box 149
Ester, AK 99725
Todd Hoener, Editor
*Dogsledding magazine*

**Musser, Tharon**
21 Cornelia St.
New York, NY 10014
*Theatrical lighting designer*

**Mustang Monthly**
Dobbs Publications, Inc.
P.O. Box 7157
Lakeland, FL 33807
Tom Corcoran, Editor
*Car magazine*

**Musto, David F.**
3530 Pine Valley Dr.
Sarasota, FL 34239
*Drug and alcohol expert*

**Mwinyi, Ali Hassan**
c/o Office of the President
Dar es Salaam, United Republic
 of Tanzania
*President of Tanzania*

**My Old Kentucky Home**
E. Stephen Foster Ave.
Bardstown, KY 40004
Alice Heaton, Park
 Superintendent
*Place where Stephen Foster
 composed*

**Myerson, Roger Bruce**
Northwestern University
 Kellogg Graduate School of
 Mgmt.
2001 Sheridan Rd.
Evanston, IL 60208
*Game theorist*

**Mystery Writers of America**
236 W. 27th St., #600
New York, NY 10001
Priscilla Ridgway, Executive
 Secretary

N

A writer lives in awe of words for they can be cruel or kind, and they can change their meanings right in front of you. They pick up flavors and odors like butter in a refrigerator.

**Nader, Ralph**
P.O. Box 19367
Washington, DC 20036
*Consumer activist*

**Naismith Memorial Basketball Hall of Fame**
P.O. Box 179
1150 W. Columbus Ave.
Springfield, MA 01101
Bob Cousy, President

**Najibullah, Major General/ Dr.**
People's Democratic Party of Afghanistan
Kabul, Afghanistan
*President of Afghanistan*

**Namaliu, Rabbie**
The Prime Minister's Office
Government Buildings
Port Moresby
Papua, New Guinea
*Prime Minister of New Guinea*

**Nance, Larry**
c/o Cleveland Cavaliers
2923 Statesboro Rd.
Richfield, OH 44286
*Professional basketball player*

**NASA Lyndon B. Johnson Space Center**
2101 NASA Rd.
Houston, TX 77058
Hal Stall, Director of Public Affairs

**Nasty Boys, The**
P.O. Box 3857
Stamford, CT 06905
*Professional "tag team" wrestlers*

**National Abortion Rights Action League**
1101 14th St., NW
Washington, DC 20005
Kate Michelman, Executive Director

**National Adoption Information Exchange System**
67 Irving Pl.
New York, NY 10003
David S. Liederman, Executive Director
*A division of the Child Welfare League*

**National AIDS Hotline**
Department of Health and
 Human Services
200 Independence Ave., SW
Washington, DC 20201
(800) 342-2437
Dr. Antonia Novello, Surgeon
 General

**National Air and Space
 Museum**
Sixth St. and Independence
 Ave., SW
Washington, DC 20560
Martin Harwit, Director

**National Alliance for the
 Mentally Ill**
2101 Wilson Blvd., #302
Arlington, VA 22201
Laurie M. Flynn, Executive
 Director

**National Anorexic Aid
 Society**
5796 Karl Rd.
Columbus, OH 43229
Arline Iannicello, Program
 Director

**National Archives**
Pennsylvania Ave. & 8th St., NW
Washington, DC 20408
Dr. Don W. Wilson, Archivist of
 the U.S.

**National Association for
 Sickle Cell Disease**
4221 Wilshire Blvd., #360
Los Angeles, CA 90010
Dorothye H. Boswell, Executive
 Director

**National Association of
 Congregational Christian
 Churches**
Box 1620
Oak Creek, WI 53154
Dr. Lloyd M. Hall, Moderator
*Religious group*

**National Association of
 Scuba Diving Schools**
641 W. Willow St.
Long Beach, CA 90806
John Geffney, Executive
 Director

**National Association of
 Youth Clubs**
5808 16th St., NW
Washington, DC 20011
Carole A. Early, Headquarters
 Secretary

**National Association on Drug
 Abuse Problems**
355 Lexington Ave.
New York, NY 10017
Warren F. Pelton, President

**National Audubon Society**
950 Third Ave.
New York, NY 10022
Harold E. Woodsum, Jr.,
 Chairman of the Board

**National Automobile
 Museum**
10 Lake St., South
Reno, NV 89501
Charles C. Hilton, Executive
 Director and CEO
*Harrah automobile collection*

**National Baseball Hall of
 Fame and Museum, Inc.**
Box 590
Cooperstown, NY 13326
Edward W. Stack, President

**National Basketball Association**
645 Fifth Ave.
New York, NY 10022
David J. Stern, Commissioner

**National Baton Twirling Association, International**
P.O. Box 266
Janesville, WI 53545
Don Sartell, President

**National Bowling Hall of Fame and Museum**
111 Stadium Plaza
St. Louis, MO 63102
R. R. Woodruff, President

**National Center for the Study of Corporal Punishment and Alternatives in the School**
Temple University
253 Ritter Annex
Philadelphia, PA 19122
Irwin A. Hyman, Director

**National Clearinghouse for Alcohol and Drug Information**
P.O. Box 2345
Rockville, MD 20852
Dr. David Rowden, Director

**National Coalition Against the Misuse of Pesticides**
530 Seventh St., SE
Washington, DC 20003
Contact Jay Feldman

**National Committee for Amish Religious Freedom**
30650 Six Mile Rd.
Livonia, MI 48152
Rev. William C. Lindholm, Chairman
*Defends Amish whose beliefs won't let them defend themselves*

**National Committee for the Prevention of Child Abuse**
332 S. Michigan Ave.
Chicago, IL 60604
Beth Waid, Executive Director

**National Council of Family Relations**
1910 W. County Road B, #147
St. Paul, MN 55113
Mary Jo Czaplewski, Ph.D., Executive Director

**National Education Association**
1201 16th St., NW
Washington, DC 20036
Keith Geiger, President

**National Energy Foundation**
5160 Wiley Post Way, #200
Salt Lake City, UT 84116
Edward A. Dalton, President and CEO

**National Federation of Parents for Drug-Free Youth**
1423 N. Jefferson
Springfield, MO 65802
Karl Bernstein, President

**National Field Archery Association**
Main Interior Bldg.
18th and C Streets, NW, Rm. 2556
Washington, DC 20240
Charles H. Collins, Executive Director

**National Football Foundation and Hall of Fame Inc., The**
Hall of Fame
King's Island, OH 45045
Dick Craig, General Manager

**National Football League**
410 Park Ave.
New York, NY 10022
Paul Tagliabue, Commissioner

**National Football League
    Player's Association**
AFL-CIO
2021 L Street, NW
Washington, DC 20036
Gene Upshaw, Executive
    Director
*Labor union for professional football
    players*

**National Forensic League**
671 Fond du Lac
Ripon, WI 54971
James Copeland, Executive
    Secretary
*Debate society*

**National Foster Parent
    Association
Information and Services
    Office**
226 Kitts Dr.
Houston, TX 77024
Gordon Evans, Director

**National Gallery of Art**
4th St. and Constitution Ave.,
    NW
Washington, DC 20565
Dr. Franklin D. Murphy,
    Chairman of the Board

**National Geographic Society**
1600 M St., NW
Washington, DC 20036
Gilbert M. Grosvenor, President
    and Chairman
*Geographic information, education
    and exploration*

**National Gerontology
    Resource Center**
1909 K St., NW
Washington, DC 20049
Paula M. Lovas, Director

**National Grange, The**
1616 H St., NW
Washington, DC 20006
Robert E. Barrow, Master

**National Hall of Fame for
    Famous American Indians**
P.O. Box 548
Anadarko, OK 73005
Allie Reynolds, President

**National Head Injury
    Foundation**
333 Turnpike Rd.
Southborough, MA 01772
Marilyn Price Spivack, President

**National Health Information
    Clearinghouse**
U.S. Department of Health and
    Human Services
P.O. Box 1133
Washington, DC 20013
Louis W. Sullivan, Secretary of
    Health and Human Services

**National Hemophilia
    Foundation**
110 Green St., Rm. 406
New York, NY 10012
Alan P. Brownstein, Executive
    Director

**National Hockey League**
650 Fifth Ave., 33rd Fl.
New York, NY 10019
William B. Wirtz, Chairman of
    the Board

**National Hot Rod Association**
2035 Financial Way
Glendora, CA 91740
Dallas Gardner, President

**National Lampoon**
155 Ave. of the Americas
New York, NY 10013
George Burkin, Editor-in-Chief
*Humor magazine*

**National League of Professional Baseball Clubs, The**
350 Park Ave.
New York, NY 10022
William White, President

**National Leather Association**
P.O. Box 17463
Seattle, WA 98107
George Nelson, Secretary
*Support network for leather/SM/ fetish community*

**National Listen America Club**
Box 100
Riverside, CA 92502
George W. French, President
*Anti-marijuana club*

**National Medical Enterprises, Inc.**
2700 Colorado Ave.
P.O. Box 4074
Santa Monica, CA 90404
Richard K. Eamer, Chairman and CEO
*Health care provider in 30 states*

**National Mental Health Association**
1021 Prince St.
Alexandria, VA 22314
Preston J. Garrison, Executive Director

**National Network of Runaway and Youth Services, Inc.**
1400 I Street, NW, #330
Washington, DC 20005
June Bucy, Executive Director

**National Organization for the Reform of Marijuana Laws (NORMAL)**
1636 R St., NW
Washington, DC 20009
Gregory Y. Porter, Acting National Director

**National Organization for Women, Inc.**
1000 16th St., NW, Suite 700
Washington, DC 20036
Patricia Ireland, President
*NOW, largest women's rights group in the U.S.*

**National Park Service**
1800 C St., NW
Washington, DC 20240
Manuel Lujan, Jr., Secretary of the Interior

**National Review**
150 E. 35th St.
New York, NY 10016
John O'Sullivan, Editor
*Political and cultural magazine*

**National Rifle Association of America**
1600 Rhode Island Ave., NW
Washington, DC 20036
Richard D. Riley, President

**National Self-Help Clearinghouse**
Graduate School and University Center
CUNY, 33 West 42nd St.
New York, NY 10036
Dr. Frank Riessman, Director

**National Semiconductor Corporation**
2900 Semiconductor Dr.
P.O. Box 58090
Santa Clara, CA 95052
Peter J. Sprague, Chairman
*Fourth largest producer of semiconductors in the U.S.*

**National Society for Prevention of Cruelty to Mushrooms**
1077 S. Airport Rd., W
Traverse City, MI 49684
Brad Brown, President

**National Speleological Society, Inc.**
Cave Ave.
Huntsville, AL 35810
John Scheltens, President
*Studies and preserves caves*

**National Trust for Historic Preservation**
1785 Massachusetts Ave., NW
Washington, DC 20036
Robert M. Bass, Chairman

**National Wild Turkey Federation, Inc.**
Wild Turkey Bldg., P.O. Box 530
Edgefield, SC 29824
Rob Keck, Executive Vice-President

**National Wildlife Federation**
1400 Sixteenth St., NW
Washington, DC 20036
George H. Hulsey, Chairman of the Board

**Natural Disasters (The Earthquake and Typhoon)**
P.O. Box 3857
Stamford, CT 06905
*Professional "tag team" wrestlers*

**Natural History Museum of Los Angeles County**
900 Exposition Blvd.
Los Angeles, CA 90007
Dr. Craig C. Black, Director

**Natural Resources Defense Council, Inc.**
40 West 20th St.
New York, NY 10011
John H. Adams, Executive Director

**Nature Conservancy, The**
1815 N. Lynn St.
Arlington, VA 22209
Frank D. Boren, President

**Naughton, James**
8899 Beverly Blvd.
Los Angeles, CA 90048
*Actor*

**Naughty by Nature**
c/o Tommy Boy Records
1747 First Ave.
New York, NY 10128
*Singing group*

**Navistar International Corporation**
455 N. Cityfront Plaza Dr.
Chicago, IL 60611
James C. Cotting, Chairman and CEO
*Formerly International Harvester, truck manufacturer*

**Navratilova, Martina**
c/o International Management Group
One Erieview Plaza
Cleveland, OH 44199
*Tennis player*

**NBC Entertainment**
a division of National
  Broadcasting, Inc.
3000 West Alameda Ave.
Burbank, CA 91523
Brandon Tartikoff, Chairman,
  NBC Entertainment Group
*Program division of NBC*

**NCNB Corporation**
One NCNB Plaza
Charlotte, NC 28255
Hugh L. McColl, Jr., Chairman
  and CEO
*Large banking corporation*

**NCR Corporation**
1700 S. Patterson Blvd.
Dayton, OH 45479
Charles E. Exley, Jr., Chairman
  and CEO
*Second largest manufacturer of
  ATMs in the U.S.*

**Ndamase, Chief Tutor
  Nyangilizwe**
Office of the President
Transkei, South Africa
*President of Transkei, South Africa*

**Neal, Patricia**
Box 1043
Edgartown, MA 02539
*Actress*

**Nebenzahl, Kenneth**
333 N. Michigan Ave.
Chicago, IL 60611
*Rare book and map dealer*

**Needham, Hal**
12711 Ventura Blvd., #440
Studio City, CA 91601
*Director and founder of Stunts
  Unlimited; owner of the fastest
  car in the world*

**Neeson, Liam**
9830 Wilshire Blvd.
Beverly Hills, CA 90212
*Actor*

**Negron, Taylor**
9000 Sunset Blvd., #1200
Los Angeles, CA 90069
*Comedian*

**Neiman, Leroy**
1 W. 67th St.
New York, NY 10023
*Artist*

**Nelligan, Kate**
8899 Beverly Blvd.
Los Angeles, CA 90048
*Actress*

**Nelson
(Matt and Gunnar)**
9130 Sunset Blvd.
Los Angeles, CA 90069
*Singing duo, third generation of
  musical Nelsons*

**Nelson, Ben**
State Capitol
Lincoln, NE 69509
*Governor of Nebraska*

**Nelson, Craig T.**
8899 Beverly Blvd.
Los Angeles, CA 90048
*Actor*

**Nelson, Harriet Hilliard**
13263 Ventura Blvd.
Studio City, CA 91604
*Actress*

**Nelson, Judd**
P.O. Box 69170
Los Angeles, CA 90069
*Actor*

**Nelson, Tracy**
9301 Wilshire Blvd., #312
Beverly Hills, CA 90210
*Actress*

**Nelson, Willie**
P.O. Box 33280
Austin, TX 78764
*Singer, songwriter*

**Nestlē Food Corporation**
100 Mahattanville Road
Purchase, NY 10577
C. A. MacDonald, President
*Candy company*

**Neuharth, Al**
*USA Today*
1000 Wilson Blvd., 14th Fl.
Arlington, VA 22229
USA Today *founder*

**Neuhaus, Richard John**
156 Fifth Ave., #400
New York, NY 10010
*Religious writer*

**Neurotics Anonymous
   International Liaison**
P.O. Box 466, Cleveland Park
   Station
Washington, DC 20008
Grover Boydston, Chairman

**New England Patriots**
Sullivan Stadium
Route 1
Foxboro, MA 02035
Patrick J. Sullivan, General
   Manager
*Professional football team*

**New Jersey Devils**
Byrne Meadowlands Arena
East Rutherford, NJ 07073
Lou Lamoriello, President/
   General Manager
*Professional hockey team*

**New Jersey Nets**
Brendan Byrne Arena
East Rutherford, NJ 07073
Bernie Mann, President
*Professional basketball team*

**New Kids on the Block**
Six St. Gregory St., #7001
Dorchester, MA 02124
*Pop group*

**New Mexico Chiles**
1501 12th Street, NW, Suite 108
Albuquerque, NM 87104
David Carr, General Manager
*Soccer team*

**New Museum of
   Contemporary Art**
583 Broadway
New York, NY 10012
Marcia Tucker, Director and
   Curator

**New Orleans Saints**
6928 Saints Ave.
Metairie, LA 70003
Jim Finks, President/General
   Manager
*Professional football team*

**New York Botanical Garden,
   The**
200th St. and Kazimiroff Blvd.
Bronx, NY 10458
James L. Ferguson, Chairman of
   the Board

**New York City Transit
   Authority**
370 Jay St.
Brooklyn, NY 11201
Alan F. Kiepper, President
*Largest subway/bus system in the
   world*

**New York Giants**
Giants Stadium
East Rutherford, NJ 07073
George Young, Vice-President/
General Manager
*Professional football team*

**New York Historical
Association**
Fenimore House
Lake Rd.
Cooperstown, NY 13326
Gates Helms Dawn, President

**New York Islanders**
Nassau Veterans Memorial
Coliseum
Hempstead Turnpike
Uniondale, NY 11553
William A. Torrey, Chairman of
the Board/General Manager
*Professional hockey team*

**New York Jets**
598 Madison Ave.
New York, NY 10022
Steve Gutman, President/COO
*Professional football team*

**New York Knickerbockers**
Four Penn Plaza
New York, NY 10001
Al Bianchi, Vice-President/
General Manager
*Professional basketball team*

**New York Life Insurance
Company**
51 Madison Ave.
New York, NY 10010
Harry G. Hohn, Chairman and
CEO
*Sixth largest life insurance company
in the U.S.*

**New York Mets**
126th and Roosevelt Ave.
Flushing, NY 11368
J. Frank Cashen, Executive Vice-
President/General Manager
*Professional baseball team*

**New York Public Library**
Astor, Lenox and Tilden
Foundations
5th Ave. and 42nd St.
New York, NY 10018
Dr. Timothy S. Healy, President

**New York Rangers**
Madison Square Garden
Four Penn Plaza
New York, NY 10001
Neil Smith, Vice-President/
General Manager
*Professional hockey team*

**New York Stock Exchange,
Inc.**
11 Wall St.
New York, NY 10005
William H. Donaldson,
Chairman and CEO
*Largest and oldest stock exchange in
the U.S.*

**New York Times Company,
The**
229 W. 43rd St.
New York, NY 10036
Arthur Ochs Sulzberger,
Chairman and CEO
*Newspaper and magazine publisher*

**New York Transit Museum**
81 Willoughby St., Rm. 602
Brooklyn, NY 11201
Terrie S. Rouse, Director
*Subway museum*

**New York Turtle and Tortoise Society**
163 Amsterdam Ave., #365
New York, NY 10023
Suzanne Dohm, President

**New York Yankees**
Yankee Stadium
Bronx, NY 10451
Harding "Pete" Peterson,
General Manager
*Professional baseball team*

**New York Zoological Park—Bronx Zoo**
185th St. and Southern Blvd.
Bronx, NY 10460
Howard Phipps, Jr., President

**New York Zoological Society**
Zoological Park, 185 St. and
Southern Blvd.
Bronx, NY 10460

**New Yorker, The**
20 W. 43rd St.
New York, NY 10036
Tina Brown, Editor
*Magazine*

**Newman, Johnny**
c/o Charlotte Hornets
Hive Dr.
Charlotte, NC 28217
*Professional basketball player*

**Newman, Paul**
9830 Wilshire Blvd.
Beverly Hills, CA 90212
*Actor, director, race car driver*

**Newton, Wayne**
6000 S. Eastern Ave., #7B
Las Vegas, NV 89119
*Entertainer*

**Newsmaker Interviews**
8217 Beverly Blvd.
Los Angeles, CA 90048
Arthur Levine, Founder
*Newsletter for radio stations to
obtain interviews*

**Newton-John, Olivia**
P.O. Box 2710
Malibu, CA 90265
*Singer, entrepreneur*

**Nez Perce National Historical Park**
P.O. Box 93
Spalding, ID 83551
Roy W. Weaver, Superintendent

**Nicholas, Denise**
9169 Sunset Blvd.
Los Angeles, CA 90069
*Actress*

**Nickelodeon/Nick at Night**
1633 Broadway
New York, NY 10019
Geraldine Laybourne, President
*Cable channel for kids*

**Nicklaus, Jack William**
Golden Bear
1208 U.S. Hwy. 1
North Palm Beach, FL 33408
*Professional golfer*

**Nickles, Don**
713 Senate Hart Office Bldg.
Washington, DC 20510
*Senator from Oklahoma*

**Nicks, Stevie**
P.O. Box 6907
Alhambra, CA 91802
*Singer*

**Nielsen, Leslie**
15760 Ventura Blvd., #1730
Encino, CA 91436
*Actor*

**Nike, Inc.**
One Bowerman Dr.
Beaverton, OR 97005
Philip H. Knight, Chairman
    and CEO
*Athletic shoe manufacturer*

**Nilsson, Birgit**
Box 527
Stockholm, Sweden
*Actress*

**Nilsson, Harry**
CL Sims Corp.
11330 Ventura Blvd.
Studio City, CA 91604
*Singer, songwriter*

**Nimoy, Leonard**
232 N. Canon Dr.
Beverly Hills, CA 90210
*Actor, director*

**Nintendo**
4820 150th Ave. NE
Redmond, WA 98052
Hiroshi Yamauchi, President
*Video game company*

**Nirvana**
9130 Sunset Blvd.
Los Angeles, CA 90069
*Rock group*

**Nixon, Marni**
9000 Sunset Blvd., #1200
Los Angeles, CA 90069
*Everybody's film singing voice*

**Nixon, Richard M.**
577 Chestnut Ridge
Woodcliffe Lake, NJ 07675
*Former President*

**Noguchi, Thomas Tsunetomi**
University of Southern
    California Medical Center
1200 N. State St., #2519
Los Angeles, CA 90033
*Author, forensic pathologist, former
    "celebrity coroner"*

**Nolte, Nick**
8899 Beverly Blvd.
Los Angeles, CA 90048
*Actor*

**Noone, Kathleen**
606 N. Larchmont Blvd., #309
Los Angeles, CA 90004
*Actress*

**Noone, Peter**
VH-1
1515 Broadway
New York, NY 10036
*"My Generation" host, Herman of
    Herman's Hermits*

**Nordstrom, Inc.**
1501 Fifth Ave.
Seattle, WA 98101
Bruce A. Nordstrom, Co-
    Chairman
John N. Nordstrom, Co-
    Chairman
*Service-oriented department store
    chain*

**Norfolk Southern
    Corporation**
Three Commercial Place
Norfolk, VA 23510
Arnold B. McKinnon,
    Chairman and CEO
*Norfolk Southern Railway and
    North American Van Lines*

**Noriega, Gen. Manuel**
2601 Bayshore, #1400
Coconut Grove, FL 33133
*Imprisoned ex-head of state*

**Norman, Greg**
IMG
One Erieview Plaza, #1300
Cleveland, OH 44114
*Professional golfer*

**Norman the Lunatic
(Makhan Singh)**
1692 Sprinter St., NW
Atlanta, GA 30318
*Professional wrestler*

**Norris, Chuck**
P.O. Box 872
Navosta, TX 77868
*Martial arts star*

**North, Oliver**
703 Kentland Dr.
Great Falls, VA 22066
*Iran-Contra participant*

**North American Association
of Ventriloquists**
800 West Littleton Blvd.
P.O. Box 420
Littleton, CO 80160
Clinton Detweiler, President

**North American Loon Fund**
RR4, Box 240C
Meredith, NH 03253
Scott Sutcliffe, Chairman

**North American Wildlife
Foundation**
102 Wilmot Rd., #410
Deerfield, IL 60015
P.A.W. Green, President

**Northrop Corporation**
1840 Century Park E.
Los Angeles, CA 90067
Kent Kresa, Chairman,
President and CEO
*Manufactures B-2 Stealth bombers*

**Northwestern Mutual Life
Insurance Co., The**
720 E. Wisconsin Ave.
Milwaukee, WI 53202
Donald J. Schuenke, Chairman
and CEO
*Tenth largest life insurance
company in the U.S.*

**Norton Simon Museum**
411 W. Colorado Blvd.
Pasadena, CA 91105
Jennifer Jones Simon, President

**Novak, Kim**
Rt. #3, Box 524
Carmel Highlands, CA 93921
*Actress*

**Novak, Robert D.**
1750 Pennsylvania Ave., NW,
1312
Washington, DC 20006
*Columnist*

**Novell, Inc.**
122 E. 1700 S.
Provo, UT 84606
Raymond J. Noorda, Chairman,
President and CEO
*Produces LANs (Local Area
Networks) for PCs*

**Novello, Don**
9200 Sunset Blvd., #408
Los Angeles, CA 90069
*Writer, comedian*

**Nugent, Nelle**
Foxboro Entertainment
133 E. 58th St., #301
New York, NY 10022
*Theater, film and TV producer*

**Nujoma, Sam Shafilshuna**
c/o Office of the President
Namibia
*President of Namibia*

**Nunn, Sam**
303 Senate Dirksen Office Bldg.
Washington, DC 20510
*Senator from Georgia*

**NWA Inc.**
Minneapolis/St. Paul
  International Airport
St. Paul, MN 55111
Alfred A. Checci, Co-Chairman
*Northwest and Eastern Airlines*

**NYNEX Corporation**
335 Madison Ave.
New York, NY 10017
William C. Ferguson, Chairman
  and CEO
*Fourth largest of the old Bell
  companies*

O

The world did not impact upon me until I got to the post office.

—CHRISTOPHER MORLEY

**Oak Ridge Boys**
329 Rockland Rd.
Hendersonville, TN 37075
*Singing group*

**Oakland Athletics**
Oakland-Alameda County
    Stadium
Oakland, CA 94621
Roy Esenhardt, Executive Vice-
    President
*Professional baseball team*

**Oates, Joyce Carol**
Princeton University
    Department of English
Princeton, NJ 08544
*Author*

**Occidental Petroleum
    Corporation**
10889 Wilshire Blvd.
Los Angeles, CA 90024
Ray R. Irani, Chairman, CEO
    and President
*"Oxy," founded by the late Armand
    Hammer*

**Ochirbat, Punsalmaagiin**
Presidential Palace
Ulan Bator
Mongolian People's Republic
*Chairman of the Presidium of the
    Great People's Khural*

**O'Connor, Carroll**
130 W. 57th St., #10A
New York, NY 10019
*Actor, restaurateur*

**O'Connor, Donald**
P.O. Box 4524
North Hollywood, CA 91607
*Famous hoofer*

**O'Connor, Sandra Day**
U.S. Supreme Court Building
1 First Street, NE
Washington, DC 20543
*Associate Justice of the Supreme
    Court*

**O'Connor, Sinéad**
13 Red Lion Square, 10 Halsey
    House
London WC1 England
*Singer*

**Octagon, The**
1799 New York Ave., NW
Washington, DC 20006
James Cramer, CEO
*Temporary White House during*
  *Madison presidency*

**O'Donnell, Rosie**
151 El Camino
Beverly Hills, CA 90212
*Comedienne, actress*

**Office Depot, Inc.**
851 Broken Sound Pkwy., NW
Boca Raton, FL 33487
David I. Fuente, Chairman and
  CEO
*Discount office supply stores*

**Ogden Corporation**
Two Pennsylvania Plaza
New York, NY 10121
Ralph E. Ablon, Chairman
*Multi-interest conglomerate*

**Oguendo, Jose**
c/o St. Louis Cardinals
Busch Stadium
St. Louis, MO 63102
*Professional baseball player*

**O'Hara, Maureen**
Box 1400
Christiansted, St. Croix, VI
  00820
*Actress*

**Ohio State University, The**
1800 Cannon Dr.
Columbus, OH 43210
Edward Jennings, Chief
  Executive
*Largest university in the U.S.*

**Okino, Betty**
c/o Karoly's Gymnastics
17203 Bamwood
Houston, TX 77090
*Gymnast*

**Olajuwon, Hakeem**
c/o Houston Rockets
The Summit
Houston, TX 77046
*Professional basketball player*

**Old Jail Center, The**
Rte. 1—Box 1
Albany, TX 76430
Nancy E. Green, Chairman
*Jail museum*

**Old Mint Museum and**
  **Public Sales**
88 Fifth and Mission Sts.
San Francisco, CA 94103
Olga K. Melko, Public Archives
  Administrator
*Money museum*

**Old World Wisconsin**
816 State St.
Madison, WI 53706
H. Nicholas Muller III, CEO
*Historic village*

**Olin, Ken**
P.O. Box 5617
Beverly Hills, CA 90210
*Actor/director*

**Oliner, Samuel and Pearl**
Humboldt State
Department of Sociology
Arcata, CA 95521
*Sociologists, authors*

**Olmos, Edward James**
10000 Santa Monica Blvd.,
  #305
Los Angeles, CA 90067
*Actor/director*


**Olsen, Ashley and Mary Kate**
c/o Robert Thorne
10100 Santa Monica Blvd.,
  #2200
Los Angeles, CA 90067
*Twins who play one character on
  "Full House"*


**Omni**
1965 Broadway
New York, NY 10023
Keith Ferrell, Editor
*Science magazine*


**O'Neal, Ryan**
8899 Beverly Blvd.
Los Angeles, CA 90048
*Actor*


**Ono, Yoko**
One W. 72nd St.
New York, NY 10023
*Singer, artist, famous widow*


**Onorati, Peter**
5750 Wilshire Blvd., #512
Los Angeles, CA 90036
*Actor*


**Oracle Systems Corporation**
500 Oracle Parkway
Redwood City, CA 94065
Lawrence J. Ellison, Chairman,
  President and CEO
*Creates database management
  systems*


**Orbach, Jerry**
1999 Ave. of the Stars, #2850
Los Angeles, CA 90067
*Actor, voice of Lumiere in* Beauty
  and the Beast


**Oregon Electric Railway
  Historical Society**
17744 SW Ivy Glenn Dr.
Beaverton, OR 97007
Gregg Bonn, President and
  Museum Director


**Orlando Magic**
Orlando Arena
One Magic Pl.
Orlando, FL 32801
Pat Williams, President/General
  Manager
*Professional basketball team*


**Orr, Bobby
(Robert Gordon)**
647 Summer St.
Boston, MA 02210
*Former hockey player*


**Orthodox Church in America**
P.O. Box 675
Syosset, NY 11791
Metropolitan Theodosius,
  Primate
*Religious group*


**Oryx Energy Company**
13155 Noel Rd.
Dallas, TX 75240
Robert P. Hauptfuhrer,
  Chairman and CEO
*Largest independent gas and oil
  producer in the world*


**Osborne, Donovan**
c/o St. Louis Cardinals
Busch Stadium
St. Louis, MO 63102
*Professional baseball player*

**Osbourne, Ozzy**
1801 Century Park W.
Los Angeles, CA 90067
*Singer*

**Oscar Getz Museum of**
  **Whiskey History**
114 N. Fifth St.
Bardstown, KY 40004
Donald Keene, Director

**Oscar Mayer**
P.O. Box 7188
Madison, WI 53707
James W. McVey, Chief
  Executive Officer
*Hot dog company*

**Osmond, Donny**
**(Donald Clark)**
151 El Camino
Beverly Hills, CA 90212
*Former teen idol, with successful*
  *new image*

**O'Toole, Peter**
151 El Camino
Beverly Hills, CA 90212
*Actor*

**Outboard Marine**
  **Corporation**
100 Sea-Horse Dr.
Waukegan, IL 60085
Charles D. Strang, Chairman
*World's largest producer of outboard*
  *motors*

**Ovitz, Michael**
9830 Wilshire Blvd.
Beverly Hills, CA 90212
*Super talent agent*

**Owens-Corning Fiberglas**
  **Corporation**
Fiberglas Tower
Toledo, OH 43659
Max O. Weber, Chairman and
  CEO
*World's largest fiberglass producer*

**Owens-Illinois, Inc.**
One SeaGate
Toledo, OH 43666
Joseph H. Lemieux, President
  and CEO
*Produces or licenses over one-half*
  *of the glass containers made*
  *worldwide*

**Ozal, Turgut**
Cumhurbaskanligi Kosku
Cankaya, Ankara, Turkey
*President of Turkey*

There are no words to express the abyss between isolation and having one ally. It may be conceded to the mathematician that four is twice two. But two is not twice one; two is two thousand times one.

—G.K. CHESTERTON

**P C Quest**
**Drew Nichols, Kim Whipkey, Steve Petree, Chad Petree**
1133 Ave. of the Americas
New York, NY 10036
*Singing group*

**P M Dawn**
14 E. Fourth St.
New York, NY 10012
*Rock group*

**Paccar Inc.**
777 106th Ave. NE
Bellevue, WA 98004
Charles M. Pigott, Chairman and CEO
*Makes Peterbilt, Kenworth and Foden heavy trucks*

**Pacific Enterprises**
633 W. Fifth St.
Los Angeles, CA 90017
James R. Ukropina, Chairman and CEO
*Owns Southern California Gas Company and Thrift discount stores*

**Pacific Gas and Electric Company**
77 Beale St.
San Francisco, CA 94106
Richard A. Clarke, Chairman and CEO
*Largest U.S. electric and natural gas utility*

**Pacific Telesis Group**
130 Kearny St.
San Francisco, CA 94108
Sam Ginn, Chairman, President and CEO
*Eighth largest U.S. telephone company*

**Pacific Whale Foundation**
101 N. Kihei Rd.
Kihei, HI 96753
Gregory D. Kaufman, President

**Packwood, Bob**
259 Senate Russell Office Bldg.
Washington, DC 20510
*Senator from Oregon*

**Paeniu, Bikenibeu**
Office of the Prime Minister
Funafuti, Tuvalu
*Prime Minister of Tuvalu*

**Pagan/Occult/Witchcraft Special Interest Group**
P.O. Box 9336
San Jose, CA 95157
Valerie Voigt, Coordinator

**Paine Webber Group, Inc.**
1285 Ave. of the Americas
New York, NY 10019
Donald B. Marron, Chairman and CEO
*Paine Webber Inc. is the nation's fourth largest brokerage firm*

**Palance, Jack**
121 N. San Vicente Blvd.
Beverly Hills, CA 90211
*Actor*

**Palm Springs Desert Museum**
P.O. Box 2288
Palm Springs, CA 92263
Marshall M. Gelfand, President

**Palmer, Arnold Daniel**
Box 52
Youngstown, PA 15696
*Professional golfer*

**Palmer, Jim**
Box 145
Brooklandville, MD 21022
*Sportscaster, former baseball player and underwear pitchman*

**Palmer, Robert**
2A Chelsea Manor
Blood St.
London SW3 England
*Singer*

**Palomar Observatory**
105–24 C.I.T.
Pasadena, CA 91125
Dr. Gerry Neugebauer, Director

**Pan Am Corporation**
Pan Am Building
200 Park Ave.
New York, NY 10166
Thomas G. Plaskett, Chairman
*Bankrupt international airline*

**Panhandle Eastern Corporation**
5400 Westheimer Ct., P.O. Box 1642
Houston, TX 77251
Dennis B. Hendrix, Chairman, President and CEO
*Operates natural gas pipeline*

**Paramount Communications, Inc.**
5555 Melrose Ave.
Hollywood, CA 90038
Martin S. Davis, Chairman/CEO
*Television and film production company*

**Parenting Magazine**
501 Second St., #110
San Francisco, CA 94107
Lornora Weiner, Editor

**Parents Anonymous**
6733 S. Sepulveda, #270
Los Angeles, CA 90045
Margot Fritz, Executive Director
*Child abuse prevention*

**Parents Magazine**
685 Third Ave.
New York, NY 10017
Ann Pleshette Murphy, Editor-in-Chief

**Parents United**
P.O. Box 952
San Jose, CA 95108
Henry Giaretto, Ph.D.,
    Executive Director
*Support group*

**Parish, Robert**
c/o Boston Celtics
150 Causeway St.
Boston, MA 02114
*Professional basketball player*

**Parker, Alan William**
9830 Wilshire Blvd.
Beverly Hills, CA 90212
*Film director, writer*

**Parker, Colonel Tom**
P.O. Box 220
Madison, TN 37118
*Elvis mentor*

**Parker, Fess**
P.O. Box 50440
Santa Barbara, CA 93150
*Actor of Daniel Boone fame*

**Parker Brothers**
50 Dunham Rd.
Beverly, MA 01915
John Moore, President
*Toy and game manufacturer*

**Parton, Dolly**
Crockett Road, Rt. #1
Brentwood, TN 37027
*Singer, actress*

**Party, The**
P.O. Box 2510
Los Angeles, CA 90078
*Pop group*

**Pastorelli, Robert**
9255 Sunset Blvd., #515
Los Angeles, CA 90069
*Actor*

**Paterno, Joseph Vincent**
Penn State University Dept. of
    Athletics
University Park, PA 16802
*Football coach*

**Patterson, Floyd**
New York Athletic Commission
P.O. Box 336
New Paltz, NY 12561
*Athletic commissioner, former
    heavyweight boxer*

**Paul, Alexandra**
190 N. Canon Dr., #201
Beverly Hills, CA 90210
*Actress*

**Pauling, Linus Carl**
Linus Pauling Institute of
    Science and Medicine
440 Page Mill Rd.
Palo Alto, CA 94306
*Vitamin C pusher*

**Pavarotti, Luciano**
941 Via Giardini
41040 Saliceta S. Giuliano
Modena, Italy
*Opera star*

**Paxson, John**
c/o Chicago Bulls
980 N. Michigan Ave.
Chicago, IL 60611
*Professional basketball player*

**Pearl, Minnie
(Sarah Ophelia Colley Cannon)**
c/o J. Halsey
3225 S. Norwood St.
Tulsa, OK 74135
*Singer, comedienne*

**Pearl Jam**
P.O. Box 4450
New York, NY 10101
*Rock group*

**Peary-MacMillan Arctic
  Museum, The**
Hubbard Hall
Bowdoin College
Brunswick, ME 04011
Dr. Susan A. Kaplan, Director

**Peck, Gregory**
P.O. Box 837
Beverly Hills, CA 90213
*Actor*

**Peck, M. Scott**
Bliss Road
New Preston, CT 06777
*Psychiatrist, author,* The Road
  Less Traveled

**Peeples, Nia**
822 S. Robertson Blvd., #200
Los Angeles, CA 90035
*Actress, singer, "Dance Party"
  hostess*

**Pelham, David**
2 Park Ave.
New York, NY 10016
*Author*

**Pell, Claiborne**
335 Senate Russell Office Bldg.
Washington, DC 20501
*Senator from Rhode Island*

**Penghlis, Thao**
9320 Wilshire Blvd., 3rd Fl.
Beverly Hills, CA 90212
*Actor*

**Penn, Sean**
P.O. Box 2630
Malibu, CA 90265
*Actor*

**Penn & Teller**
P.O. Box 1196
New York, NY 10185
*Comedy magicians*

**Penny, Joe**
151 El Camino
Beverly Hills, CA 90212
*Actor*

**Pennzoil Company**
Pennzoil Pl.
P.O. Box 2967
Houston, TX 77252
J. Hugh Liedtke, Chairman
*19th largest U.S. oil company*

**People Magazine**
Time Inc.
Time and Life Building
Rockefeller Center
New York, NY 10020
Landon Y. Jones, Jr., Editor

**Peppard, George**
P.O. Box 1643
Beverly Hills, CA 90213
*Actor*

**Pepsico, Inc.**
Anderson Hill Rd.
Purchase, NY 10577
D. Wayne Calloway, Chairman
  and CEO
*Soft drink company*

**Peregrine Fund, Inc., The**
5666 West Flying Hawk Ln.
Boise, ID 83709
Roy E. Disney, Chairman of the
  Board
*Bird preservation*

**Perkins, Elizabeth**
9830 Wilshire Blvd.
Beverly Hills, CA 90212
*Actress*

**Perlman, Itzhak**
40 W. 57th St.
New York, NY 10019
*Violinist*

**Perot, H. Ross**
12377 Merit Dr.
Dallas, TX 75251
*Moneyed non-politician, politician*

**Perry, Luke**
1801 Ave. of the Stars, #1250
Los Angeles, CA 90067
*Actor*

**Person, Chuck**
c/o Indiana Pacers
300 E. Market St.
Indianapolis, IN 46204
*Professional basketball player*

**Pesci, Joe**
9830 Wilshire Blvd.
Beverly Hills, CA 90212
*Actor*

**Pescow, Donna**
P.O. Box 9375
Los Angeles, CA 90093
*Actress*

**Peter, Paul and Mary**
853 Seventh Ave.
New York, NY 10019
*Singing group*

**Peter Kiewit Sons Inc.**
1000 Kiewit Plaza
Omaha, NE 68131
Walter Scott, Jr., Chairman,
    President and CEO
*Heavy construction contractor*

**Petty, Richard**
Rte. 3, Box 631
Randleman, NC 27317
*Race car driver*

**Pfeiffer, Michelle**
8899 Beverly Blvd.
Los Angeles, CA 90048
*Actress*

**Pfizer Inc.**
235 E. 42nd St.
New York, NY 10017
Edmund T. Pratt, Jr., Chairman
*Drug company*

**Pheasants Forever, Inc.**
P.O. Box 75473
St. Paul, MN 55175
Robert Brengman, President
*Pheasant preservation*

**Phelps Dodge Corporation**
2600 N. Central Ave.
Phoenix, AZ 85004
Douglas C. Yearley, Chairman
    and CEO
*Largest copper producer in North
    America*

**Philadelphia Eagles**
Veterans Stadium
Broad St. and Pattison
Philadelphia, PA 19148
Harry Gamble, President/COO
*Professional football team*

**Philadelphia Flyers**
The Spectrum—Pattison Place
Philadelphia, PA 15219
Bobby Clark, Vice-President/
    General Manager
*Professional hockey team*

**Philadelphia Museum of Art**
P.O. Box 7646
Philadelphia, PA 19101
Robert Montgomery Scott,
  President and CEO

**Philadelphia Phillies**
P.O. Box 7575
Philadelphia, PA 19101
David Montgomery, Executive
  Vice-President
*Professional baseball team*

**Philadelphia 76ers**
Veterans Stadium
P.O. Box 25040
Philadelphia, PA 19147
John Nash, General Manager
*Professional basketball team*

**Philbin, Regis**
ABC Television Network
77 W. 66th St.
New York, NY 10023
*Talk show host*

**Philip Morris Companies,
  Inc.**
120 Park Ave.
New York, NY 10017
Michael A. Miles, Chairman
  and CEO
*Kraft, General Foods, Oscar Mayer,
  Miller Brewing, Benson &
  Hedges*

**Phillips, Julianne**
232 N. Canon Dr.
Beverly Hills, CA 90210
*Actress*

**Phillips, Lou Diamond**
1999 Ave. of the Stars, #2850
Los Angeles, CA 90067
*Actor*

**Phillips, Michelle**
301 N. Canon Dr., #305
Beverly Hills, CA 90210
*Actress, singer*

**Phillips, Wendy**
9301 Wilshire Blvd., #312
Beverly Hills, CA 90210
*Actress*

**Phillips Petroleum Company**
Phillips Bldg.
Bartlesville, OK 74004
C. J. Silas, Chairman and CEO
*Ninth largest integrated petroleum
  company in the U.S.*

**Phoenix Art Museum**
1625 N. Central Ave.
Phoenix, AZ 85004
James K. Ballinger, CEO

**Phoenix Cardinals**
P.O. Box 888
Phoenix, AZ 85001
Joe Rhein, Executive Vice-
  President
*Professional football team*

**Phoenix House Foundation**
164 W. 74th St.
New York, NY 10023
Mitchell S. Rosenthal, M.D.,
  President
*Drug rehab*

**Phoenix, River**
P.O. Box 520
Royal Palm Beach, FL 33411
*Actor*

**Phoenix Society**
11 Rust Hill Rd.
Levittown, PA 19056
Alan Jeffry Breslau, Executive
  Director
*Burn victim support group*

**Phoenix Suns**
2910 North Central
P.O. Box 1369
Phoenix, AZ 85001
Jerry Colangelo, President/CEO
*Professional basketball team*

**Pike, Christopher**
c/o Pocket/Archway
1230 Ave. of the Americas
New York, NY 10020
*Author*

**Pinchot, Bronson**
9200 Sunset Blvd., #428
Los Angeles, CA 90069
*Actor*

**Pink Floyd**
43 Portland Road
London W11 England
*Rock group*

**Pinnacle West Capital Corporation**
400 E. Van Buren St., Suite 700
Phoenix, AZ 85004
Richard Snell, Chairman,
    President and CEO
*Largest electric utility in Arizona*

**Pippen, Scottie**
c/o Chicago Bulls
980 N. Michigan Ave.
Chicago, IL 60611
*Professional basketball player*

**Pitney Bowes Inc.**
Stamford, CT 06926
George B. Harvey, Chairman,
    President and CEO
*Postage machine and business
    equipment manufacturers*

**Pittsburgh Penguins**
Gate Number 9, Civic Arena
Pittsburgh, PA 15219
Craig Patrick, General Manager
*Professional hockey team*

**Pittsburgh Pirates**
600 Stadium Circle
Pittsburgh, PA 15212
Larry Doughty, Senior Vice-
    President/General Manager
*Professional baseball team*

**Pittsburgh Steelers**
Three Rivers Stadium
300 Stadium Circle
Pittsburgh, PA 15212
Daniel M. Rooney, President
*Professional football team*

**Plainsman Museum**
210 16th St.
Aurora, NE 68818
Wesley C. Huenefeld, President
*Old West museum*

**Planned Parenthood
    Federation of America, Inc.**
810 Seventh Ave.
New York, NY 10019
Anne M. Saunier, Chairperson

**Plant, Robert Anthony**
c/o Atlantic Records
75 Rockefeller Plaza
New York, NY 10019
*Singer, composer*

**Platters, The**
P.O. Box 39
Las Vegas, NV 89101
*Singers*

**Playbill**
Playbill Inc.
71 Vanderbilt Ave., Suite 320
New York, NY 10169
Joan Alleman, Editor
*Theater magazine*

**Playboy**
680 N. Lakeshore Dr.
Chicago, IL 60611
Christine Hefner, Publisher
*Magazine*

**Playskool Inc.**
110 Pitney Rd.
Lancaster, PA 17602
S. Erman, Director
*Toy manufacturer*

**Pleshette, Suzanne**
P.O. Box 1492
Beverly Hills, CA 90213
*Actress*

**Plimpton, George Ames**
541 E. 72nd St.
New York, NY 10021
*Writer, editor, TV host*

**Plumb, Eve**
280 S. Beverly Dr., #400
Beverly Hills, CA 90212
*Actress, original Brady Bunch kid*

**PNC Financial Corp**
5th Ave. and Wood St.
Pittsburgh, PA 15222
Thomas H. O'Brien, Chairman,
   President and CEO
*Bank and investment company*

**Pointer Sisters**
10100 Santa Monica Blvd.,
   #1600
Los Angeles, CA 90067
*Singers*

**Poison**
1750 North Vine St.
Hollywood, CA 90028
*Rock group*

**Poitier, Sidney**
9830 Wilshire Blvd.
Beverly Hills, CA 90212
*Actor, director, 1992 AFI Lifetime
   Achievement award*

**Polaroid Corporation**
549 Technology Sq.
Cambridge, MA 02139
I. MacAllister Booth, Chairman,
   President and CEO
*Instant camera producers*

**Pollack, Cheryl**
P.O. Box 5617
Beverly Hills, CA 90210
*Actress*

**Pollan, Tracy**
9301 Wilshire Blvd., #312
Beverly Hills, CA 90210
*Actress*

**Polygram Records, Inc.**
3800 W. Alameda Ave., #1500
Burbank, CA 91505
Peter Takiff, Executive Vice-
   President, Administration
*Recording company*

**Pop Warner Football**
1315 Walnut St., #1632
Philadelphia, PA 19107
David Glenn Warner Tomlin,
   President
*Various leagues for various age
   groups, 7–16*

**Pope John Paul II (Karol Wojtyla)**
Apostolic Palace
Vatican City
*Religious leader*

**Popov, Dmitar**
Office of the Prime Minister
Sofia, Bulgaria
*Prime Minister of Bulgaria*

**Popular Mechanics**
Hearst Corp.
224 W. 57th St., 3rd Fl.
New York, NY 10019
Joe Oldham, Editor

**Population Crisis Committee**
1120 19th St., NW, #550
Washington, DC 20036
J. Joseph Speidel, M.D., M.P.H.,
    President

**Porter, Alisan**
131 S. Rodeo Dr., #300
Beverly Hills, CA 90212
*Actress*

**Porter, Terry**
c/o Portland Trail Blazers
700 NE Multnomah St.
Portland, OR 97232
*Professional basketball player*

**Portland Timbers**
10725 SW Barbur Blvd., Suite
    390
Portland, OR 97219
Art Dixon, President
*Soccer team*

**Portland Trail Blazers**
700 NE Multnomah St.
Suite 600, Lloyd Bldg.
Portland, OR 97232
Harry Glickman, President
*Professional basketball team*

**Post, Markie**
151 El Camino
Beverly Hills, CA 90212
*Actress*

**Potts, Annie**
10100 Santa Monica Blvd.,
    16th Fl.
Los Angeles, CA 90067
*Actress*

**Pouncey, Peter**
Amherst College
Amherst, MA 01002
*College president*

**Poundstone, Paula**
9000 Sunset Blvd., #1200
Los Angeles, CA 90069
*Comedienne*

**Powell, General Colin**
The Pentagon
Room 2E872
Washington, DC 20301
*Army boss*

**Powell, Laurence**
c/o Police Protective League
600 E. 8th St.
Los Angeles, CA 90014
*Officer involved in the Rodney King
    incident*

**Powers, Dr. James B.**
American Baptist Assn.
4605 N. State Line
Texarkana, TX 75503
*Religious group leader*

**Powers, Stefanie**
8899 Beverly Blvd.
Los Angeles, CA 90048
*Actress*

**PPG Industries Inc.**
One PPG Place
Pittsburgh, PA 15272
Vincent A. Sarni, Chairman and
    CEO
*World's largest automotive and
    industrial finishes supplier*

**Prager, Dennis**
6020 Washington Blvd., #2
Culver City, CA 90262
*Radio commentator, author, lecturer*

**Prelutsky, Jack**
c/o Alfred A. Knopf, Inc.
201 E. 50th St.
New York, NY 10022
*Author*

**Premadasa, Ranasinghe**
Office of the President
Republic Square
Colombo 1, Sri Lanka
*President of Sri Lanka*

**Premark International, Inc.**
1717 Deerfield Rd.
Deerfield, IL 60015
Warren L. Batts, Chairman and
    CEO
*Tupperware*

**Premiere**
Murdoch Publications, Inc.
    2 Park Ave., 4th Fl.
New York, NY 10016
Susan Lyne, Editor
*Entertainment magazine*

**Presbyterian Church (U.S.A.)**
100 Witherspoon St.
Louisville, KY 40202
C. Kenneth Hall, Contact
*Religious group*

**President's Council on
    Physical Fitness and Sports**
450 5th Street, NW, Suite 7103
Washington, DC 20001
Steve Guback, Director of
    Information

**Presley, Priscilla Beaulieu**
151 El Camino
Beverly Hills, CA 90212
*Actress*

**Pressler, Larry**
133 Senate Hart Office Bldg.
Washington, DC 20501
*Senator from South Dakota*

**Pressman Toy Corporation**
200 Fifth Ave., #1052
New York, NY 10010
James R. Pressman, President
*Toy manufacturer*

**Preston, Kelly**
9320 Wilshire Blvd., 3rd Fl.
Beverly Hills, CA 90212
*Actress*

**Price, Frank**
Columbia Studios
10202 W. Washington Blvd.
Culver City, CA 90232
*Film executive, producer*

**Price, Rt. Hon. George Cadle**
c/o House of Representatives
Belmopan, Belize
*Prime Minister of Belize*

**Price Company, The**
4649 Morena Blvd.
San Diego, CA 92117
Robert E. Price, Chairman and
    CEO
*Price Clubs, membership discount
    stores*

**Price Waterhouse**
Southwark Towers
32 London Bridge St.
London SE1 9SY England
*One of the top three accounting
firms in the U.S. and the world;
counts Oscar ballots*

**Pride, Charley**
c/o Chardon Inc.
3198 Royal Ln., #204
Dallas, TX 75229
*Country and western singer*

**Priestley, Jason**
2121 Ave. of the Stars, #950
Los Angeles, CA 90067
*Actor*

**Prime Computer, Inc.**
Prime Park
Natick, MA 01760
Russell E. Planitzer, Chairman
*Computer and software
manufacturer*

**Prime Ticket Network**
10000 Santa Monica Blvd.
Los Angeles, CA 90067
John Severino, President
*Sports cable network*

**Primerica Corporation**
65 E. 55th St.
New York, NY 10022
Sanford I. Weill, Chairman and
CEO
*Diversified financial services firm*

**Prince**
3300 Warner Blvd.
Burbank, CA 91510
*Musician, actor, director*

**Prince Hans Adam II**
Schloss Vaduz
Principality of Liechtenstein
*Ruler of the Principality of
Liechtenstein*

**Prince Rainier III**
Palais de Monaco
Boîte Postale 518
98015 Monte Carlo, Monaco
*Ruler of Monaco*

**Princess Diana
(Spencer Windsor)**
Kensington Palace
London W8 England
*Princess Di, Princess of Wales*

**Principal, Victoria**
10000 Santa Monica Blvd.,
#400
Los Angeles, CA 90067
*Actress, entrepreneur*

**Prison Families Anonymous**
353 Fulton Ave.
Hempstead, NY 11550
Sharon Brand, Executive
Director

**Private Pilot**
Fancy Publications Corp.
Box 6050
Mission Viejo, CA 92690
Mary F. Silitch, Editor
*Magazine for owner/pilots of
private aircraft*

**Pro Football Hall of Fame**
2121 George Halas Dr., NW
Canton, OH 44708
Peter R. Elliott, President/
Executive Director

**Pro Rodeo Hall of Fame and Museum of the American Cowboy**
101 Pro Rodeo Dr.
Colorado Springs, CO 80919
Lewis A. Cryer, CEO and President

**Procter & Gamble Company, The**
One Procter & Gamble Plaza
Cincinnati, OH 45202
Edwin L. Artzt, Chairman and CEO
*Personal care, laundry and food products*

**Professional Bowhunters Society**
P.O. Box 20066
Charlotte, NC 28202
Fred Richter, President

**Professional Bowler's Association of America**
1720 Merriman Rd.
P.O. Box 5118
Akron, OH 44313
John Petraglia, President

**Professional Golfers' Association Hall of Fame**
P.O. Box 109601
100 Ave. of the Champions
Palm Beach Gardens, FL 33418
Gary Wiren, Director

**Professional Pilot**
Queensmith Communications
3014 Colvin St.
Alexandria, VA 22314
Clifton Stroud, Editor
*Magazine*

**Professional Surfing Association of America**
530 Sixth St.
Hermosa Beach, CA 90254
L. Malek, Marketing Director

**Pronzini, William**
P.O. Box 1349
Sonoma, CA 95476
*Author*

**Prudential Insurance Co. of America**
751 Broad St.
Newark, NJ 07102
Robert C. Winters, Chairman and CEO
*The rock*

**Pryor, David H.**
267 Senate Russell Office Bldg.
Washington, DC 20510
*Senator from Arkansas*

**Public Broadcasting Service (PBS)**
Executive Headquarters
1320 Braddock Pl.
Alexandria, VA 22314
Bruce Christensen, President/CEO
*Viewer-supported noncommercial television network*

**Public Enemy**
c/o Columbia Records
1801 Century Park West
Los Angeles, CA 90067
*Rap group*

**Public Service Enterprise Group Inc.**
80 Park Plaza, P.O. Box 1171
Newark, NJ 07101
E. James Ferland, Chairman, President and CEO
*Parent company of PSE&G, electric and gas company*

**Publix Super Markets, Inc.**
P.O. Box 407, 1936 George
　Jenkins Blvd.
Lakeland, FL 33802
Charles H. Jenkins, Jr.,
　Chairman of the Executive
　Committee of the Board
*Largest grocery chain in Florida*


**Puett, Tommy**
9000 Sunset Blvd., #1200
Los Angeles, CA 90069
*Actor*

**Pulliam, Keshia Knight**
P.O. Box 866
Teaneck, NJ 07666
*Actress*

**Puppeteers of America**
Five Cricklewood Path
Pasadena, CA 91107
Paul Eide, President

**Puttnam, David Terence**
13/15 Queen's Gate Place Mews
London SW7 5BG England
*Film producer*

Real letter-writing makes writing into a different process because the letter is to somebody—a significant other—and not just a pronouncement to an imaginary world, a generalized other.

**Qaddafi, Colonel Muammar el**
Office of the President
Tripoli, Libya
*Libyan Head of State*

**Quaid, Dennis**
9830 Wilshire Blvd.
Beverly Hills, CA 90212
*Actor*

**Quail Unlimited, Inc.**
P.O. Box 10041
Augusta, GA 30903
M. McNiell Hollowy, President

**Quaker Oats Company, The**
Quaker Tower
P.O. Box 9001, 321 N. Clark St.
Chicago, IL 60604
William D. Smithburg,
    Chairman and CEO
*Cereal and pet food company*

**Quayle, J. Danforth**
Admiral House
34th and Massachusetts
Washington, DC 20005
*Former Vice-President of the United
    States*

**Québec Nordiques**
Colisée de Québec
2205 Avenue du Colisée
Québec, Québec G1L 4W7
    Canada
Martin Madden, General
    Manager
*Professional hockey team*

**Queen Beatrix
(Wilhelmina Armagard)**
Binnen Huf 19
The Hague 2513 AA, The
    Netherlands
*Queen of The Netherlands*

**Queen Emma Summer Palace**
2913 Pali Hwy.
Honolulu, HI 96817
Mildred Nolan, CEO
*King Kamehameha's base when he
    unified Hawaii*

**Queen Mary Museum and
    Spruce Goose (Howard
    Hughes's Flying Boat)**
Pier "J," P.O. Box 8
Long Beach, CA 90801
Keith Kambak, Vice-President
*Two big boats to visit*

**Quinn, Aidan**
9830 Wilshire Blvd.
Beverly Hills, CA 90212
*Actor*

**Quinn, Martha**
c/o MTV
1515 Broadway
New York, NY 10019
*MTV hostess*

An intention to write never turns into a letter. A letter must happen to one like a surprise, and one may not know where in the day there was room for it to come into being. So it is that my daily intentions have nothing to do with this fulfillment of today.

—RAINER MARIA RILKE,
*letter to F. von Bülow*

**Rabbit, Roger**
c/o Touchstone Pictures
500 S. Buena Vista St.
Burbank, CA 91521
*Cartoon rabbit*

**Rabin, Yitzhak**
Office of the Prime Minister
Hakirya, Ruppin Street
Jerusalem, Israel
*Prime Minister of Israel*

**Rachel Carson Council, Inc.**
8940 Jones Mill Rd.
Chevy Chase, MD 20815
Dr. Samuel S. Epstein, President
*International environmental
    clearinghouse*

**Rachins, Alan**
9000 Sunset Blvd., #1200
Los Angeles, CA 90069
*Actor*

**Rae, Charlotte**
P.O. Box 49991
Los Angeles, CA 90049
*Actress*

**Raffi**
**(Cavoukian)**
c/o Jensen Communications
120 S. Victory Blvd., #201
Burbank, CA 91502
*Singer*

**Rafsanjani, Hashemi**
c/o Islamic Republican Party
Dr. Al Shariati Avenue
Teheran, Iran
*President of Iran*

**Ragghianti, Marie**
3630 Pine Valley Dr.
Sarasota, FL 34239
*Former chairperson of Paroles and
    Pardons in Tennessee, subject of
    book and film*

**Rails-to-Rails Conservancy**
1400 16th St., NW, #300
Washington, DC 20036
Louise Sazlyn, President
*Railroad conservation group*

**Rainforest Alliance**
270 Lafayette St., #512
New York, NY 10012
Daniel R. Katz, President

**Raitt, Bonnie**
P.O. Box 626
Los Angeles, CA 90078
*Singer*

**Ralston Purina Company**
Checkerboard Sq.
St. Louis, MO 63164
William P. Stiritz, Chairman,
CEO and President
*Chuck Wagon, Eveready, Batman
cereal and Beech-Nut baby food*

**Ramaema, Colonel E. P.**
The Military Council
Maseru, Lesotho
*Lesotho Head of Government*

**Rambo, Dack**
Rambo Horse Farm
Earlimart, CA 93219
*Actor, AIDS activist*

**Ramos, Fernando**
Office of the President
Malacanong
Manila, Philippines
*President of the Philippines*

**Rampal, Jean-Pierre Louis**
15 Avenue Mozart
75016 Paris, France
*Flutist*

**Ramushwana, Colonel
Gabriel Mutheiwana**
Council of National Unity
Thohoyandou, Venda, South
Africa
*Chairman of the Council of
National Unity for Venda, South
Africa*

**Rancho Santa Ana Botanic
Garden**
1500 N. College Ave.
Claremont, CA 91711
Ernest A. Bryant, Chairman

**Randall, Ethan**
261 S. Robertson Blvd.
Beverly Hills, CA 90211
*Actor*

**Rao, P. V. Narasimha**
Lok Sabha
New Delhi, India
*Prime Minister of India*

**Raphael, Sally Jessy**
510 West 57th St.
New York, NY 10019
*Talk show host*

**Rasche, David**
P.O. Box 5617
Beverly Hills, CA 90210
*Actor*

**Raskin, Marcus Goodman**
Institute of Policy Studies
1601 Connecticut Ave., NW
Washington, DC 20009
*Writer*

**Rathbun, Melissa**
Fort Bliss
El Paso, TX 79907
*First woman soldier captured in the
Gulf War*

**Ratsiraka, Didier**
Présidence de la République
Antananarivo, Madagascar
*President and Head of State of
Madagascar*

**Rattle, Simon**
c/o H. Holt
31 Sinclair Rd.
London W14 ONS England
*Conductor*

**Rawlings, Flight Lt. Jerry John**
Office of the Head of State
The Castle
Accra, Ghana
*Chairman of the Provisional Defense Council of Ghana*

**Raytheon Company**
141 Spring St.
Lexington, MA 02173
Dennis J. Picard, Chairman and CEO
*Maker of the Patriot missile*

**RCA Records**
a division of BMG Music
1133 Ave. of the Americas
New York, NY 10036
Joe Galante, President
*Recording company*

**Reader's Digest Association, Inc., The**
Pleasantville, NY 10570
George V. Grune, Chairman and CEO
*Magazine, book and video publisher*

**Reagan, Ronald and Nancy**
668 St. Cloud Rd.
Los Angeles, CA 90077
*Ex-President and ex-First Lady*

**Real Santa Barbara**
105 E. De La Guerra, #4
Santa Barbara, CA 93101
C. Paul Davis, General Manager
*Soccer team*

**Reckell, Peter**
10100 Santa Monica Blvd., #700
Los Angeles, CA 90067
*Actor*

**Red Hot Chili Peppers**
75 Rockefeller Plaza, 20th Fl.
New York, NY 10019
*Rock group*

**Redbook Magazine**
224 W. 57th St.
New York, NY 10019
Diane Salvatore, Senior Editor

**Redford, Robert**
Rt. 3, Box 837
Provo, UT 84601
*Actor, director, activist*

**Reebok International Ltd.**
100 Technology Center Dr.
Stoughton, MA 02072
Paul B. Fireman, Chairman, President and CEO
*Second largest domestic producer of athletic shoes*

**Reed, Shanna**
15301 Ventura Blvd., #345
Sherman Oaks, CA 91403
*Actress*

**Reeve, Christopher**
P.O. Box 461
New York, NY 10024
*"Superman" actor*

**Reeves, Keanu**
9830 Wilshire Blvd.
Beverly Hills, CA 90212
*Actor*

**Reformed Episcopal Church in America**
2001 Frederick Rd.
Baltimore, MD 21228
Franklin Sellers, Presiding Bishop
*Religious group*

**Regalbuto, Joe**
5750 Wilshire Blvd., #512
Los Angeles, CA 90036
*Actor*

**Rehnquist, William H.**
U.S. Supreme Court Bldg.
One First Street, NE
Washington, DC 20543
*Chief Justice of the Supreme Court*

**Reid, Harry M.**
324 Senate Hart Office Bldg.
Washington, DC 20510
*Senator from Nevada*

**Reiner, Rob**
335 N. Maple Dr., #135
Beverly Hills, CA 90210
*Director, actor*

**Reitman, Ivan**
Universal Studios
100 Universal City Plaza
Universal City, CA 91608
*Film director, producer*

**Reliance Electric Company**
6065 Parkland Blvd.
Cleveland, OH 44124
H. Virgil Sherrill, Chairman
*Produces electrical, mechanical and
    telecommunication products*

**R.E.M.**
P.O. Box 8032
Athens, GA 30603
*Rock band*

**Remarried Parents, Inc.**
102–20 67th Dr.
Forest Hills, NY 11375
Jack Pflaster, Founder
*Information and support for newly
    combined families*

**Rene, France Albert**
The State House
Victoria, Mahe, Seychelles
*President of Seychelles*

**Renegade Warriors, The
(Chris and Mark Youngblood)**
1692 Sprinter St., NW
Atlanta, GA 30318
*Professional "tag-team" wrestlers*

**Reorganized Church of Jesus
    Christ of Latter Day Saints**
The Auditorium, P.O. Box 1059
Independence, MO 64051
Wallace B. Smith, President
*Religious group*

**Reptile & Amphibian
    Magazine**
RD 3, P.O. Box 3709
Pottsville, PA 17901
Norman Frank, Editor

**Republican Party**
310 First St., SE
Washington, DC 20003
Clayton Yeutter, Chairman

**Rescue 911**
Arnold Shapiro Productions
5800 Sunset Blvd., Bldg. #12
Hollywood, CA 90028
Arnold Shapiro, Executive
    Producer
*Life-saving reality TV series*

**Reynolds, Burt**
4000 Warner Blvd.
Burbank, CA 91522
*Actor, producer*

**Reynolds, Gene**
8439 Sunset Blvd., #402
Los Angeles, CA 90069
*Writer, producer, director*

**Reynolds, Dr. Herbert H.**
Baylor University
Waco, TX 76798
*University CEO*

**Reynolds Metals Company**
6601 W. Broad St., P.O. Box
27003
Richmond, VA 23261
William O. Bourke, Chairman
and CEO
*Second largest U.S. producer of
aluminum*

**Rhoads, Dr. Jonathan Evans**
3400 Spruce St.
Philadelphia, PA 19104
*Surgeon*

**Rhodes, Richard Lee**
Janklow & Nesbit
598 Madison Ave.
New York, NY 10022
*Writer*

**Ricardo, Joaquin Balaguer**
Oficina del Presidente
Santo Domingo, D.N.,
Dominican Republic
*President of the Dominican
Republic*

**Rice, Anne**
c/o Knopf
201 E. 50th St.
New York, NY 10022
*Witchcraft/vampire author*

**Rice, Glen**
c/o Miami Heat
Miami Arena
Miami, FL 33136
*Professional basketball player*

**Richards, Ann**
State Capitol
Austin, TX 78711
*Governor of Texas*

**Richards, Keith**
Raindrop Services
1776 Broadway
New York, NY 10019
*Musician*

**Richardson, Elliot Lee**
1825 I St., NW, #900
Washington, DC 20006
*Lawyer*

**Richie, Lionel**
P.O. Box 1862
Encino, CA 91426
*Singer, composer*

**Richmond, Mitch**
c/o Golden State Warriors
The Oakland Coliseum Arena
Oakland, CA 94621
*Professional basketball player*

**Ricker, Dr. Robert S.**
Baptist General Conference
2002 S. Arlington Heights Rd.
Arlington, IL 60005
*Religious leader*

**Riegle, Donald W., Jr.**
105 Senate Dirksen Office Bldg.
Washington, DC 20510
*Senator from Michigan*

**Rigg, Diana**
130 W. 57th St., #10A
New York, NY 10019
*Actress, PBS hostess*

**Righteous Brothers**
5218 Almont St.
Los Angeles, CA 90032
*Singers*

**Riklis Family Corporation**
725 Fifth Ave.
New York, NY 10022
Meshulam Riklis, Chairman
*Wheeler-dealer variety store
  company*

**Riley, Jeannie C.**
P.O. Box 454
Brentwood, TN 37027
*Singer*

**Riley, Pat**
c/o New York Knickerbockers
4 Pennsylvania Plaza
New York, NY 10001
*Basketball coach*

**Ringling Brothers Circus**
P.O. Box 2366
L'Enfant Plaza St.
Washington, DC 20026
Kenneth Feld, President

**Rio Grande Industries, Inc.**
Southern Pacific Transportation
  Co.
Pacific Bldg., One Market Plaza
San Francisco, CA 94105
Philip F. Anschutz, Chairman,
  President and CEO
*Railroad company*

**Rite Aid Corporation**
431 Railroad Ave.
Shiremanstown, PA 17011
Alex Grass, Chairman and CEO
*Discount drug store chain*

**Ritter, John**
10100 Santa Monica Blvd.,
  16th Fl.
Los Angeles, CA 90067
*Actor*

**Rivera, Geraldo**
481 Broadway
New York, NY 10013
*Talk show host, investigative
  reporter*

**RJR Nabisco Inc.**
9 West 57th St., 48th Fl.
New York, NY 10019
Louis V. Gerstner, Jr., CEO/
  Chairman of the Board
*Cookies, crackers, nuts and snack
  food manufacturer*

**Road King Magazine**
Box 250
Park Forest, IL 60466
George Friend, Editor
*Truck driver leisure magazine*

**Roadway Services, Inc.**
1077 Gorge Blvd., P.O. Box 88
Akron, OH 44309
Joseph M. Clapp, Chairman,
  President and CEO
*Transportation company*

**Robb, Charles G.**
483 Senate Russell Office Bldg.
Washington, DC 20501
*Senator from Virginia*

**Robbins, Tim**
8899 Beverly Blvd.
Los Angeles, CA 90048
*Actor*

**Roberson Center for the Arts
  & Sciences**
30 Front St.
Binghamton, NY 13905
Robert W. Aber, Executive
  Director
*Science, technology, art, music,
  ballet and film in one museum*

**Robert Frost Farm**
P.O. Box 1075
Derry, NH 03038
Hannah Martin, Head of
  Trustees

**Robert H. Lowie Museum of Anthropology**
103 Kroeber Hall, University of California
Berkeley, CA 94720
Burton Benedict, Director

**Robert Louis Stevenson House**
530 Houston St.
Monterey, CA 93940
Johnathan Williams, Supervising Ranger

**Roberts, Barbara**
State Capitol
Salem, OR 97310
*Governor of Oregon*

**Roberts, Julia**
8899 Beverly Blvd.
Los Angeles, CA 90048
*Actress*

**Robertson, Alvin**
c/o Milwaukee Bucks
1001 N. 4th St.
Milwaukee, WI 53203
*Professional basketball player*

**Robertson, Rev. Pat**
CBN Center
Virginia Beach, VA 23463
*Proponent of mixing church and state*

**Robinson, Holly**
8899 Beverly Blvd.
Los Angeles, CA 90048
*Actress*

**Rockefeller, John D. IV**
109 Senate Hart Office Bldg.
Washington, DC 20501
*Senator from West Virginia*

**Rockefeller Foundation, The**
1133 Ave. of the Americas
New York, NY 10036
John R. Evans, Chairman
*Philanthropic organization*

**Rockwell International Corporation**
2230 E. Imperial Hwy.
El Segundo, CA 90245
Donald R. Beall, Chairman and CEO
*Space shuttle manufacturer*

**Rodgers, Bill (William Henry)**
353T N. Marketplace, Faneuil Hall
Boston, MA 02109
*Professional runner*

**Rodriguez, Carlos Andres Perez**
c/o Oficina del Presidente
Palacio de Miraflores
Caracas, Venezuela
*President of Venezuela*

**Rodriguez, General Andres**
Casa Presidencial
Avenida Mariscal Lopez
Asuncion, Paraguay
*President of Paraguay*

**Rogers, Kenny**
Box 100, Rte. #1
Colbert, GA 30628
*Singer*

**Rogers, Mimi**
9830 Wilshire Blvd.
Beverly Hills, CA 90212
*Actress*

**Rogers, Roy (Leonard Slye)**
15650 Seneca Rd.
Victorville, CA 92392
*Singing cowboy on the comeback trail*

**Rolling Stones, The**
1776 Broadway, #507
New York, NY 10019
*Granddaddies of rock and roll*

**Roman Catholic Church
(U.S.)**
3211 Fourth St., NE
Washington, DC 20017
Pope John Paul II
*Largest religious denomination in
the U.S.*

**Romanian Orthodox
Episcopate of America**
2522 Grey Tower Rd.
Jackson, MI 49201
Nathaniel Popp, Bishop
*Religious group*

**Romer, Roy**
136 State Capitol
Denver, CO 80203
*Governor of Colorado*

**Ronstadt, Linda**
5750 Wilshire Blvd., #590
Los Angeles, CA 90036
*Singer*

**Rose, Beatrice Schroeder**
Houston Symphony
Jones Hall
Houston, TX 77002
*Harpist, educator*

**Rosenblueth, Emilio**
Instituto de Ingenieria
Ciudad Universidad
Mexico City 04510 Mexico
*Earthquake engineer*

**Ross, Diana**
780 Third Ave.
New York, NY 10017
*Singer, actress*

**Ross, Herbert David**
9830 Wilshire Blvd.
Beverly Hills, CA 90212
*Film director*

**Ross, Marion**
10000 Santa Monica Blvd.,
    #305
Los Angeles, CA 90067
*Actress*

**Ross, Stanley Ralph**
Neila Inc.
7865 Willoughby Ave.
Los Angeles, CA 90046
*Writer, producer, CEO Comedy
    Software Inc.*

**Rotary International**
One Rotary Center
1560 Sherman Ave.
Evanston, IL 60201
Spencer Robinson, Jr., General
    Secretary
*Oldest and most international
    service organization in the U.S.*

**Roth, Philip**
c/o Simon & Schuster
1230 Ave. of the Americas
New York, NY 10020
*Author*

**Roth, William V., Jr.**
104 Senate Hart Office Bldg.
Washington, DC 20510
*Senator from Delaware*

**Rothstein, Ron**
c/o Detroit Pistons
2 Championship Dr.
Auburn Hills, MI 48326
*Basketball coach*

**Rourke, Mickey**
8439 Sunset Blvd., #107
Los Angeles, CA 90069
*Actor*

**Roxette**
**Marie Fredrikson, Per Gessle**
1800 N. Vine St.
Hollywood, CA 90028
*Singing duo from Sweden*

**Rubbermaid Inc.**
1147 Akron Rd.
Wooster, OH 44691
Walter W. Williams, Chairman
and CEO
*Rubber and plastic goods
manufacturer*

**Rudenstine, Neil**
Harvard University
Cambridge, MA 02138
*University CEO*

**Ruehl, Mercedes**
8899 Beverly Blvd.
Los Angeles, CA 90048
*Actress*

**Run D.M.C.**
296 Elizabeth St.
New York, NY 10012
*Rappers*

**Rush Limbaugh Fan Club**
197 W. Utica St.
Buffalo, NY 14222

**Rushdie, Salman**
c/o Rogers Ltd.
49 Blenheim Crescent
London W11 England
Satanic Verses *author in hiding*

**Rushford, Michael**
Criminal Justice Legal
Foundation
P.O. Box 1199
Sacramento, CA 95812
*Anti-crime activist*

**Russell, Kurt**
9830 Wilshire Blvd.
Beverly Hills, CA 90212
*Actor*

**Russell, Theresa**
232 N. Canon Dr.
Beverly Hills, CA 90210
*Actress*

**Ryan, Meg**
8899 Beverly Blvd.
Los Angeles, CA 90048
*Actress*

**Ryan, Nolan**
Box 670
Alvin, TX 77512
*Baseball player*

**Ryder System, Inc.**
3600 NW 82nd Ave.
Miami, FL 33166
M. Anthony Burns, Chairman,
President and CEO
*Rent-a-truck company*

**Ryder, Winona**
**(Horowitz)**
8899 Beverly Blvd.
Los Angeles, CA 90048
*Actress*

# S

Probably the disembodied abstractness of a letter permits the reader to impute to the writer whatever qualities the reader is already listening for . . .

—SHANA ALEXANDER, "The Feminine Eye"

**Sabatini, Gabriela**
c/o Proserv
11010 Wilson Blvd., #1800
Arlington, VA 22209
*Professional tennis player*

**Sacramento Kings**
1515 Sports Drive
Sacramento, CA 95834
Joe Axelson, Executive Vice-
    President
*Professional basketball team*

**Sacramento Senators**
4010 Foothill Boulevard, Suite
    104
Roseville, CA 95678
Greg McKeown, Chairman
*Soccer team*

**Safeway Inc.**
Fourth and Jackson Sts.
Oakland, CA 94660
Peter A. Magowan, Chairman,
    President and CEO
*Grocery store chain*

**Safire, William**
*The New York Times*
1627 Eye Street, NW
Washington, DC 20006
*Journalist*

**Sagan, Dr. Carl**
Cornell University
Space-Science Bldg.
Ithaca, NY 14853
*Space scientist*

**Saget, Bob**
8899 Beverly Blvd.
Los Angeles, CA 90048
*Actor, comedian, TV host*

**Saibou, General Ali**
Office of the Chairman of the
    High Council for National
    Orientation
Niamey, Niger
*Chief of State of Niger*

**Said, Qabboos Bin**
The Palace
Muscat, Sultanate of Oman
*Sultan of Oman*

**St. Louis Blues**
The Arena
5700 Oakland Ave.
St. Louis, MO 63110
Jack Quinn, President
*Professional hockey team*

**St. Louis Cardinals**
250 Stadium Plaza
St. Louis, MO 63102
Dal Maxvill, Vice-President/
    General Manager
*Professional baseball team*

**Saint James, Susan**
854 Genessee Ave.
Los Angeles, CA 90048
*Actress*

**Salazar, Alberto**
c/o International Management
    Group
One Erieview Plaza, #1300
Cleveland, OH 44114
*Professional runner*

**Saldana, Theresa**
10637 Burbank Blvd.
N. Hollywood, CA 91601
*Actress, victims' rights activist*

**Saleh, Ali Abdullah**
Office of the President
San'a', Republic of Yemen
*President of the Republic of Yemen*

**Salinger, J. D.**
RR #3, Box 176
Cornish Flat, NH 03746
*Author*

**Salisbury, Harrison Evans**
c/o HarperCollins
10 E. 53rd St.
New York, NY 10022
*International political writer*

**Salomon Brothers, Inc.**
One New York Plaza
New York, NY 10004
Warren E. Buffett, Chairman
    and CEO
*International investment banking
    and securities trading firm*

**Salt Lake City**
c/o Salt Lake City Trappers
1301 SW Temple
Salt Lake City, UT 84115
Mark Hugo, General Manager
*Soccer team*

**Salvation Army, The**
799 Bloomfield Ave.
Verona, NJ 07044
James Osborne, National Chief
    Secretary

**Samaritans**
500 Commonwealth Ave.
Boston, MA 02215
Shirley Karnovsky, Executive
    Director
*Suicide prevention*

**Samms, Emma**
1999 Ave. of the Stars, #2850
Los Angeles, CA 90067
*Actress*

**Sampras, Pete**
c/o Proserv
11010 Wilson Blvd., #1800
Arlington, VA 22209
*Professional tennis player*

**San Antonio Spurs**
600 East Market, Suite 102
San Antonio, TX 78205
Russ Bookbinder, Executive
    Vice-President
*Professional basketball team*

**San Diego Chargers**
Jack Murphy Stadium
P.O. Box 20666
San Diego, CA 92120
Steve Ortmayer, Director of
   Football Operations
*Professional football team*

**San Diego Museum of
   Contemporary Art**
700 Prospect St.
La Jolla, CA 92037
Hugh M. Davies, Director and
   CEO

**San Diego Nomads**
1298 Prospect St.
La Jolla, CA 92037
James Jessel, General Manager
*Soccer team*

**San Diego Padres**
P.O. Box 2000
San Diego, CA 92120
Dick Freeman, President
*Professional baseball team*

**San Diego Wild Animal Park**
15500 San Pasqual Valley Rd.
Escondido, CA 92027
Douglas Myers, Executive
   Director

**San Diego Zoo**
P.O. Box 551
San Diego, CA 92112
Doug Myers, Executive Director

**San Francisco Bay
   Blackhawks**
3820 Blackhawk Road
Danville, CA 94506
Terry Fisher, General Manager
*Soccer team*

**San Francisco 49ers**
4949 Centennial Boulevard
Santa Clara, CA 95054
Edward J. DeBartolo, Jr.,
   Owner/President
*Professional football team*

**San Francisco Giants**
Candlestick Park
San Francisco, CA 94124
Al Rosen, President/General
   Manager
*Professional baseball team*

**San Giacomo, Laura**
11726 San Vicente Blvd., #300
Los Angeles, CA 90049
*Actress*

**San Joaquin County
   Historical Museum**
P.O. Box 21
Lodi, CA 95241
Michael W. Bennett, Director
*Farming and mining museum*

**San Menem, Carlos**
Casa de Gobierno
Balcarce 50, 1064 Buenos Aires
Argentina
*President of Argentina*

**Sanders, Barry**
c/o Detroit Lions
P.O. Box 4200
Pontiac, MI 48057
*Professional football player*

**Sanford, Terry**
Senate Hart Office Bldg.
Washington, DC 20510
*Senator from North Carolina*

**Santa Fe Pacific Corporation**
1700 E. Golf Rd.
Schaumburg, IL 60173
Robert D. Krebs, Chairman,
  President and CEO
*Atchison, Topeka & Santa Fe*

**Santana**
P.O. Box 26671
San Francisco, CA 94126
*Rock group*

**Sara Lee Corporation**
3 First National Plaza
Chicago, IL 60602
John H. Bryan, Jr., Chairman
  and CEO
*Goodies manufacturer*

**Sarandon, Susan**
8899 Beverly Blvd.
Los Angeles, CA 90048
*Actress*

**Sarbanes, Paul S.**
309 Senate Hart Office Bldg.
Washington, DC 20510
*Senator from Maryland*

**Sasser, Jim**
363 Senate Russell Office Bldg.
Washington, DC 20501
*Senator from Tennessee*

**Sassou-Neguessou, Colonel
  Denis**
Office du Président
Comité Militaire du Parti
  Congolais du Travail
Brazzaville, Congo People's
  Republic
*President of the Congo*

**Saturday Evening Post, The**
1100 Waterway Blvd.
Indianapolis, IN 46202
Cory SerVaas, Editor
*Magazine*

**Savage, Fred**
9830 Wilshire Blvd.
Beverly Hills, CA 90212
*Actor*

**Save Our Streams**
1401 Wilson Blvd., Level B
Arlington, VA 22209
Karen Firehock, Coordinator

**Save the Dolphins Project**
Earth Island Institute
300 Broadway, #28
San Francisco, CA 94133
David Phillips, Contact

**Save the Dunes Council**
444 Barker Rd.
Michigan City, IN 46360
Thomas Serynek, President

**Save-the-Redwoods League**
114 Sansome St., #605
San Francisco, CA 94104
Bruce S. Howard, President

**Sawyer, Amos**
Office of the President
Monrovia, Liberia
*President of Liberia*

**Sayles, John T.**
5555 Melrose Ave.
Los Angeles, CA 90038
*Writer, filmmaker*

**Sbarge, Raphael**
1999 Ave. of the Stars, #2850
Los Angeles, CA 90067
*Actor*

**Scacchi, Greta**
8899 Beverly Blvd.
Los Angeles, CA 90048
*Actress*

**Scalia, Antonin**
U.S. Supreme Court Bldg.
One First Street, NE
Washington, DC 20543
*Associate Justice of the Supreme
    Court*


**Scalia, Jack**
8899 Beverly Blvd.
Los Angeles, CA 90048
*Actor*


**SCECORP**
2244 Walnut Grove Ave.
Rosemead, CA 91770
John E. Bryson, Chairman and
    CEO
*Parent company of Southern
    California Edison, electric utility*


**Scenic America**
216 Seventh St., SE
Washington, DC 20003
Carroll Shaddock, President


**Schaefer, William Donald**
State House
Annapolis, MD 21404
*Governor of Maryland*


**Schering-Plough Corporation**
1 Giralda Farms
Madison, NJ 07940
Robert P. Luciano, Chairman
    and CEO
*Coppertone, Dr. Scholl's and
    pharmaceuticals*


**Schickel, Richard**
Time Life Bldg.
Rockefeller Center
New York, NY 10020
*Film critic*


**Schifrin, Lalo**
Glendale Symphony Orchestra
401 Brand Blvd., #520
Glendale, CA 91203
*Composer*


**Schisgal, Murray Joseph**
40 W. 57th St.
New York, NY 10019
*Playwright*


**Schlafly, Phyllis**
68 Fairmont
Alton, IL 62002
*Conservative leader*


**Schlatter, Charlie**
9830 Wilshire Blvd.
Beverly Hills, CA 90212
*Actor*


**Schlickau, George Hans**
Rte. 2, Box 125
Haven, KS 67543
*Cattle breeder*


**Schlumberger NV**
277 Park Ave.
New York, NY 10172
D. Euan Baird, Chairman,
    President and CEO
*Worldwide leader in oil and gas
    exploration*


**Schluter, Poul Holmskov**
Prime Minister's Office
Christianborg, Prins Jorgens
    Gaardii
1218 Copenhagen K, Denmark
*Prime Minister of Denmark*


**Schonberg, Harold Charles**
*The New York Times*
229 W. 43rd St.
New York, NY 10036
*Music critic*

**Schultes, Richard Evans**
Botanical Museum
Harvard University
Cambridge, MA 02138
*Ethnobotanist*

**Schulz, Charles Monroe**
One Snoopy Place
Santa Rosa, CA 95401
*"Peanuts" cartoonist*

**Schwarzenegger, Arnold**
c/o Oak Productions
321 Hampton Dr., #20
Venice, CA 90291
*Actor, director, Special Olympics
trainer*

**Schwarzkopf, Norman H.**
8899 Beverly Blvd.
Los Angeles, CA 90048
*Retired army general, hero of
Desert Storm*

**SCI Systems, Inc.**
2101 W. Clinton Ave.
Huntsville, AL 35805
Olin B. King, Chairman and
CEO
*Printed circuit-board assembler*

**Scieszka, Jon**
c/o Viking Press
375 Hudson St.
New York, NY 10014
*Author*

**Scoon, Sir Paul**
Governor General's House
St. George's, Grenada
*Governor General of Grenada*

**Scorsese, Martin**
9830 Wilshire Blvd.
Beverly Hills, CA 90212
*Film director*

**Scott, Byron**
c/o Los Angeles Lakers
P.O. Box 10
Inglewood, CA 90306
*Professional basketball player*

**Scott Paper Company**
Scott Plaza
Philadelphia, PA 19113
Philip E. Lippincott, Chairman
and CEO
*World's leading manufacturer of
tissue products*

**Screw**
P.O. Box 432
Old Chelsea Station
New York, NY 10113
Manny Neuhaus, Managing
Editor
*Magazine*

**Scripps, E. W., Company, The**
1105 N. Market St.
Wilmington, DE 19801
Charles E. Scripps, Chairman
*Eighth largest U.S. newspaper
publisher*

**Sea World, Inc.**
1720 South Shores Rd.
San Diego, CA 92109
Robert K. Gault, Jr., President

**Seagate Technology, Inc.**
920 Disc Drive
Scotts Valley, CA 95066
Gary B. Filler, Chairman
*Manufactures computer hard drives*

**Search Reports, Inc./A
Central Registry of the
Missing**
396 Route 17, N.
Hasbrouck Heights, NJ 07604
Charles A. Sutherland,
President
*Missing children registry*

**Sears, Roebuck & Co.**
Sears Tower
Chicago, IL 60684
Edward A. Brennan, Chairman,
  President and CEO
*Catalog department store chain*

**Seattle Art Museum**
Volunteer Park
Seattle, WA 98112
C. Calvert Knudsen, Chairman
  of the Board

**Seattle Mariners**
P.O. Box 4100
Seattle, WA 98104
Woody Woodward, Vice-
  President/General Manager
*Professional baseball team*

**Seattle Seahawks**
11220 NE 53rd Street
Kirkland, WA 98033
Tom Flores, General Manager
*Professional football team*

**Seattle Storm**
2815 Second Avenue, Suite 590
Seattle, WA 98121
David Gillett, General Manager
*Soccer team*

**Seattle Supersonics**
C-Box 900911
Seattle, WA 98109
Bob Whitsitt, President
*Professional basketball team*

**Seaver, Tom**
**(George Thomas)**
c/o M. Mendola
185 E. 85th St., #18G
New York, NY 10028
*Former baseball star*

**Security Pacific Corporation**
333 S. Hope St.
Los Angeles, CA 90071
Richard J. Flamson III,
  Chairman
*Banking corporation undergoing
  merger with Bank of America*

**Sega, Inc.**
**(Sega-Genesis)**
573 Forbes Blvd.
South San Francisco, CA 94080
Thomas Kalinske, President
*Video games manufacturer*

**Segal, Erich**
Wolfson College
Oxford OX2 66D, England
*"Love Means Never Having to Say
  You're Sorry" author*

**Seignoret, Sir Clarence**
The President's Office
Roseau, Commonwealth of
  Dominica, West Indies
*President of Commonwealth of
  Dominica, West Indies*

**Seko, Mobutu Sese**
Présidence de la République
Kinshasa, Zaire
*President of Zaire*

**Seles, Monica**
c/o International Management
  Group
One Erieview Plaza, Suite 1300
Cleveland, OH 44114
*Professional tennis player*

**Self-Help Center**
1600 Dodge Ave., Suite S-122
Evanston, IL 60201
Daryl Isenberg, Ph.D., Acting
  Director
*Clearinghouse*

**Sellecca, Connie**
151 El Camino
Beverly Hills, CA 90212
*Actress*

**Selleck, Tom**
9021 Melrose Ave., #207
Los Angeles, CA 90069
*Actor*

**Sendak, Maurice Bernard**
c/o HarperCollins
10 East 53rd St.
New York, NY 10022
*Children's book illustrator/author*

**Serbian Orthodox Church for the U.S.A. and Canada**
Box 519
Libertyville, IL 60048
Rt. Rev. Georgijie, Bishop
*Religious group*

**Service Merchandise Company, Inc.**
7100 Service Merchandise Dr.
Brentwood, TN 37027
Raymond Zimmerman,
   Chairman, President and
   CEO
*Largest retail catalog store in the U.S.*

**Sesame Street**
Children's TV Workshop
One Lincoln Plaza
New York, NY 10023
Dulcy Singer, Executive
   Producer
*PBS series*

**Seventeen**
Triangle Communications
850 Third Ave.
New York, NY 10022
Midge Richardson, Editor-in-
   Chief
*Magazine*

**Seven-Up Company**
8144 Walnut Hill Lane
Dallas, TX 75231
John R. Albers, Chief Executive
   Officer
*Soft drink company*

**Seymour, Anne**
National Victim Center
2111 Wilson Blvd., #300
Arlington, VA 22101
*Anti-crime activist*

**Seymour, Jane**
9320 Wilshire Blvd., 3rd Fl.
Beverly Hills, CA 90212
*Actress*

**Seymour, John**
902 Senate Hart Office Bldg.
Washington, DC 20510
*Senator from California*

**Shackelford, Ted**
9830 Wilshire Blvd.
Beverly Hills, CA 90212
*Actor*

**Shaffer, Paul**
NBC
30 Rockefeller Plaza
New York, NY 10112
*Musician, "Late Night" bandleader*

**Shaffer, Peter (Leon)**
c/o Macnaughton-Lowe
200 Fulham Rd.
London SW10 England
*Playwright, novelist*

**Shaker Village, Inc.**
288 Shaker Rd.
Canterbury, NH 03224
Scott T. Swank, Director
*1792 Shaker community*

**Shandling, Garry**
9830 Wilshire Blvd.
Beverly Hills, CA 90212
*Comedian*

**Shange, Ntozake**
c/o St. Martin's Press
175 Fifth Ave.
New York, NY 10010
*Writer*

**Shangkun, General Yang**
Office of the President
Beijing, People's Republic of
    China
*President of People's Republic of
    China*

**Sharper Image Corporation**
650 Davis St.
San Francisco, CA 94111
Richard Thalheimer, Chairman,
    President and CEO
*Gadget and high tech "toy" store*

**Shatner, William**
345 N. Maple St., #183
Beverly Hills, CA 90210
*Actor*

**Shaud, Grant**
11726 San Vicente Blvd., #300
Los Angeles, CA 90049
*Actor*

**Shear, Rhonda**
c/o "USA Up All Night"
1230 Ave. of the Americas
New York, NY 10020
*Late night hostess, actress*

**Sheedy, Ally**
P.O. Box 6327
Malibu, CA 90264
*Actress*

**Shelby, Richard C.**
313 Senate Hart Office Bldg.
Washington, DC 20510
*Senator from Alabama*

**Sheldon, Sidney**
c/o William Morrow
1350 Ave. of the Americas
New York, NY 10020
*TV and film writer turned novelist*

**Shepard, Sam**
40 W. 57th St.
New York, NY 10019
*Actor, playwright*

**Sheridan, Nicollette**
P.O. Box 25578
Los Angeles, CA 90025
*Actress*

**Sherlock Holmes Society**
221B Baker St.
London W1 England

**Sherwin-Williams Company,
    The**
101 Prospect Ave., NW
Cleveland, OH 44115
John G. Breen, Chairman and
    CEO
*Paint manufacturer and paint store
    chain*

**Shire, David Lee**
2049 Century Park E., #3700
Los Angeles, CA 90067
*Composer*

**Shoemaker, Bill**
2545 Fairfield Pl.
San Marino, CA 91108
*Retired "winningest" jockey,
    quadriplegic horse trainer*

**Short, Martin**
9830 Wilshire Blvd.
Beverly Hills, CA 90212
*Actor, comedian*

**Showtime Networks, Inc.**
1633 Broadway
New York, NY 10019
Winston H. Cox, Chairman/
  CEO
*Premium cable channel*

**Shue, Elisabeth**
9830 Wilshire Blvd.
Beverly Hills, CA 90212
*Actress*

**Shulweiss, Harold**
Valley Beth Shalom
15739 Ventura Blvd.
Encino, CA 91436
*Rabbi*

**Sider, Rev. Harvey R.**
Brethren in Christ Church
P.O. Box 245
Upland, CA 91785
*President, religious organization*

**Sidey, Hugh**
*Time* Magazine
1050 Connecticut Ave., NW
Washington, DC 20071
*Journalist, writer on the presidency*

**Sierra Club**
730 Polk St.
San Francisco, CA 94109
Susan Merrow, President
*Environmental organization*

**Sihanouk, Prince Sandech
  Preah Norodom**
Pyongyang,
Democratic People's
Republic of Korea
*President of Provisional
  Government of Cambodia*

**Sikking, James B.**
9320 Wilshire Blvd., #512
Los Angeles, CA 90036
*Actor*

**Silent Network, The**
American Disability Network
1777 NE Loop 410, #1401
San Antonio, TX 78212
Dr. Bill Nichols, President
*Network for the deaf and hearing-
  impaired*

**Silverman, Jonathan**
10390 Santa Monica Blvd.,
  #300
Los Angeles, CA 90025
*Actor*

**Simmonds, Kennedy
  Alphonse**
Office of the Prime Minister
Basseterre, St. Kitts, West Indies
*Prime Minister of St. Kitts*

**Simon, Neil**
10100 Santa Monica Blvd.,
  #400
Los Angeles, CA 90067
*Playwright*

**Simon, Paul**
1619 Broadway, #500
New York, NY 10019
*Singer, songwriter*

**Simon, Paul**
462 Senate Dirksen Office Bldg.
Washington, DC 20510
*Senator from Illinois*

**Simon Wiesenthal Center Holocaust Museum**
9760 W. Pico Blvd.
Los Angeles, CA 90035
Rabbi Marvin Hier, CEO

**Simpson, Alan K.**
261 Senate Dirksen Office Bldg.
Washington, DC 20510
*Senator from Wyoming*

**Simpsons, The**
**(Homer, Marge, Lisa, Maggie and Bart)**
10201 West Pico Blvd.
Los Angeles, CA 90035
*Cartoon family*

**Single Parent, The**
Parents Without Partners, Inc.
8807 Colesville Rd.
Silver Spring, MD 20910
Allan N. Glennon, Editor
*Magazine*

**Single Parent Resource Center**
1165 Broadway, Rm. 504
New York, NY 10001
Suzanne Jones, Executive Director

**Singleton, John**
9830 Wilshire Blvd.
Beverly Hills, CA 90212
*Film director*

**Sinner, George A.**
600 East Boulevard, State Capitol, Ground Fl.
Bismarck, ND 58505
*Governor of North Dakota*

**Siskel & Ebert**
**(Gene and Roger)**
630 McClurg Ct.
Chicago, IL 60611
*Film critics*

**Sisterhood of Black Single Mothers**
1360 Fulton St., #423
Brooklyn, NY 11216
Daphne Busby, Executive Director
*Self-help organization*

**Skid Row**
9229 Sunset Blvd., #710
Los Angeles, CA 90069
*Rock group*

**Skidmore, Owings & Merrill**
33 W. Monroe
Chicago, IL 60603
David M. Childs, Partner Contact
*Until 1990, world's largest architectural/engineering firm*

**Slater, Christian**
9830 Wilshire Blvd.
Beverly Hills, CA 90212
*Actor*

**Slater, Helen**
151 El Camino
Beverly Hills, CA 90212
*Actress*

**Slaughter, Sgt.**
P.O. Box 3857
Stamford, CT 06905
*Professional wrestler*

**Slavin, Neal**
62 Greene St.
New York, NY 10012
*Photographer*

**Slezak, Erika**
8899 Beverly Blvd.
Los Angeles, CA 90048
*Actress*

**Smiley, John**
c/o Pittsburgh Pirates
600 Stadium Circle
Pittsburgh, PA 15212
*Professional baseball player*

**Smith, Bryn**
c/o St. Louis Cardinals
Busch Stadium
St. Louis, MO 63102
*Professional baseball player*

**Smith, Charles**
c/o Los Angeles Clippers
3939 S. Figueroa
Los Angeles, CA 90037
*Professional basketball player*

**Smith, Jaclyn**
151 El Camino
Beverly Hills, CA 90212
*Actress*

**Smith, Kenny**
c/o Houston Rockets
The Summit
Houston, TX 77046
*Professional basketball player*

**Smith, Lacey Baldwin**
Northwestern University
Department of History
Evanston, IL 60201
*Educator, historian, author*

**Smith, Lee**
c/o St. Louis Cardinals
Busch Stadium
St. Louis, MO 63102
*Professional baseball player*

**Smith, Robert C.**
332 Senate Dirksen Office Bldg.
Washington, DC 20510
*Senator from New Hampshire*

**Smith, William Kennedy**
100 E. 42nd St., #1850
New York, NY 10017
*Controversial ex-defendant*

**Smithsonian Institution**
1000 Jefferson Dr., SW
Washington, DC 20560
Dr. Robert McCormick, CEO,
   Chairman and President

**Smits, Jimmy**
9830 Wilshire Blvd.
Beverly Hills, CA 90212
*Actor*

**Smothers Brothers**
8489 W. Third St., #1020
Los Angeles, CA 90048
*Comic musicians*

**Snap-On Tools Corporation**
2801 80th St.
Kenosha, WI 53141
Robert A. Cornog, Chairman,
   President and CEO
*Tool manufacturers*

**Snead, Sam**
P.O. Box 777
Hot Springs, VA 24445
*Ex-champion golfer*

**Snipes, Wesley**
9830 Wilshire Blvd.
Beverly Hills, CA 90212
*Actor*

**Soap Opera Digest**
News America
45 W. 25 St.
New York, NY 10010
Meredith Berlin, Editor
*Magazine*

**Soares, Mario**
Presidencia da Republica
Palacio de Belem
1300 Lisbon, Portugal
*President of Portugal*

**Sober Times**
**The Recovery Magazine**
3601 30th St.
San Diego, CA 92104
J. S. Rudolf, Ph.D., Editor

**Society for the Preservation**
**and Enhancement of the**
**Recognition of Millard**
**Fillmore, Last of the Whigs**
P.O. Box 712
Cascade, CO 80909
Phil Akrow, Vice-President
*Gives a medal of mediocrity in*
*memory of the dullest and*
*unluckiest President*

**Society of the Preservation of**
**New England Antiquities—**
**Harrison Grary Otis**
**House, The**
141 Cambridge St.
Boston, MA 02114
Nancy R. Coolidge, Director

**Society of Tympanuchus**
**Cupido Pinnatus Ltd.**
930 Elm Grove Rd.
Elm Grove, WI 53122
Bernard J. Westfahl
*Preserves the prairie chicken*

**Society to Curtail Ridiculous,**
**Outrageous and**
**Ostentatious Gift Exchange**
**(SCROOGE)**
1447 Westwood Rd.
Charlottesville, VA 22901
Charles G. Langham, Executive
Director
*Strives to de-emphasize the*
*commercialization of Christmas*

**Soglo, Nicephore**
Office of the President
Cotonou, Benin
*President of Benin*

**Sokol, Dr. Robert James**
Wayne State University School
of Medicine
540 E. Canfield
Detroit, MI 48201
*Obstetrician, gynecologist, educator*

**Soldier of Fortune**
**The Journal of Professional**
**Adventurers**
Omega Group, Ltd.
P.O. Box 693
Boulder, CO 80306
John W. Coleman, Managing
Editor

**Solomon R. Guggenheim**
**Museum**
1071 Fifth Ave.
New York, NY 10128
Peter O. Lawson-Johnston,
President

**Somers, Suzanne**
190 N. Canon Dr., #201
Beverly Hills, CA 90210
*Actress, singer*

**Sondheim, Stephen Joshua**
c/o F. Roberts
65 E. 55th St., #702
New York, NY 10022
*Composer*

**Sons of the Pioneers**
12403 W. Green Mountain
Lakewood, CO 80228
*Singing cowboys*

**Souter, David H.**
U.S. Supreme Court Building
One First Street, NE
Washington, DC 20543
*Associate Justice of the Supreme Court*

**South Carolina Confederate Relic Room and Museum**
World War Memorial Blvd.
920 Sumter St.
Columbia, SC 29201
John A. Martin, Jr., CEO and Director

**Southern Company, The**
64 Perimeter Center E.
Atlanta, GA 30346
Edward L. Addison, President and CEO
*Second largest U.S. electric utility*

**Southland Corporation, The**
2711 N. Haskell Ave.
Dallas, TX 75204
Masatoshi Ito, Chairman
*7-Eleven*

**Southwest Airlines Co.**
P.O. Box 36611, Love Field
Dallas, TX 75235
Herbert D. Kelleher, Chairman, President and CEO
*Low fare, no frills airline*

**Southwest Museum**
234 Museum Dr.
Los Angeles, CA 90045
Jerome R. Selmer, CEO, Executive Director

**Southwestern Bell Corporation**
One Bell Center
St. Louis, MO 63101
Edward E. Whitacre, Jr., Chairman and CEO
*Local telephone company for five states*

**Space Camp/Space Academy**
The Space & Rocket Center
One Tranquility Base
Huntsville, AL 35807

**Spacek, Sissy**
9830 Wilshire Blvd.
Beverly Hills, CA 90212
*Actress*

**Spacey, Kevin**
9830 Wilshire Blvd.
Beverly Hills, CA 90212
*Actor*

**Speaker's Connection**
3530 Pine Valley Dr.
Sarasota, FL 34239
Gerry Tausch, Director
*Speaker's bureau*

**Special Olympics International**
1350 New York Ave., NW, #500
Washington, DC 20005
Eunice Kennedy Shriver, Chairperson

**Specter, Arlen**
303 Senate Hart Office Bldg.
Washington, DC 20510
*Senator from Pennsylvania*

**Spelling, Tori**
1450 Belfast Dr.
Los Angeles, CA 90069
*Actress*

**Spencer, John**
9200 Sunset Blvd., #625
Los Angeles, CA 90069
*Actor*

**Spielberg, Steven**
P.O. Box 6190
Malibu, CA 90264
*Director, producer*

**Spinelli, Jerry**
c/o Little, Brown and Company
205 Lexington Ave.
New York, NY 10016
*Author, 1991 Newbery Award
   Winner*

**Sports Channel**
1545 26th St.
Santa Monica, CA 90404
Lynn Woodard, President
*Cable premium sports channel*

**Sports Hall of Shame**
P.O. Box 31867
Palm Beach Gardens, FL 33420
Bruce M. Nash, Co-Founder
*Collection of big goofs*

**Springfield, Rick**
9200 Sunset Blvd., PH15
Los Angeles, CA 90069
*Singer, actor*

**Springs Industries, Inc.**
P.O. Box 70, 205 N. White St.
Fort Mill, SC 29715
Walter Y. Elisha, Chairman,
   CEO, and President
*Largest manufacturer of sheets and
   bedding in the U.S.*

**Spy**
Spy Publishing Partners
Five Union Sq. W., 8th Fl.
New York, NY 10003
K. Andersen, Editor
*Satirical non-fiction magazine*

**Square D Company**
1415 S. Roselle
Palatine, IL 60067
Didier Pineau-Valencienne,
   Chairman and CEO
*Manufacturer of electrical products*

**Stafford, Nancy**
1999 Ave. of the Stars, #2850
Los Angeles, CA 90067
*Actress*

**Stallone, Sylvester**
9830 Wilshire Blvd.
Beverly Hills, CA 90211
*Actor, writer, producer*

**Stamos, John**
151 El Camino
Beverly Hills, CA 90212
*Actor*

**Stanford University**
Office of Admissions
Old Union, Leland Stanford, Jr.,
   University
Stanford, CA 94305
Donald Kennedy, President

**Stanley Works, The**
1000 Stanley Dr., P.O. Box 7000
New Britain, CT 06050
Richard H. Ayers, Chairman,
   President and CEO
*Hardware manufacturer*

**Stapleton, Jean**
5750 Wilshire Blvd.
Los Angeles, CA 90036
*Actress*

**Starr, Ringo**
Tittenhurst Park
Ascot, Surrey, England
*Musician*

**State Farm Mutual**
  **Automobile Insurance**
  **Company**
One State Farm Plaza
Bloomington, IL 61710
Edward B. Rust, Jr., Chairman,
  President and CEO

**Statler Brothers**
P.O. Box 2703
Staunton, VA 24401
*Singers*

**Statue of Liberty Collectors'**
  **Club**
P.O. Box 535
Chautauqua, NY 14722
Iris November, Contact

**Stearns Collection of Musical**
  **Instruments**
University of Michigan School
  of Music
Ann Arbor, MI 48109
William P. Malm, Director

**Steel, Danielle**
Box 1637, Murray Hill Station
New York, NY 10156
*Author*

**Steen, Jessica**
10100 Santa Monica Blvd.,
  16th Fl.
Los Angeles, CA 90067
*Actress*

**Steenburgen, Mary**
8899 Beverly Blvd.
Los Angeles, CA 90048
*Actress*

**Steinem, Gloria**
118 E. 73rd St.
New York, NY 10021
*Feminist, writer, editor*

**Stepfamily Foundation, Inc.**
333 West End Ave.
New York, NY 10003
Jeannette Lofas, Executive
  Director
*Information and counseling for a
  newly created family*

**Stephens, Olin James II**
79 Madison Ave.
New York, NY 10016
*Yacht designer*

**Stephens, Stan**
State Capitol
Helena, MT 59620
*Governor of Montana*

**Stern, David**
League Office
645 Fifth Ave.
New York, NY 10022
*NBA commissioner*

**Stern, Howard**
600 Madison Ave.
New York, NY 10022
*Disc jockey*

**Stern, Isaac**
40 W. 57th St.
New York, NY 10019
*Violinist*

**Stevens, John Paul**
U.S. Supreme Court Building
1 First Street, NE
Washington, DC 20543
*Associate Justice of the Supreme
  Court*

**Stevens, Ted**
522 Senate Hart Office Bldg.
Washington, DC 20510
*Senator from Alaska*

**Stewart, James**
P.O. Box 90
Beverly Hills, CA 90213
*Actor*

**Stewart, Patrick**
8899 Beverly Blvd.
Los Angeles, CA 90048
*Actor*

**Stiers, David Ogden**
121 N. San Vicente Blvd.
Beverly Hills, CA 90211
*Actor*, Beauty and the Beast *voice*

**Sting**
2 the Grove
Highgate Village
London N16 England
*Singer, actor*

**Stockwell, Dean**
P.O. Box 6248
Malibu, CA 90265
*Actor*

**Stone, Michael**
606 S. Olive St., 10th Fl.
Los Angeles, CA 90017
*Defense attorney in Rodney King
   incident*

**Stone, Oliver**
1180 S. Beverly Dr., #320
Los Angeles, CA 90035
*Controversial director/writer*

**Stone, Sharon**
232 N. Canon Dr.
Beverly Hills, CA 90210
*Actress*

**Stop & Shop Companies,
   Inc., The**
P.O. Box 369
Boston, MA 02101
Lewis G. Schaeneman, Jr.,
   Chairman and CEO
*Supermarket chain*

**Stoppard, Tom**
Peters, Fraser, Dunlop
The Chambers, 5th Fl.
Chelsea Harbor
London SW10 OXF England
*Playwright*

**Storage Technology
   Corporation**
2270 S. 88th St.
Louisville, CO 80028
Ryal R. Poppa, Chairman, CEO
   and President
*Computer data storage and retrieval
   storage company*

**Stowe-Day Foundation**
77 Forest St.
Hartford, CT 06105
Joseph S. Van Why, Director and
   CEO
*Harriet Beecher Stowe Museum*

**Strategic Air Command
   Museum**
2510 Clay St.
Bellevue, NE 68005
Jack L. Allen, Director
*Missile museum*

**Straub, Peter**
1 Beachside Common
Westport, CT 06880
*Author*

**Strawberry, Darryl**
c/o Los Angeles Dodgers
1000 Elysian Park Ave.
Los Angeles, CA 90012
*Professional baseball player*

**Stray Cats**
113 Wardour St.
London W1 England
*Rock group*

**Streisand, Barbra**
**(Barbara Joan)**
9830 Wilshire Blvd.
Beverly Hills, CA 90212
*Actress, director, singer*

**Stroh Companies, Inc.**
100 River Pl.
Detroit, MI 48207
Peter W. Stroh, Chairman
*Beer company*

**Struthers, Sally**
181 N. Saltair
Los Angeles, CA 90045
*Actress, children's activist*

**Studd, Diamond**
P.O. Box 105366
Atlanta, GA 30348
*Professional wrestler*

**Students Against Driving**
  **Drunk**
**(SADD)**
P.O. Box 800
Marlboro, MA 01752
Robert Anastas, Executive
  Director/Founder

**Students and Youth Against**
  **Racism**
P.O. Box 1819, Madison Square
  Station
New York, NY 10159
Jelayne Miles, Spokesperson

**Students to Offset Peer**
  **Pressure (STOPP)**
STOPP Consulting Services
P.O. Box 103
Hudson, NH 03051
Peter M. Jean, Executive
  Director

**Suharto**
Office of the President
15 Jalan Merdeka Utara
Jakarta, Indonesia
*President of Indonesia*

**Sullivan, Mike**
State Capitol
Cheyenne, WY 82002
*Governor of Wyoming*

**Sun Company, Inc.**
100 Matsonford Rd.
Radnor, PA 19087
Robert McClements, Jr.,
  Chairman
*11th largest petroleum refiner in the*
  *U.S.*

**Sun Microsystems, Inc.**
2550 Garcia Ave.
Mountain View, CA 94043
Scott G. McNealy, Chairman,
  President and CEO
*World's leading supplier of*
  *computer workstations*

**Sundlun, Bruce**
State House
Providence, RI 02903
*Governor of Rhode Island*

**Sung, Marshal Kim Il**
Office of the President
Pyongyang
Democratic People's Republic of
  Korea
*President, Democratic People's*
  *Republic of Korea*

**Suntrust Banks, Inc.**
25 Park Place, NE
Atlanta, GA 30303
James B. Williams, Chairman
and CEO
*17th largest publicly traded
banking concern in the U.S.*

**Super Dave**
**(Bob Einstein)**
8955 Beverly Blvd.
Los Angeles, CA 90048
*Comic stuntman*

**Superman**
DC Comics, Inc.
355 Lexington Ave.
New York, NY 10017
Julius Schwartz, Publisher
*Superhero comic book*

**Supermarkets General**
**Holdings Corp.**
301 Blair Rd.
Woodbridge, NJ 07095
Jack Futterman, Chairman,
President and CEO
*Retail supermarket chain*

**Superstation TBS**
Turner Broadcasting,
Incorporated
One CNN Center
P.O. Box 105366
Atlanta, GA 30348–5366
R. E. Turner, Chairman of the
Board/President
*Television superstation*

**Super Valu Stores, Inc.**
P.O. Box 990
Minneapolis, MN 55440
Michael W. Wright, Chairman,
President and CEO
*Food wholesaler*

**Sutherland, Kiefer**
9200 Sunset Blvd., #25
Los Angeles, CA 90069
*Actor*

**Swaggert, Jimmy**
P.O. Box 2550
Baton Rouge, LA 70821
*TV evangelist*

**Swann, Lynn Curtis**
c/o M. O'Brien
1720 Kelton Ave.
Los Angeles, CA 90024
*Sportscaster, retired dancing
football player*

**Swayze, Patrick**
8436 W. Third St., #650
Los Angeles, CA 90048
*Actor, dancer*

**Sweeney, D. B.**
131 S. Rodeo Dr., #300
Beverly Hills, CA 90212
*Actor*

**Sweetin, Jodie**
6212 Banner Ave.
Hollywood, CA 90038
*Actress*

**Swensens**
P.O. Box 9008
Andover, MA 01810
Richard Smith, Chairman
*Ice cream store chain*

**Symington, Fife**
State House
Phoenix, AZ 85007
*Governor of Arizona*

**Symms, Steve**
509 Senate Hart Office Bldg.
Washington, DC 20510
*Senator from Idaho*

**Syntex Corporation**
3401 Hillview Ave.
Palo Alto, CA 94304
Paul E. Freiman, Chairman and
   CEO
*Pharmaceutical company*

**Syrian Orthodox Church of
   Antioch, Archdiocese of
   the U.S.A. and Canada**
45 Fairmount Ave.
Hackensack, NJ 07601
Archbishop Mar-Athansius Y.
   Samuel, Primate
*Religious group*

**Sysco Corporation**
1390 Enclave Pkwy.
Houston, TX 77077
John E. Baugh, Senior
   Chairman of the Board
*Food product distributor*

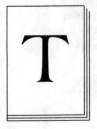

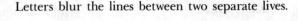
Letters blur the lines between two separate lives.

**Tabai, Ieremia**
Office of the President
Tarawa, Kiribati
*President of Kiribati*

**Tabone, Dr. Vincent**
Office of the President
The Palace
Valletta, Malta
*President of Malta*

**Taco Bell Corp.**
17901 Von Karman
Irvine, CA 92714
John E. Martin, President
*Fast food chain*

**Takei, George**
3800 Barham Blvd., #303
Los Angeles, CA 90068
*Actor, original "Star Trek" cast*

**Talking Heads**
1775 Broadway, #700
New York, NY 10019
*Rock group*

**Tallon Termite & Pest Control**
1949 E. Market St.
Long Beach, CA 90805
Jay Tallon, President
*Environmentally safe pest control*

**Tampa Bay Buccaneers**
One Buccaneer Plaza
Tampa, FL 33607
Hugh F. Culverhouse, Owner
*Professional football team*

**Tandem Computers Inc.**
19333 Vallco Pkway.
Cupertino, CA 95014
Thomas J. Perkins, Chairman
*Eighth largest midrange computer manufacturer in the world*

**Tandy, Jessica**
8899 Beverly Blvd.
Los Angeles, CA 90048
*Actress*

**Tandy Corporation**
1800 One Tandy Center
Fort Worth, TX 76102
John V. Roach, Chairman, CEO and President
*Computer manufacturer and owner of Radio Shack stores*

**Tanumafili, Malietoa II**
Government House
Vailima, Apia
Western Samoa, South Pacific
*Head of State of Western Samoa*

**Tarkenton, Francis Asbury**
3340 Peachtree Rd. NE, #1100
Atlanta, GA 30326
*Retired football player, sports
commentator*

**Taya, Col. Maaouye Ould Sidi
Ahmed**
Présidence de la République
B.P. 184, Nouachchott
Mauritania
*Chief of State and Head of
Government of Mauritania*

**Taylor, Elizabeth**
151 El Camino
Beverly Hills, CA 90212
*Actress, entrepreneur, activist*

**Taylor, Lawrence**
c/o New York Giants
Giants Stadium
E. Rutherford, NJ 07073
*Professional football player*

**Teachers Insurance**
730 Third Ave.
New York, NY 10017
Clifton R. Wharton, Jr.,
Chairman and CEO
*Insurance company for employees of
educational institutions*

**Teamsters
(International Brotherhood of
Teamsters, Chauffeurs,
Warehousemen and Helpers
of America)**
25 Louisiana Ave., NW
Washington, DC 20001
William J. McCarthy, General
President
*Largest and most diverse U.S. labor
union*

**Tears for Fears**
50 New Bond St.
London W1 England
*Rock group*

**Teen**
Petersen Publishing Company
8490 Sunset Blvd.
Los Angeles, CA 90069
Robert F. MacLeod, Editorial
Director and Executive
Publisher
*Fashion and beauty magazine for
teenage girls*

**Teen Association of Model
Railroading**
Lone Eagle Payne
1028 Whaley Rd., RD #4
New Carlisle, OH 45344
Stan Ujka, President
*Promotes building and operating of
model railroads*

**Teen Beat Magazine**
215 Lexington Ave.
New York, NY 10016
Karen L. Williams, Editor
*Youth-oriented magazine*

**Teen Machine**
Sterling's Magazines
355 Lexington Ave.
New York, NY 10017
Marie Therese Morreale, Editor
*Fan magazine*

**Teenage Mutant Ninja
Turtles**
c/o New Line Cinema
116 N. Robertson Blvd., #200
Los Angeles, CA 90048
*Michelangelo, Donatello, Leonardo
and Raphael, superheroes on a
half shell*

**Tele-Communications, Inc.**
4643 S. Ulster St.
Denver, CO 80237
Bob Magness, Chairman
*Nation's largest cable systems operator*

**Teledyne, Inc.**
1901 Ave. of the Stars
Los Angeles, CA 90067
George A. Roberts, Chairman
*Technology-oriented conglomerate*

**Teng-Hui, Li**
Office of the President
Taipei, Taiwan, Republic of China
*President of Taiwan*

**Tenneco, Inc.**
Tenneco Bldg., P.O. Box 2511
Houston, TX 77252
James L. Ketelsen, Chairman and CEO
*Farm and construction equipment, gas pipelines*

**Teresa, Mother
(Agnes Gonxha Bojaxhia)**
54A Lower Circular Rd.
Calcutta, India 700016
*Missionary, Nobel Peace Prize winner*

**Terkel, Studs Louis**
303 E. Wacker
Chicago, IL 60601
*Author*

**Terlesky, John**
P.O. Box 5617
Beverly Hills, CA 90210
*Actor*

**Tesh, John**
5555 Melrose Ave.
Los Angeles, CA 90038
*Celebrity interviewer, musician*

**Tewkesbury, Joan F.**
9830 Wilshire Blvd.
Beverly Hills, CA 90212
*Film director, writer*

**Texaco Inc.**
2000 Westchester Ave.
White Plains, NY 10650
James W. Kinnear, President and CEO
*Third largest integrated oil company in the U.S.*

**Texas Instruments Inc.**
13500 N. Central Expressway,
P.O. Box 655474
Dallas, TX 75265
Jerry R. Junkins, Chairman, President and CEO
*The company that invented the pocket calculator*

**Texas Rangers**
1250 Copeland Rd., #1100
Arlington, TX 76011
Thomas A. Grieve, Vice-President/General Manager
*Professional baseball team*

**Texas Utilities Company**
2001 Bryan Tower
Dallas, TX 75201
Jerry S. Farrington, Chairman and CEO
*America's ninth largest electric utility*

**Textron Inc.**
40 Westminster St.
Providence, RI 02903
B. F. Dolan, Chairman
*Aerospace, financial services and commercial products*

**Tharp, Twyla**
American Ballet Theatre
890 Broadway
New York, NY 10003
*Dancer, choreographer*

**Theodore Roosevelt National Park**
Visitor Center
Medora, ND 58645
Pete Hark, Park Superintendent

**Theus, Reggie**
c/o New Jersey Nets
Meadowlands Arena
E. Rutherford, NJ 07073
*Professional basketball player*

**Thiokol Corporation**
2475 Washington Blvd.
Ogden, UT 84401
U. Edwin Garrison, Chairman, President and CEO
*U.S. producer of solid fuel systems for rockets*

**Thomas, Clarence**
U.S. Supreme Court Building
One First Street, NE
Washington, DC 20543
*Associate Justice of the Supreme Court*

**Thomas, Derrick**
c/o Kansas City Chiefs
One Arrowhead Dr.
Kansas City, MO 64129
*Professional football player*

**Thomas, Isiah**
c/o Detroit Pistons
One Championship Dr.
Auburn Hills, MI 48057
*Professional basketball player*

**Thomas, Jay**
10351 Santa Monica Blvd., #211
Los Angeles, CA 90025
*Actor, D.J.*

**Thomas, Thurman**
c/o Buffalo Bills
1 Bills Dr.
Orchard Park, NY 14127
*Professional football player*

**Thomas Jefferson Institute for the Study of Religious Freedom**
P.O. Box 1777
Fredericksburg, VA 22402
Dr. Kurt F. Leidecker, President

**Thomas Wolfe Memorial**
48 Spruce St.
Asheville, NC 28801
Steve Hill, Site Manager

**Thompson, Hunter S.**
Box 220
Woody Creek, CO 81656
*Gonzo journalist*

**Thompson, Lea**
232 N. Canon Dr.
Beverly Hills, CA 90210
*Actress*

**Thompson, Tommy G.**
State Capitol
Madison, WI 53707
*Governor of Wisconsin*

**Thomson, Gordon**
10100 Santa Monica Blvd., #700
Los Angeles, CA 90067
*Actor*

**Thornley, Stew**
982 15th Ave. SE
Minneapolis, MN 55414
*Baseball historian and author*

**Thorpe, Otis**
c/o Houston Rockets
The Summit
Houston, TX 77046
*Professional basketball player*

**Thurmond, Strom**
217 Senate Russell Office Bldg.
Washington, DC 20501
*Senator from South Carolina*

**Timakata, Fred**
Office of the President
Port Vila, Vanuatu
*President of Vanuatu*

**Time Warner Inc.**
75 Rockefeller Plaza
New York, NY 10019
Steven J. Ross, Chairman and
Co-CEO
*Largest media and entertainment
company in the world*

**Times Mirror Company, The**
Times Mirror Square
Los Angeles, CA 90053
Robert F. Erburu, Chairman
and CEO
*Newspaper and magazine publisher*

**Timmerman, Bonnie**
445 Park Ave., 7th Fl.
New York, NY 10022
*Casting director*

**Titanic Historical Society**
Box 53
Indian Orchard, MA 01151
*Sunken ship society*

**TLC**
6 W. 57th St.
New York, NY 10019
*Musical group*

**TLC Beatrice International
Holdings**
9 W. 57th St.
New York, NY 10019
Reginald F. Lewis, Chairman
and CEO
*Wholesale and retail food
distribution company*

**Toastmasters International**
2200 N. Grand Ave.
Santa Ana, CA 92711
Greg Giesen, Manager,
Membership and Club
Extension
*Public speaking group*

**Toffler, Alvin**
201 E. 50th St., 3rd Fl.
New York, NY 10022
*Future Shocker*

**Tom Petty and the
Heartbreakers**
1755 Broadway, 8th Fl.
New York, NY 10019
*Rock group*

**Tomlin, Lily**
P.O. Box 27700
Los Angeles, CA 90027
*Comedienne, actress*

**Tong, Goh Chok**
Prime Minister's Office
Istana, Singapore 0923
*Prime Minister of Singapore*

**Tonka Corporation**
6000 Clearwater Dr.
Minnetonka, MN 55343
Stephen G. Shank, CEO
*Best toy trucks*

**Tony the Tiger**
c/o Kellogg Company
235 Porter
Battle Creek, MI 49017
*Kellogg's mascot*

**Tootsie Roll**
7401 Cicero Ave.
Chicago, IL 60629
M. J. Gordon, President
*Candy company*

**Toronto Blue Jays**
300 The Esplanade W., #3200
Toronto, Ontario M5 V3 B3
　Canada
Paul Beeston, President/COO
*Professional baseball team*

**Toronto Maple Leafs**
Maple Leaf Gardens
60 Carlton St.
Toronto, Ontario M5B 1L1
　Canada
Harold E. Ballard, President
*Professional hockey team*

**Toto**
P.O. Box 7308
Carmel, CA 93921
*Rock group*

**Touch America Program**
U.S. Forest Service
P.O. Box 96090
Washington, DC 20090
Don Hansen, Director, Human
　Resource Programs
*Volunteer conservation programs*

**Touchstone Pictures**
500 S. Buena Vista St.
Burbank, CA 91521
David Hoberman, President
*Movie production company*

**Toughlove**
P.O. Box 1069
Doylestown, PA 18901
Gwen Olitsky, Managing
　Director
*Deals with problem kids*

**Toure, Lt. Co. Amadou
　Toumani**
c/o Cabinet du Président
Comité militaire de libération
　nationale
B.P. 1463, Bamako, Mali
*President of Mali*

**Toy Manufacturers of
　America, Inc.**
200 Fifth Ave.
New York, NY 10010
Walter Armatys, Executive
　Director
*Tests toys*

**Toy Train Museum**
Paradise Ln.
Strasburg, PA 17579
Betty Perini, Director/Curator

**Toys "Я" Us**
4 Fromm Rd.
Paramus, NJ 07652
Charles Lazarus, Chairman and
　CEO
*Toy store chain*

**Traci Lords Fan Club**
Rte. 1, Box 18
Berger, MO 63014
Dennis Rylee, President
*Former teenage porn queen's fan
　club*

**Trammell, Terry**
1801 N. Senate Blvd., #200
Indianapolis, IN 46202
*Orthopedic surgeon specializing in
race car drivers*

**Trammell Crow Company**
3500 Trammell Crow Center
2001 Ross Ave.
Dallas, TX 75201
Trammell Crow, Chairman
*Nation's largest real estate developer*

**Trans World Airlines, Inc.**
100 S. Bedford Rd.
Mt. Kisco, NY 10549
Carl C. Icahn, Chairman and
    CEO
*Troubled international airline*

**Transamerica Corporation**
600 Montgomery St.
San Francisco, CA 94111
James R. Harvey, Chairman
*Financial services company*

**Traveler's Corporation, The**
One Tower Sq.
Hartford, CT 06183
Edward H. Budd, Chairman
    and CEO
*Ninth largest U.S. insurance
    company*

**Travis, Randy**
P.O. Box 121712
Nashville, TN 37212
*Singer*

**Treepeople**
12601 Mulholland Dr.
Beverly Hills, CA 90210
Andy Lipkus, President
*Urban tree planters*

**Tribune Company**
435 N. Michigan Ave.
Chicago, IL 60611
Stanton R. Cook, Chairman
*Media giant*

**Tri-Star Pictures**
3400 Riverside Dr.
Burbank, CA 91505
Mike Medavoy, Chairman
*Movie production company*

**Tropical Fish Hobbyist**
TFH Publications, Inc.
211 W. Sylvania Ave.
Neptune City, NJ 07753
Ray Hunziker, Editor
*Fish magazine*

**Trovoada, Miguel Anjos de
    Cunha Lisboa**
Office of the President
Sao Tome, Sao Tome and
    Principe
*President of Sao Tome*

**True Confessions**
Macfadden Holdings, Inc.
233 Park Ave., South
New York, NY 10003
H. Marie Atkocius, Editor
*Magazine*

**Trujillo, Cesar Gaviria**
Office of the President
Casa de Narino
Carrera 8A, No. 7–26, Bogota,
    Colombia
*President of Colombia*

**Trump, Donald**
725 Fifth Ave.
New York, NY 10022
*Businessman*

**Trumpeter Swan Society, The**
3800 County Rd. 24
Maple Plain, MN 55359
R. W. McKelvey, President
*Swan preservation*

**Trust for the Public Land, The**
116 New Montgomery St., 4th Fl.
San Francisco, CA 94105
Martin J. Rosen, President

**TRW Inc.**
1900 Richmond Rd.
Cleveland, OH 44124
Joseph T. Gorman, Chairman and CEO
*Civilian version of the IRS; credit information company that plays God*

**Tsongas, Paul**
1 Post Office Sq.
Boston, MA 02109
*Ex-Senator, ex-presidential candidate*

**Tucker, Michael**
10100 Santa Monica Blvd., 16th Fl.
Los Angeles, CA 90067
*Actor*

**Tucker, Tanya**
P.O. Box 15245
Nashville, TN 37215
*Singer*

**Tupou, King Taufa'ahau, IV**
The Palace
P.O. Box 6
Nuku'alofa, Tonga
*Sovereign of Tonga*

**Tureck, Rosalind**
c/o Columbia Artists Mgmt.
165 W. 57th St.
New York, NY 10019
*Harpsichordist*

**Turner, Janine**
9255 Sunset Blvd., #515
Los Angeles, CA 90069
*Actress*

**Turner, Kathleen**
232 N. Canon Dr.
Beverly Hills, CA 90210
*Actress*

**Turner, Lana**
10100 Santa Monica Blvd., #700
Los Angeles, CA 90067
*Actress*

**Turner, Ted**
P.O. Box 4064
Atlanta, GA 30302
*Entrepreneur*

**Turner, Tina**
Lindenallee 86
D-5000 Koln 51, Germany
*Singer*

**Turner Network Television (TNT)**
One CNN Center, P.O. Box 105336
Atlanta, GA 30348
Scott Sassa, President, Turner Entertainment Networks
*Cable television network*

**Turtle Mountain Chippewa Heritage Center**
Hwy. 5, P.O. Box 257
Belcourt, NC 58316
Denise Lajimodierre, CEO and
  Chairman
*Indian historical center*

**Tutu, Bishop Desmond**
Box 31190
Johannesburg, South Africa
*Human rights activist*

**TW Holdings, Inc.**
P.O. Box 3800, 203 E. Main St.
Spartanburg, SC 29304
Paul E. Tierney, Chairman
*Denny's, El Pollo Loco, Hardee's*

**Twentieth Century-Fox, Inc.**
10201 W. Pico Blvd.
Los Angeles, CA 90035
Barry Diller, Chairman/CEO
*Television and film production
  company*

**Tyco Toys, Inc.**
6000 Midlantic Dr.
Mt. Laurel, NJ 08054
Richard E. Grey, President/
  Chairman/CEO
*Game manufacturer*

**Tyson, Mike**
#922335, Regional Diagnostic
  Center
Plainfield, IN 46168
*Incarcerated boxer*

**Tyson Food, Inc.**
2210 W. Oaklawn
Springdale, AR 72764
Don Tyson, Chairman and CEO
*World's largest producer, processor
  and marketer of poultry-based
  food products*

It gives me the greatest pleasure to realize I have one more invisible friend at the other end of the post office. Nearly every week a new one turns up, and I feel like I am having a party, and the postman is a sort of Santa Claus every day, with letters from my new friends.

—VACHEL LINDSAY TO ALICE HENDERSON, 1913

**UAL Corporation**
1200 Algonquin Rd.
Elk Grove Township, IL 60007
Stephen M. Wolf, Chairman,
    President and CEO
*United Airlines*

**Ueberroth, Peter**
P.O. Box 2649
Los Angeles, CA 90053
*Entrepreneur, in charge of
    rebuilding Los Angeles*

**UFO Magazine**
California UFO
P.O. Box 1053
Sunland, CA 91041
Vicki Cooper, Sherie Stark, Co-
    Publishers

**Ugly Kid Joe**
825 Eighth Ave.
New York, NY 10019
*Rock group*

**Ukrainian Orthodox Church
    in America**
90–34 139th St.
Jamaica, NY 11435
Rev. Bishop Vsevolod, Primate
*Religious group*

**Ullman, Tracey**
9830 Wilshire Blvd.
Beverly Hills, CA 90212
*Comedienne, actress*

**Ultimate Warrior**
P.O. Box 3857
Stamford, CT 06905
*Professional wrestler*

**Underwood, Blair**
9830 Wilshire Blvd.
Beverly Hills, CA 90212
*Actor*

**Union Carbide Corporation**
39 Old Ridgebury Rd.
Danbury, CT 06817
Robert D. Kennedy, Chairman
    and CEO
*Fourth largest U.S. chemical
    company*

**Union of American Hebrew
    Congregations (Reform)**
838 Fifth Ave.
New York, NY 10021
Rabbi Alexander M. Schindler,
    President
*Religious group*

**Union of Concerned Scientists**
26 Church St.
Cambridge, MA 02238
Howard Ris, Executive Director

**Union of Orthodox Jewish Congregations of America**
45 W. 36th St.
New York, NY 10018
Sidney Kwestel, President
*Religious group*

**Union Pacific Corporation**
Martin Tower
8th and Eaton Aves.
Bethlehem, PA 18018
Drew Lewis, Chairman,
   President and CEO
*Second largest U.S. railroad system*

**Unisys Corporation**
Township Line and Union
   Meeting Rds.
Blue Bell, PA 19424
James A. Unruh, Chairman and
   CEO
*Third largest computer maker in the
U.S.*

**United Nations Environment Programme**
P.O. Box 30552
Nairobi, Kenya
Mostafa K. Tolba, Executive
   Director

**United Parcel Service of America, Inc.**
Greenwich Office Park 5
Greenwich, CT 06831
Kent C. (Oz) Nelson, Chairman
   and CEO
*Familiar brown trucks*

**United States Amateur Confederation of Roller Skating**
P.O. Box 6579
1500 S. 70th St.
Lincoln, NE 68506
Len Taylor, Public Information
   Director

**United States Baseball Federation**
2160 Greenwood Ave.
Trenton, NJ 08609
Scott Bollwage, Development
   Director
*International baseball tournaments*

**United States Chamber of Commerce**
1615 H St., NW
Washington, DC 20062
Dr. Richard L. Lesher, President

**United States Committee for UNICEF**
331 E. 38th St.
New York, NY 11235
Lawrence Bruce, President

**United States Diving, Inc.**
201 S. Capitol Ave., #430
Indianapolis, IN 46225
Todd B. Smith, Executive
   Director

**United States Fencing Association**
1750 E. Boulder St.
Colorado Springs, CO 80909
Carla-Mae Richards, Executive
   Director

## United States Figure Skating Association
20 First St.
Colorado Springs, CO 80906
Ian Anderson, Executive
  Director

## United States Gymnastics Federation
Pan American Plaza
201 S. Capitol, #300
Indianapolis, IN 46225
Mike Jacki, Executive Director

## United States International Speedskating Association
240 Oneida St.
Syracuse, NY 13204
John Byrne, Executive Officer

## United States Judo, Inc.
P.O. Box 10013
El Paso, TX 79991
Frank Fullerton, President

## United States Lifesaving Association
425 E. McFetridge Dr.
Chicago, IL 60605
Ray Colonna, Executive Director
*Association of lifeguards*

## United States Luge Association
P.O. Box 651
Lake Placid, NY 12946
Lin Hancock, Junior
  Development Director

## U.S. Marine Corps
Arlington Annex
Washington, DC 20380
General Carl E. Mundy, Jr.,
  Commandant

## United States Paddle Tennis Association
Box 30
Culver City, CA 90232
Greg Lawrence, President

## United States Shoe Corporation, The
1 Eastwood Dr.
Cincinnati, OH 45227
Philip C. Barach, Chairman
*Amalfi, Capezio, Joyce, Red Cross, etc.*

## United States Ski Association
P.O. Box 100
Park City, UT 84060
Howard Peterson, Executive
  Officer

## United States Soccer Federation
1835 Union Ave., #190
Memphis, TN 38104
Mavis Derflinger, Chairman

## United States Surfing Federation
P.O. Box 495
Huntington Beach, CA 92648
Janice Aragon, Executive
  Director

## United States Swimming, Inc.
1750 E. Boulder St.
Colorado Springs, CO 80909
Ray B. Essick, Executive
  Director

## United States Synchronized Swimming, Inc.
201 S. Capitol Ave., #510
Indianapolis, IN 46225
Betty Watanabe, Executive
  Director

**United States Table Tennis Association**
1750 E. Boulder St.
Colorado Springs, CO 80909
*Ping-Pong group*

**United States Tae Kwon Do Union**
1750 E. Boulder St.
Colorado Springs, CO 80909
Kay Flora, Business Director

**United States Team Handball Federation**
1750 E. Boulder St.
Colorado Springs, CO 80909
Mike Cavanaugh, Executive Director

**United States Tennis Association**
707 Alexander Rd.
Princeton, NJ 08540
Beth Brainard, Coordinator of Program Development

**United States Tourist Council**
Drawer 1875
Washington, DC 20013
Stanford West, Executive Director

**United States Twirling Association**
P.O. Box 24488
Seattle, WA 98124
Kathy Forsythe, Administrative Coordinator

**United States Volleyball Association**
1750 E. Boulder St.
Colorado Springs, CO 80909
Clifford T. McPeak, Executive Director

**United States Weightlifting Federation**
1750 E. Boulder St.
Colorado Springs, CO 80909
George Greenway, Executive Director

**United Synagogue of America (Conservative)**
155 Fifth Ave.
New York, NY 10010
Alan Tichnor, President
*Religious group*

**United Technologies Corporation**
United Technologies Bldg.
Hartford, CT 06101
Robert F. Daniell, Chairman, President, CEO and COO
*Manufactures helicopters, jet engines, elevators, etc.*

**United Telecommunications, Inc.**
2330 Shawnee Mission Pkwy.
Westwood, KS 66205
William T. Esrey, Chairman and CEO
*Largest U.S. telephone company*

**United Way of America**
701 N. Fairfax St.
Alexandria, VA 22314
John F. Akers, Chairman
*Nonprofit service agency that raises funds for other nonprofit organizations*

**Universal Corporation**
P.O. Box 25099, Hamilton St. at Broad
Richmond, VA 23260
Gordon L. Crenshaw, Chairman
*World's largest tobacco dealer*

**University Art Museum, Berkeley**
2625 Durant Ave.
Berkeley, CA 94720
John Bransten, President, Board of Trustees

**University Museum, The**
University of Arkansas
Museum Building
Fayetteville, AR 72701
Dr. Johnnie L. Gentry, Director

**University of Alaska Museum**
907 Yukon Dr.
Fairbanks, AK 99775
Wallace A. Steffan, Director

**University of Chicago**
5801 S. Ellis Ave.
Chicago, IL 60637
Hanna H. Gray, President

**University of Texas at Austin, The**
UT Station
Austin, TX 78713
Louis A. Beecherl, Jr.,
Chairman of Board of Regents

**Unocal Corporation**
1201 W. Fifth St.
Los Angeles, CA 90017
Richard J. Stegemeier,
Chairman, President and CEO
*11th largest U.S. petroleum company*

**Unser, Al**
7625 Central NW
Albuquerque, NM 87105
*Race car driver*

**Upjohn Company, The**
7000 Portage Rd.
Kalamazoo, MI 49001
Theodore Cooper, Chairman
and CEO
*Pharmaceutical company*

**Urich, Robert**
822 S. Robertson Blvd., #200
Los Angeles, CA 90035
*Actor*

**Uris, Leon**
c/o Doubleday
245 Park Ave.
New York, NY 10017
*Author*

**USA Amateur Boxing Federation**
1750 E. Boulder St.
Colorado Springs, CO 80909
Bruce Mathis, Associate
Executive Director

**USA Karate Federation, The**
1300 Kenmore Blvd.
Akron, OH 44314

**USA Network**
1230 Ave. of the Americas
New York, NY 10020
Kay Koplovitz, President/CEO
*Cable television network*

**USA Wrestling**
255 S. Academy Blvd.
Colorado Springs, CO 80901
David C. Miller, Executive
Director

**USAIR Group, Inc.**
2345 Crystal Dr.
Arlington, VA 22227
Edwin I. Colodny, Chairman
*Airline*

## USF&G Corporation
100 Light St.
Baltimore, MD 21202
Norman P. Blake, Jr., Chairman,
 President and CEO
*Property/casualty insurance
 company*

## USG Corporation
101 S. Wacker Dr.
Chicago, IL 60606
Eugene B. Connolly, Chairman
 and CEO
*Largest manufacturer of gypsum in
 North America*

## U.S. West, Inc.
7800 E. Orchard Rd.
Englewood, CO 80111
Jack A. MacAllister, Chairman
*Telephone company*

## U.S.S. Arizona Memorial
#1 Arizona Memorial Dr.
Honolulu, HI 96818
William K. Dickinson,
 Superintendent
*Pearl Harbor memorial*

## USX Corporation
600 Grant St.
Pittsburgh, PA 15219
Charles A. Corry, Chairman
 and CEO
*Nation's largest steelmaker*

## Utah Jazz
5 Triad Center
Salt Lake City, UT 84180
Frank Layden, President
*Professional basketball team*

## U2
4 Windmill Lane
Dublin 4, Ireland
*Rock group*

La Letter, l'épitre, qui n' est pas un genre mais tous les genres, la littérature même.

The letter, the epistle, which is not a genre but all the genres, literature itself.

—JACQUES DERRIDA, "La Carte Postale"

**Valentine, Scott**
151 El Camino
Beverly Hills, CA 90212
*Actor*

**Valli, Frankie**
8899 Beverly Blvd.
Los Angeles, CA 90048
*Singer*

**Van Ark, Joan**
151 El Camino
Beverly Hills, CA 90212
*Actress*

**Van Buren, Abigail**
9200 Sunset Blvd., #1003
Los Angeles, CA 90069
*"Dear Abby"*

**Van Damme, Jean Claude**
P.O. Box 4149
Chatsworth, CA 91313
*Actor*

**Van Halen**
3300 Warner Blvd.
Burbank, CA 91510
*Rock group*

**Vancouver Canucks**
Pacific Coliseum
100 North Renfrew Street
Vancouver, British Columbia
V5K 3N7 Canada
Pat Quinn, President/General
Manager
*Professional hockey team*

**Vandeweghe, Kiki**
c/o New York Knickerbockers
4 Pennsylvania Plaza
New York, NY 10001
*Professional basketball player*

**Vanilla Ice**
8730 Sunset Blvd., 5th Fl. W.
Los Angeles, CA 90069
*Rapper*

**Vanity**
151 El Camino
Beverly Hills, CA 90212
*Singer, actress*

**Vanity Fair**
350 Madison Ave.
New York, NY 10017
E. Graydon Carter, Editor-in-
Chief

**Variety**
475 Park Ave. S.
New York, NY 10016
Peter Bart, Editor
*Weekly trade paper*

**Vassiliou, Dr. George**
Presidential Palace
Nicosia, Cyprus
*President of Cyprus*

**VelJohnson, Reginald**
9229 Sunset Blvd., #607
Los Angeles, CA 90069
*Actor*

**V. F. Corporation**
1047 N. Park Rd.
Wyomissing, PA 19610
Lawrence R. Pugh, Chairman,
President and CEO
*World's second largest clothing
company*

**Viacom Inc.**
1515 Broadway
New York, NY 10036
Sumner M. Redstone, Chairman
*MTV, VH-1 and Nickelodeon*

**Video Hits 1
(VH-1)**
MTV Networks
1515 Broadway
New York, NY 10036
Edward A. Bennett, President

**Vieira, Joao Bernardo**
Conselho de Estado
Bissau, Guinea-Bissau
*President of the Council of State of
Guinea-Bissau*

**Villechaize, Herve**
P.O. Box 1305
Burbank, CA 91507
*Troublesome diminutive actor*

**Vincent, Francis T., Jr.**
Commissioner's Office
350 Park Ave.
New York, NY 10022
*Commissioner of baseball*

**Vinton, Bobby
(Stanley Robert)**
c/o T. Cassidy
417 Marawood Dr.
Woodstock, IL 60098
*Singer*

**Virgin Records America, Inc.**
9247 Alden Dr.
Beverly Hills, CA 90210
Jeff Ayeroff, Co-Managing
Director
*Record label*

**Voinovich, George V.**
State House
Columbus, OH 43215
*Governor of Ohio*

**Von Stade, Frederica**
165 W. 57th St.
New York, NY 10019
*Opera star*

**Vongvichit, Phuomi**
Office of the President
Vientiane, Laos
*President of Laos*

**Vons Companies, Inc., The**
618 Michillinda Ave.
Arcadia, CA 91007
Roger E. Stangeland, Chairman
and CEO
*Tenth largest supermarket chain in
the U.S.*

**Voss, Sammi Davis**
151 El Camino
Beverly Hills, CA 90212
*Actress*

**Vulcan Materials Company**
One Metroplex Dr.
Birmingham, AL 35209
Herbert A. Sklenar, President
and CEO
*Gravel, sand and rock producer*

Dear Pamela, the value of a letter can't be measured quantitatively. If you haven't time to write what you call a "real" letter, then write a few lines. I don't expect anyone to compose longwinded epistles, as I sometimes do. I write letters because I enjoy doing it. It doesn't matter too much whether the recipient takes pleasure in reading what I write; I've had my pleasure.

—"In Absentia"

**Wagner, Lindsay**
P.O. Box 188
Pacific Palisades, CA 90272
*Actress*

**Wagner, Robin**
890 Broadway
New York, NY 10003
*Stage and set designer*

**Waihee, John D.**
State Capitol
Honolulu, HI 96813
*Governor of Hawaii*

**Waits, Tom**
**(Thomas Alan)**
c/o E. Smith
305 E. 72nd St., #4BN
New York, NY 10021
*Singer, composer, actor*

**Waldheim, Kurt**
Präsidentschaftskanzlei
Hofburg, 1014 Vienna, Austria
*Former President of Austria*

**Walesa, Lech**
Kancelaria Presydenta RP,
Ul Wiejska 4/8
00-902 Warsaw, Poland
*President of Poland*

**Walgreen Co.**
200 Wilmot Rd.
Deerfield, IL 60015
Charles R. Walgreen III,
    Chairman and CEO
*Drugstore chain*

**Walker, Alice Malsenior**
c/o Harcourt Brace Jovanovich
111 Fifth Ave.
New York, NY 10003
*Author*

**Wallace, George**
Troy State University
P.O. Box 4419
Montgomery, AL 36195
*Controversial ex-governor of
    Alabama and sometime
    presidential candidate*

**Wallace, Mike**
CBS News
524 W. 57th St.
New York, NY 10019
*TV journalist*

**Wallendas, The Great**
138 Frog Hollow Rd.
Churchville, PA 18966
*Family of trapeze artists*

**Wallop, Malcolm**
237 Senate Russell Office Bldg.
Washington, DC 20501
*Senator from Wyoming*

**Wal-Mart Stores, Inc.**
702 SW 8th St.
Bentonville, AR 72716
Sam M. Walton, Chairman
*Fastest growing retailer in the U.S.*

**Walt Disney Company**
500 S. Buena Vista St.
Burbank, CA 91521
Michael D. Eisner, Chairman
    and CEO
*The house that mouse built*

**Walt Whitman Association**
P.O. Box 1493
Camden, NJ 08101
John C. Milley, President

**Walters, Barbara**
c/o ABC News
1330 Sixth Ave.
New York, NY 10019
*Television journalist, co-host of
    "20/20"*

**Walters, David**
State Capitol, Rm. 212
Oklahoma City, OK 73105
*Governor of Oklahoma*

**Wang Laboratories, Inc.**
One Industrial Ave.
Lowell, MA 01851
Richard W. Miller, Chairman
    and CEO
*Computer and software
    manufacturer*

**Wangchuk, King Jigme
    Singye**
Royal Palace
Thimphu, Bhutan
*Ruler of Bhutan*

**Ward, David S.**
9830 Wilshire Blvd.
Beverly Hills, CA 90212
*Screenwriter, film director*

**Ward, Rachel**
10100 Santa Monica Blvd.,
    #1600
Los Angeles, CA 90067
*Actress*

**Ward, Sela**
8899 Beverly Blvd.
Los Angeles, CA 90048
*Actress*

**Warfield, Marsha**
P.O. Box 691713
Los Angeles, CA 90069
*Actress, comedienne*

**Warlock, Billy**
9200 Sunset Blvd., #625
Los Angeles, CA 90069
*Actor*

**Warlord**
P.O. Box 3857
Stamford, CT 06905
*Professional wrestler*

**Warner, John W.**
225 Senate Russell Office Bldg.
Washington, DC 20501
*Senator from Virginia*

**Warner, Malcolm Jamal**
8230 Beverly Blvd., #23
Los Angeles, CA 90048
*Actor*

**Warner Brothers Collections**
Dept. TS
P.O. Box 60049
Tampa, FL 33660
*Mail order for Warner Brothers
collectibles*

**Warner Brothers Records**
75 Rockefeller Plaza, 20th Fl.
New York, NY 10019
Mo Ostin, Chairman
*Recording company*

**Warner-Lambert Company**
201 Tabor Rd.
Morris Plains, NJ 07950
Joseph D. Williams, Chairman
  and CEO
*Listerine, Rolaids, Certs, Chiclets*

**Warrell, Todd**
c/o St. Louis Cardinals
Busch Stadium
St. Louis, MO 63102
*Professional baseball player*

**Warwick, Dionne**
December Twelve
144 S. Beverly Dr., #503
Beverly Hills, CA 90212
*Singer, activist*

**Washington, Denzel**
8899 Beverly Blvd.
Los Angeles, CA 90048
*Actor*

**Washington Blade, The**
724 Ninth St., NW, 8th Fl.
Washington, DC 20001
Lisa M. Keen, Senior Editor
*Weekly news tabloid for the gay and
  lesbian community*

**Washington Bullets**
One Harry S. Truman Dr.
Landover, MD 20786
Bob Ferry, Vice-President/
  General Manager
*Professional basketball team*

**Washington Capitals**
Capitol Center
Landover, MD 20786
David Poile, Vice-President/
  General Manager
*Professional hockey team*

**Washington Post Company,
  The**
1150 15th St., NW
Washington, DC 20071
Katharine Graham, Chairman
*Newspaper and magazine publisher*

**Washington Redskins**
P.O. Box 17247
Dulles International Airport
Washington, DC 20041
John Kent Cooke, Executive
  Vice-President
*Professional football team*

**Waste Management, Inc.**
3003 Butterfield Rd.
Oak Brook, IL 60521
Dean L. Buntrock, Chairman
  and CEO
*Largest waste collection, disposal
  and recycling company in the
  world*

**Water Pollution Control
  Federation**
601 Wythe St.
Alexandria, VA 22314
Charles B. Kaiser, Jr., President

**Waterston, Sam**
9000 Sunset Blvd., #1200
Los Angeles, CA 90069
*Actor*

**Watley, Jody**
8439 Sunset Blvd., #103
Los Angeles, CA 90069
*Singer*

**Watt, James Gaius**
755 E. Paintbrush Dr., Box 3705
Jackson, WY 83001
*Controversial former Secretary of the Interior*

**Wayans, Keenan Ivory**
P.O. Box 900
Beverly Hills, CA 90213
*Executive Producer and star of "In Living Color"*

**Weaver, Dennis**
P.O. Box 983
Malibu, CA 90265
*Actor*

**Weber, Dr. Arnold R.**
Northwestern University
Evanston, IL 60208
*University president*

**Wedgeworth, Ann**
822 S. Robertson Blvd., #200
Los Angeles, CA 90035
*Actress*

**Weicker, Lowell Jr.**
State Capitol
Hartford, CT 06106
*Governor of Connecticut*

**Weinberger, Caspar**
60 Fifth Ave.
New York, NY 10011
*Foreign affairs expert, former Secretary of Defense*

**Weisberg, Stanley**
Los Angeles Superior Court
111 N. Hill St.
Los Angeles, CA 90012
*Judge in the Rodney King beating trial*

**Welch, Raquel**
151 El Camino
Beverly Hills, CA 90212
*Actress, author*

**Weld, William F.**
State House
Boston, MA 02133
*Governor of Massachusetts*

**Weller, Peter**
8205 Santa Monica Blvd., #1-262
Los Angeles, CA 90046
*Robocop actor*

**Wells Fargo & Company**
420 Montgomery St.
San Francisco, CA 94163
Carl E. Riechardt, Chairman and CEO
*California bank*

**Wellstone, Paul D.**
702 Senate Hart Office Bldg.
Washington, DC 20510
*Senator from Minnesota*

**Welty, Eudora**
1119 Pinehurst St.
Jackson, MS 39202
*Writer*

**Wendy's International, Inc.**
4288 West Dublin Granville Rd.
Dublin, OH 43017
R. David Thomas, Founder
*Fast food chain named for the founder's daughter*

**Western Museum of Mining and Industry**
1025 N. Gate Rd.
Colorado Springs, CO 80921
Daniel League, Jr., Chairman

**Western Soccer League**
2815 Second Ave., #300
Seattle, WA 98121
William C. Sage, Chairman
*Association of soccer teams*

**Westinghouse Electric Corporation**
Westinghouse Bldg., Gateway Center
Pittsburgh, PA 15222
Paul E. Lego, Chairman and CEO
*Group W, Longines-Wittnauer Watches, Westinghouse Electric*

**Westling, Jon**
Boston University
Boston, MA 02215
*University CEO*

**Wetlands for Wildlife, Inc.**
P.O. Box 344
West Bend, WI 53095
Lambert Neuburg, President

**Weyerhaeuser Company**
Tacoma, WA 98477
George H. Weyerhaeuser, Chairman
*Fourth largest forest products company in the world*

**Wheaton, Wil**
P.O. Box 12567
La Crescenta, CA 91214
*Actor*

**Whipple, Fred Lawrence**
60 Garden St.
Cambridge, MA 02138
*Astronomer*

**Whirlpool Corporation**
2000 M-63
Benton Harbor, MI 49022
David Whitwam, Chairman, President and CEO
*Household appliance manufacturer*

**White, Betty**
P.O. Box 3713
Granada Hills, CA 91344
*Actress*

**White, Byron R.**
U.S. Supreme Court Building
One First Street, NE
Washington, DC 20543
*Associate Justice of the Supreme Court*

**White, Jaleel**
1450 Belfast Dr.
Los Angeles, CA 90069
*Actor*

**White, Dr. John**
General Association of Regular Baptist Churches
1300 N. Meacham Rd.
Schaumburg, IL 60173
*Association chairman*

**White, Norval Crawford**
CCNY School of Architecture
138th St. and Covent Ave.
New York, NY 10031
*Architect, author*

**White, Vanna**
345 N. Maple Dr., #185
Beverly Hills, CA 90210
*Game show letter turner*

**Whitetails Unlimited, Inc.**
P.O. Box 422
Sturgeon Bay, WI 54235
Jeffrey B. Schinkten, President
*Deer conservation*

**Whitman Corporation**
III Crossroads of Commerce
3501 Algonquin Rd.
Rolling Meadows, IL 60006
James W. Cozad, Chairman and
  CEO
*Soft drink and tire company*

**Whitney, Phyllis A.**
666 Fifth Ave.
New York, NY 10103
*Novelist*

**Whitworth, Kathryne Ann**
c/o LPGA
2570 Valusia Ave.
Daytona Beach, FL 32114
*Professional golfer*

**Who, The**
48 Harley House
Marylebone Rd.
London NW1 England
*Rock band*

**Whooping Crane
  Conservation Association,
  Inc.**
3000 Meadlowlark Dr.
Sierra Vista, AZ 85635
C. Eugene Knoder, President

**Wicker, Tom**
229 W. 43rd St.
New York, NY 10036
*Journalist*

**Wild Canid Survival and
  Research Center/Wolf
  Sanctuary**
P.O. Box 760
Eureka, MO 63025
Gary Schoenberger, President
*Wolf preservation society*

**Wild Horse Organized
  Assistance, Inc. (WHOA)**
Box 555
Reno, NV 89504
Dawn Y. Lappin, Executive
  Director

**Wild Thing
(Stevie Ray)**
1692 Sprinter St., NW
Atlanta, GA 30318
*Professional wrestler*

**Wilder, Gene**
9830 Wilshire Blvd.
Beverly Hills, CA 90212
*Actor*

**Wilder, L. Douglas**
State Capitol
Richmond, VA 23219
*Governor of Virginia*

**Wilderness Society, The**
900 17th St., NW
Washington, DC 20006
Alice M. Rivlin, Chair

**Wildlife Society, The**
5410 Grosvenor Ln.
Bethesda, MD 20814
Richard J. Mckie, President

**Wilkins, Dominique**
c/o Atlanta Hawks
1 CNN Center
Atlanta, GA 30303
*Professional basketball player*

**Will, George**
1150 50th St.
Washington, DC 20036
*Political columnist*

**Will Rogers Memorial**
P.O. Box 157
Claremore, OK 74018
Joseph H. Carter, CEO

**William Holden Wildlife
    Foundation**
P.O. Box 67981
Los Angeles, CA 90067

**William S. Hart County Park
    and Museum**
24151 San Fernando Rd.
Newhall, CA 91321
Craig C. Black, Director
*Film cowboy museum*

**Williams, Barry**
1930 Century Park West, #403
Los Angeles, CA 90067
*Actor, author, original Brady Bunch
    kid*

**Williams, Buck**
c/o Portland Trail Blazers
700 NE Multnomah St.
Portland, OR 97232
*Professional basketball player*

**Williams, Hank, Jr.**
P.O. Box 850
Paris, TN 38242
*Singer*

**Williams, John**
301 Massachusetts Ave.
Boston, MA 02115
*Conductor, composer*

**Williams, Montel**
151 El Camino
Beverly Hills, CA 90212
*Talk show host*

**Williams, Robin**
9830 Wilshire Blvd.
Beverly Hills, CA 90212
*Actor, comedian*

**Williams, Vanessa**
Rt. #100
Millwood, NY 10546
*Singer*

**Williams, Willie**
Los Angeles Police Department
Office of the Chief, Parker
    Center
Los Angeles, CA 90012
*New L.A. police chief (Why would
    anybody want this job?)*

**Willis, Bruce**
1122 S. Robertson Blvd., #15
Los Angeles, CA 90035
*Actor*

**Willis, Gordon**
c/o R. Taft
18 W. 55th St.
New York, NY 10019
*Cinematographer*

**Willis, Kevin**
c/o Atlanta Hawks
1 CNN Center
Atlanta, GA 30303
*Professional basketball player*

**Wilson, August**
c/o E. Kretschmer
Savoie Bldg.
126 N. Third St., #400
Minneapolis, MN 55401
*Playwright*

**Wilson, Gahan**
HMH Publications
919 N. Michigan Ave.
Chicago, IL 60611
*Cartoonist*

**Wilson, Pete**
State Capitol
Sacramento, CA 95814
*Governor of California*

**Wilson Phillips
(Chynna Phillips, Carnie
Wilson, Wendy Wilson)**
1290 Ave. of the Americas
New York, NY 10104
*Pop singing group*

**Wind, Timothy**
c/o Police Protective League
600 E. 8th St.
Los Angeles, CA 90014
*Officer involved in the Rodney King
incident*

**Windstar Foundation, The**
2317 Snowmass Creek Rd.
Snowmass, CO 81654
John Denver, President
*Environmental action group*

**Winfield, Paul**
10000 Santa Monica Blvd.,
#305
Los Angeles, CA 90067
*Actor*

**Winfrey, Oprah**
P.O. Box 909715
Chicago, IL 60690
*Talk show host, children's activist*

**Winger, Debra**
8436 W. Third St., #650
Los Angeles, CA 90048
*Actress*

**Winn-Dixie Stores, Inc.**
P.O. Box B, 5050 Edgewood Ct.
Jacksonville, FL 32203
A. Dano Davis, Chairman and
Principal Executive Officer
*Supermarket chain*

**Winningham, Mare**
9830 Wilshire Blvd.
Beverly Hills, CA 90212
*Actress*

**Winnipeg Jets**
Winnipeg Arena
15-1430 Maroons Road
Winnipeg, Manitoba R3G 0L5
Canada
Barry Shenkarow, President
*Professional hockey team*

**Winters, Jonathan**
11151 Ophir Dr.
Los Angeles, CA 90024
*Comedian*

**Winters, Shelley**
8899 Beverly Blvd.
Los Angeles, CA 90048
*Actress, author, raconteur*

**Wirth, Timothy E.**
380 Senate Russell Office Bldg.
Washington, DC 20510
*Senator from Colorado*

**Witt, Katarina**
Reichenheimer Str. D-(0)
9023 Chemnitz
Germany
*Ice skater*

**Wm. Wrigley Jr. Company**
410 N. Michigan Ave.
Chicago, IL 60611
William Wrigley III, CEO/
President
*Chewing gum manufacturer*

**Wolfe, Tom**
(Thomas Kennerly, Jr.)
c/o Farrar, Straus & Giroux
19 Union Sq. West
New York, NY 10003
*Author*

**Wolfman Jack**
Rt. 1, Box 56
Belvidere, NC 27919
*Perennial D.J.*

**Women's Army Corps Museum**
U.S. Army Military Police &
Chemical Schools/Training
Center
Fort McLellan, AL 36205
Colonel Bettie J. Morden,
President

**Women's Christian Temperance Union**
1730 Chicago Ave.
Evanston, IL 60201
Frances Bateman, National
Executive Director

**Women's International Bowling Congress, Inc.**
5301 S. 76th St.
Greendale, WI 53129
Gladys Banker, President

**Women's Professional Rodeo Association**
Route 5, Box 698
Blanchard, OK 73010
Lydia Moore, Secretary-
Treasurer

**Woo, Roh Tae**
Chong Wa Dae
1 Sejongno, Chougnogu
Seoul 110-050, Republic of
Korea
*President of the Republic of Korea*

**Woodcraft Rangers**
2111 Park Grove Ave.
Los Angeles, CA 90007
James Van Hoven, Executive
Director
*A scouting-type program*

**Woodmen Rangers**
Woodmen of the World
1700 Farnam St.
Omaha, NE 68102
Larry R. Wegener, Manager,
National Youth Activities
*Forest fans*

**Woods, James**
9830 Wilshire Blvd.
Beverly Hills, CA 90212
*Actor*

**Woodward, Joanne**
40 W. 57th St.
New York, NY 10019
*Actress*

**Woolridge, Orlando**
c/o Denver Nuggets
1635 Clay St.
Denver, CO 80204
*Professional basketball player*

**Woolworth Corporation**
233 Broadway
New York, NY 10279
Harold E. Sells, Chairman and
CEO
*Kinney Shoes, Footlocker,
granddaddy of the five and dime
stores*

**Working Mother Magazine**
Lang Communications
230 Park Ave.
New York, NY 10169
Judsen Culbreth, Editor

**World Championship Wrestling, Inc.**
(a subsidiary of Turner Broadcasting)
P.O. Box 105366
Atlanta, GA 30348-5366
Ted Turner, CEO

**World Federalist Association**
P.O. Box 15250
Washington, DC 20003
Anthony Allen, Youth Director
*Supports the United Nations with 70 youth and adult chapters*

**World Figure Skating Hall of Fame and Museum, The**
20 First St.
Colorado Springs, CO 80906
Ian Anderson, Executive Director

**World Vision**
919 W. Huntington Dr.
Monrovia, CA 91016
Robert A. Seiple, President
*Christian relief organization*

**World Wildlife Fund-U.S.**
1250 24th St., NW
Washington, DC 20037
Russell E. Train, Chairman of the Board

**World Wrestling Federation**
c/o Titan Sports
1055 Summer St.
P.O. Box 3857
Stamford, CT 06905
Vincent K. McMahon, President/CEO

**Worldwatch Institute**
1776 Massachusetts Ave., NW
Washington, DC 20036
Lester R. Brown, President
*Environmental group*

**Worthy, James**
c/o L.A. Lakers
P.O. Box 10
Inglewood, CA 90306
*Basketball player*

**Wrangler**
P.O. Box 21488
Greensboro, NC 27420
Mackey McDonald, President
*Jeans/clothing manufacturer*

**Wright, Robin**
P.O. Box 2630
Malibu, CA 90265
*Actress*

**Writer's Digest**
F & W Publications, Inc.
1507 Dana Ave.
Cincinnati, OH 45207
Peter Blocksom, Editor
*Magazine*

**Wuorinen, Charles**
c/o H. Stokar
870 W. End Ave.
New York, NY 10025
*Composer*

**Wyeth, Andrew**
c/o General Delivery
Chadds Ford, PA 19317
*Artist*

**Wynnona**
3907 Alameda Ave., 2nd Fl.
Burbank, CA 91505
*Singer*

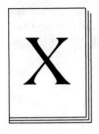

I see you understand the pleasure that can be got from writing letters. In other centuries this was taken for granted. Not any longer. Only a few people carry on true correspondences. No time, the rest will tell you. Quicker to telephone. Like saying a photograph is more satisfying than a painting. There wasn't all that much time for writing letters in the past, either, but time was found, as it generally can be for whatever gives pleasure.

**Xerces Society, The**
10 SW Ash St.
Portland, OR 97204
Edward O. Wilson, President
*Preserves invertebrates*

**Xerox Corporation**
P.O. Box 1600, 800 Long Ridge Rd.
Stamford, CT 06904
Paul A. Allaire, Chairman and CEO
*Leading manufacturer of copier machines*

But I want music and intellectual companionships and affection. Well, perhaps I'll get all that one day. And in the meantime there are little things to look forward to, letters and the unexpected.

**Yankovic, "Weird" Al**
8842 Hollywood Blvd.
Los Angeles, CA 90069
*Composer, singer, comedian*

**Yeager, Gen. Chuck**
Box 128
Cedar Ridge, CA 95924
*Retired test pilot*

**Yellow Freight System**
10990 Roe Ave., P.O. Box 7563
Overland Park, KS 66207
George E. Powell, Jr., Chairman
*Trucking company*

**Yeltsin, Boris**
The Kremlin
Moscow, Russia
*President of Russia*

**Yetnikoff, Walter**
Trump Tower
721 Fifth Ave.
New York, NY 10022
*Music executive*

**YMCA of the USA**
101 N. Wacker Dr.
Chicago, IL 60606
Solon B. Cousins, Executive
    Director
*Various programs available for
    children and adults*

**York, Michael**
8899 Beverly Blvd.
Los Angeles, CA 90048
*Actor*

**Yothers, Tina**
9000 Sunset Blvd., #1200
Los Angeles, CA 90069
*Actress, activist*

**Young, Neil**
506 Santa Monica Blvd.
Santa Monica, CA 90401
*Musician, songwriter*

**Young, Steve**
c/o San Francisco 49ers
4949 Centennial Blvd.
Santa Clara, CA 95054
*Professional football player*

## Young Actors Guild
125 South 4th Street
Connellsville, PA 15425
Aaron White, President
*Protects child actors*

## Young Americans for Freedom
380 Maple Ave., W
Vienna, VA 22180
Thomas C. Lizardo, Executive Director
*Oldest conservative political youth organization*

## Young & Rubicam Inc.
285 Madison Ave.
New York, NY 10017
Alexander S. Kroll, Chairman and CEO
*Largest independent advertising agency*

## Young Communist League of the United States of America
235 W. 23rd St., 6th Fl.
New York, NY 10011
John Bachtell, Chairman

## Young Democrats of America
c/o Democratic National Committee
430 S. Capitol St., SE
Washington, DC 20003
Kathy McGough, Spokesperson
*The youth organization for the Democratic Party*

## Young Republican National Federation
310 First St., SE
Washington, DC 20003
Terry Campo, National Chairman
*The youth organization of the Republican Party*

## Young Socialist Alliance
191 Seventh Ave., 2nd Fl.
New York, NY 10011
Greg McCarten, National Organization Secretary
*Promotes socialist ideas*

## Young Women's Christian Association of the United States of America (YWCA)
726 Broadway
New York, NY 10003
Gwendolyn Calvert Baker, Executive Director

## Youth Against War and Facism
46 W. 21st St.
New York, NY 10010
Kathy Durkin, Corresponding Secretary

## Youth Suicide National Center
204 E. 2nd Ave., #203
San Mateo, CA 94401
Charlotte Rose, Executive Director
*Suicide prevention for kids*

# Z

I have now attained the true art of letter writing, which, we are always told, is to express on paper exactly what one would say to the same person by word of mouth; I have been talking to you almost as fast as I could the whole of this letter.

—JANE AUSTEN

**Zamora, Jaime Paz**
Palacio de Gobierno
Plaza Murillo
La Paz, Bolivia
*President of Bolivia*

**Zanuck, Richard Darryl**
202 N. Canon Dr.
Beverly Hills, CA 90210
*Film producer*

**Zapf, Hermann**
2 Hammarskjold Plaza ITC
New York, NY 10017
*Book and type designer*

**Zappas**
**(Frank, Moon Unit, Dweezil)**
P.O. Box 5265
N. Hollywood, CA 91616
*Musicians, personalities, etc.*

**Zeffirelli, Franco**
Via Appia Pignatelli 448
Rome, Italy
*Film director, Shakespeare adaptor*

**Zeman, Jacklyn**
9113 Sunset Blvd.
Los Angeles, CA 90069
*Actress*

**Zenawi, Meles**
c/o Ethiopian People's
  Revolutionary Democratic
  Front
Addis Ababa, Ethiopia
*President of Ethiopia*

**Zenith Electronics**
  **Corporation**
1000 Milwaukee Ave.
Glenview, IL 60025
Jerry K. Pearlman, Chairman,
  President and CEO
*Developer of high-definition
  television*

**Zero Population Growth, Inc.**
1400 16th St., NW, #320
Washington, DC 20036
Timothy B. Lovain, President

**Zia, Begum Khaleda**
Office of the Prime Minister
Dhaka, Bangladesh
*Prime Minister of Bangladesh*

**Ziering, Ian**
335 N. Maple Dr., #360
Beverly Hills, CA 90210
*Actor*

**Zimbalist, Stephanie**
10100 Santa Monica Blvd.,
  #1600
Los Angeles, CA 90067
*Actress*

**Zinneman, Fred**
128 Mount St.
London W1 England
*Film director, producer, activist*

**Zipprodt, Patricia**
29 King St.
New York, NY 10014
*Costume designer*

**Zmeskal, Kim**
c/o Karoly's Gymnastics
17203 Bamwood
Houston, TX 77090
*Gymnast*

**Zsigmond, Vilmos**
9229 Sunset Blvd., #700
Los Angeles, CA 90069
*Cinematographer*

**Zumwalt, Elmo Russell, Jr.**
1500 Wilson Blvd.
Arlington, VA 22209
*Retired admiral*

**Zuniga, Daphne**
P.O. Box 1249
White River Junction, VT 05001
*Actress*

**ZZ Top**
P.O. Box 19744
Houston, TX 77024
*Rock group*

# Celebrity Birthday List

| | | | |
|---|---|---|---|
| Hank Aaron | 2/5/34 | Shirley Booth | 8/30 |
| Andre Agassi | 4/29/70 | Bjorn Borg | 6/7/56 |
| Alan Alda | 1/28/36 | Tom Bosley | 10/1 |
| Jane Alexander | 10/28 | Marlon Brando | 4/3/24 |
| Muhammad Ali | 1/18/42 | Beau Bridges | 2/5 |
| Woody Allen | 12/1 | Jeff Bridges | 12/4/49 |
| Herb Alpert | 3/31 | Charles Bronson | 11/3/22 |
| Loni Anderson | 8/5 | Mel Brooks | 6/28 |
| Julie Andrews | 10/1/35 | Dr. Joyce Brothers | 10/20/28 |
| Jennifer Anglin | 10/4 | Carol Burnett | 4/26/33 |
| Paul Anka | 7/30 | Raymond Burr | 5/25/13 |
| Ann-Margret | 4/28/41 | George Bush | 6/12/24 |
| Desi Arnaz, Jr. | 1/19/53 | Michael Caine | 3/14/33 |
| James Arness | 5/26/23 | Kirk Cameron | 10/12 |
| Bea Arthur | 5/13 | John Candy | 10/31 |
| Elizabeth Ashley | 8/30 | Art Carney | 11/14/18 |
| Armand Assante | 10/4 | Leslie Caron | 7/1/31 |
| Gene Autry | 9/29/07 | Diahann Carroll | 7/17/35 |
| Lauren Bacall | 9/16/24 | Johnny Carson | 10/23/25 |
| Joan Baez | 1/19/41 | Jimmy Carter | 10/1/24 |
| Scott Baio | 9/22/61 | Fidel Castro | 8/13/27 |
| Brigitte Bardot | 9/28 | Richard Chamberlain | 3/31/35 |
| Mikhail Baryshnikov | 12/27/47 | Chevy Chase | 10/8 |
| Warren Beatty | 3/30/37 | Chubby Checker | 10/3 |
| Boris Becker | 11/22/67 | Cher | 5/20/46 |
| James Belushi | 6/15 | Julie Christie | 4/14/41 |
| Tom Berenger | 5/31 | Eric Clapton | 3/30/45 |
| Candice Bergen | 4/9/46 | Dick Clark | 11/30/29 |
| Valerie Bertinelli | 4/23/60 | Natalie Cole | 2/8 |
| Jacqueline Bisset | 9/13/44 | Jimmy Connors | 9/2/52 |
| Bill Bixby | 1/22/34 | Bill Cosby | 7/11/37 |
| Linda Blair | 1/22 | Kevin Costner | 1/18 |
| Peter Bogdanovich | 7/30/39 | Jacques Cousteau | 6/11/10 |
| Sonny Bono | 2/16/40 | David Crosby | 8/14/41 |

| | | | |
|---|---|---|---|
| Billy Crystal | 3/14 | Soleil Moon Frye | 8/6/76 |
| Jamie Lee Curtis | 1/22/58 | James Garner | 4/7/28 |
| Tony Danza | 4/21/51 | Leif Garrett | 11/6/61 |
| James Darren | 6/9/36 | Steve Garvey | 12/22/48 |
| Doris Day | 4/1/24 | Barry Gibb | 9/1 |
| Peter DeLuise | 11/6 | Melissa Gilbert- | |
| Elizabeth Dennehy | 10/1 | Brinkman | 5/8/64 |
| John Denver | 12/31/43 | Sharon Gless | 5/31/43 |
| Johnny Depp | 7/9 | Louis Gossett, Jr. | 5/27 |
| Susan Dey | 12/10 | Lee Grant | 10/31/29 |
| Neil Diamond | 1/24/41 | Linda Gray | 9/12/41 |
| Angie Dickinson | 9/30/31 | Dick Gregory | 10/12/32 |
| Bo Diddley | 12/30/27 | Merv Griffin | 7/6/25 |
| Fats Domino | 2/26/28 | Andy Griffith | 6/2/26 |
| Phil Donahue | 12/21 | Pedro Guerrero | 6/29/56 |
| Michael Douglas | 9/25 | Sir Alec Guinness | 4/11 |
| Hugh Downs | 2/14 | Bryant Gumbel | 9/29 |
| Richard Dreyfuss | 10/29/47 | Barbara Hale | 4/18 |
| Patrick Duffy | 3/17 | Daryl Hall | 10/11/49 |
| Faye Dunaway | 1/14/41 | Mark Hamill | 9/25/51 |
| Bob Dylan | 5/24/41 | Harry Hamlin | 10/30 |
| Sheena Easton | 4/27/59 | Tom Hanks | 7/9/55 |
| Clint Eastwood | 5/29/30 | Valerie Harper | 8/22 |
| Buddy Ebsen | 4/2 | Richard Harris | 10/1 |
| Barbara Eden | 5/31 | George Harrison | 2/25/43 |
| Blake Edwards | 7/26/22 | Hugh Hefner | 4/9/26 |
| Anita Ekberg | 9/29 | Florence Henderson | 2/14 |
| Linda Evans | 11/18/42 | Doug Henning | 5/3/47 |
| Chris Evert | 12/21/54 | Charlton Heston | 10/4 |
| Douglas Fairbanks, Jr. | 12/9 | Judd Hirsch | 3/15 |
| Peter Falk | 9/16/27 | Dustin Hoffman | 8/8/37 |
| Debrah Farentino | 9/30 | Hal Holbrook | 2/17 |
| Farrah Fawcett | 2/2 | Bob Hope | 5/29/03 |
| Jose Feliciano | 9/10/45 | Dennis Hopper | 5/17/36 |
| Albert Finney | 5/9/36 | Ron Howard | 3/1/54 |
| Carrie Fisher | 10/21 | C. Thomas Howell | 12/9/66 |
| Nina Foch | 4/20 | Tab Hunter | 7/1/31 |
| Jane Fonda | 12/21/37 | Lauren Hutton | 11/17/43 |
| Peter Fonda | 2/23/39 | Timothy Hutton | 8/16 |
| Harrison Ford | 7/13/42 | Kate Jackson | 10/29/49 |
| Jodie Foster | 11/19/62 | Michael Jackson | 8/29/58 |
| Michael J. Fox | 6/9/61 | Mick Jagger | 7/26/54 |
| Aretha Franklin | 3/25/42 | Bruce Jenner | 10/28/49 |

| | | | |
|---|---|---|---|
| Billy Joel | 5/9/49 | Robert Mitchum | 8/6/17 |
| Elton John | 3/25/47 | Elizabeth Montgomery | 4/15/33 |
| James Earl Jones | 1/17/31 | Demi Moore | 11/11 |
| Shirley Jones | 3/31 | Roger Moore | 10/14/27 |
| Madeline Kahn | 9/29 | Martin Mull | 8/18/43 |
| Donna Karan | 10/2 | Bill Murray | 9/21/49 |
| Diane Keaton | 1/15 | Patricia Neal | 1/20/26 |
| Edward Kennedy | 2/22/32 | Harriet Nelson | 7/18 |
| Carole King | 2/9/42 | Willie Nelson | 4/30/33 |
| Gladys Knight | 5/28/44 | Paul Newman | 1/26/25 |
| Patti LaBelle | 10/4 | Wayne Newton | 4/3/42 |
| Angela Lansbury | 10/16 | Olivia Newton-John | 9/26/47 |
| Cyndi Lauper | 6/22/53 | Leslie Nielsen | 2/11 |
| Jack Lemmon | 2/8/25 | Birgit Nilsson | 7/15/63 |
| Janet Lennon | 6/15/46 | Leonard Nimoy | 3/26 |
| Michael Levine | 4/17/54 | Nick Nolte | 2/8/40 |
| Jerry Lewis | 3/16/26 | Kim Novak | 2/13/33 |
| Jerry Lee Lewis | 9/29/35 | John Oates | 4/7/49 |
| Larry Linville | 9/29 | Carroll O'Connor | 8/2 |
| Emily Lloyd | 9/29 | Donald O'Connor | 8/28/25 |
| Rob Lowe | 3/17/63 | Maureen O'Hara | 8/17 |
| George Lucas | 5/14/44 | Ryan O'Neal | 4/20/41 |
| Dolph Lundgren | 10/16 | Donny Osmond | 12/9/57 |
| Shirley MacLaine | 4/24/34 | Carre Otis | 9/28 |
| Madonna | 4/16/58 | Peter O'Toole | 8/2/32 |
| Henry Mancini | 4/16 | Jack Palance | 2/18 |
| Barry Manilow | 6/17 | Fess Parker | 8/26 |
| Ed Marinaro | 3/31 | Dolly Parton | 1/3/46 |
| Penny Marshall | 10/15 | Pope John Paul II | 5/18/20 |
| Marsha Mason | 4/3 | Minnie Pearl | 10/25 |
| Marcello Mastroianni | 9/28 | George Peppard | 10/1 |
| Tim Matheson | 12/31/47 | H. Ross Perot | 6/27 |
| Johnny Mathis | 9/30 | Lou Diamond Phillips | 2/17/62 |
| Walter Matthau | 10/1 | Suzanne Pleshette | 1/31/37 |
| Paul McCartney | 6/18/42 | George Plimpton | 3/18/27 |
| Marilyn McCoo | 9/30 | Sidney Poitier | 2/20 |
| Ted McGinley | 5/30/58 | Stefanie Powers | 11/2/42 |
| Nancy McKeon | 4/5/66 | Priscilla Presley | 5/24 |
| Rod McKuen | 4/29/33 | Charley Pride | 3/18 |
| Kristy McNichol | 9/11/62 | Prince | 6/7/58 |
| Zubin Mehta | 4/29/36 | Dennis Quaid | 4/9 |
| John Mellencamp | 10/7/51 | Randy Quaid | 10/1 |
| Lee Ann Meriwether | 5/27/35 | Charlotte Rae | 4/22 |

| | | | |
|---|---|---|---|
| Ronald Reagan | 2/6/11 | Dean Stockwell | 3/5/36 |
| Robert Redford | 8/18/37 | Daryl Strawberry | 3/12/62 |
| Christopher Reeve | 9/25/52 | Barbra Streisand | 4/24/42 |
| Duncan Regehr | 10/3 | Sally Struthers | 7/28 |
| Rob Reiner | 3/6 | Mary Ellen Stuart | 10/4 |
| Burt Reynolds | 2/11/36 | Fran Tarkenton | 2/3/40 |
| Madlyn Rhue | 10/3 | Elizabeth Taylor | 2/27/32 |
| Diana Rigg | 7/20/38 | Shirley Temple Black | 4/22/28 |
| John Ritter | 9/17/48 | Victoria Tennant | 9/30 |
| Kenny Rogers | 8/21/41 | Tiffany | 10/2 |
| Roy Rogers | 11/15/12 | Lily Tomlin | 9/1/36 |
| Linda Ronstadt | 7/15 | Tanya Tucker | 10/10 |
| Diana Ross | 3/26/44 | Lana Turner | 2/8/20 |
| Kurt Russell | 3/17/51 | Tina Turner | 11/26/39 |
| Nolan Ryan | 1/31/47 | Gore Vidal | 10/3 |
| Susan Saint James | 8/14 | Herve Villechaize | 4/23/43 |
| Susan Sarandon | 10/4 | Bobby Vinton | 4/16/41 |
| Tom Seaver | 11/17/44 | Jack Wagner | 10/3 |
| Connie Sellecca | 5/25/55 | Lindsay Wagner | 6/22 |
| William Shatner | 3/22/31 | Barbara Walters | 9/25/31 |
| Sam Shepard | 11/5/43 | Dennis Weaver | 6/5/24 |
| Paul Simon (Singer) | 10/13/41 | Racquel Welch | 9/5/40 |
| Helen Slater | 12/15/63 | Jill Whelan | 9/29 |
| Jaclyn Smith | 10/26/47 | Betty White | 1/17 |
| Dick Smothers | 11/20/39 | Gene Wilder | 6/11 |
| Tom Smothers | 2/2/37 | Barry Williams | 9/5/54 |
| Suzanne Somers | 10/16 | Robin Williams | 7/21/52 |
| Sissy Spacek | 12/25/49 | Debra Winger | 5/16/55 |
| Rick Springfield | 8/23/49 | Jonathan Winters | 11/11/25 |
| Sylvester Stallone | 7/6 | Shelley Winters | 8/18/22 |
| Jean Stapleton | 1/19/23 | Joanne Woodward | 2/27/31 |
| Ringo Starr | 7/7/40 | Tina Yothers | 5/5/73 |
| James Stewart | 5/20/08 | Moon Zappa | 9/28 |
| Sting | 10/21/51 | | |

# Write to Me

*The Address Book* is updated every two years, and you can play an active role in this procedure. If you are notable in any field, or know someone who is, send the name, mailing address, and some documentation of the notability (newspaper clippings are effective) for possible inclusion in our next edition.

Also, we are very interested in learning of any success stories resulting from *The Address Book*.

During the last few years, I have received tens of thousands of letters, ranging from loving to vituperative, from owners of *The Address Book*. Despite the overwhelming task of answering this mail, I really enjoy the letters.

But, please, remember a couple of rules if you write:

- Remember to include a *self-addressed stamped envelope*. For reasons of both time and expense, this is the only way I can respond to mail; so, unfortunately, I've had to draw the line—no S.A.S.E., no reply.
- I need your comments. While I confess I'm partial to success stories, comments from purchasers of the book have helped me a great deal for future editions; so fire away.
- Many people have written to request addresses of people not listed in the book. As much as I would like to, I simply can't open up this can of worms. Requests for additional addresses are carefully noted and considered for future editions.

Receiving a photo from someone who writes adds an entirely new dimension to the letter, so feel free. That's right, enclose a photo of yourself. After all, from the photo on the back cover, you know what I look like, and I'm rather anxious to see you.

Keep those cards and letters coming.

Michael Levine
8730 Sunset Blvd., Sixth Floor
Los Angeles, CA 90069

# Address Book Poll
## Salutation Surveys

In doing research for *The Address Book* I thought it would be interesting to study people and their letters. Do certain closings stand out as all-around favorites? Well, off I went with this in mind and this is what I found out:

- Sincerely—24%
- No closing used at all—17%
- Yours, yours truly—6%
- Warm regards, best regards, etc.—5%
- Cheers, in a tie with Love (3% each)
- Wishes, warm, with all good, etc.—2%
- The real winner for all-time favorite letter closing, however, may not fit in any category at all, since 40% of the examples ended with closings that were too unique—one or two of a kind, reflecting the originality of the letter writers.

Some of the more unique ones include:

- Pen-fully yours
- May you live all the days of your life
- Pen-sively yours
- Catching up
- Keep the bilge pumped and the motor running
- Yours till the last stamp is licked
- Yours because His (a common letter ending among Christians)
- With a grin and a chortle
- Red roses
- With as much optimism as I can muster
- Happy Trails
- Stand up for America!
- With standards in mind

**Michael Levine's comprehensive address books provide access to the inaccessible.**

## THE ADDRESS BOOK

Used by everyone from the White House staff to Barbara Walters, this volume contains the most confidential mailing addresses of thousands of the world's most powerful, interesting, and influential people.

## THE ENVIRONMENTAL ADDRESS BOOK

A powerful tool to help concerned citizens take part in the fight to save the planet, with listings for more than 2,000 leading environmental figures and organizations, concerned celebrities, and some of the worst polluters.

## THE KID'S ADDRESS BOOK

A fun-filled, information-packed collection of addresses geared specifically to the needs and interests of children aged six through fifteen.

These books are available at your bookstore or wherever books are sold, or for your convenience, we'll send them directly to you. Just call 1-800-631-8571, or fill out the coupon below and send it to:

The Putnam Publishing Group
390 Murray Hill Parkway, Dept. B
East Rutherford, NJ 07073

|  |  | Price | |
|---|---|---|---|
|  |  | U.S. | Canada |
| _____ The Address Book | 399-51793-6 | $ 9.95 | $12.95 |
| _____ The Environmental Address Book | 399-51660-3 | 14.95 | 19.50 |
| _____ The Kid's Address Book | 399-51783-9 | 8.95 | 11.75 |
| Subtotal | | $ _____ | |
| Postage and handling* | | $ _____ | |
| Sales tax (CA, NJ, NY, PA) | | $ _____ | |
| Total amount due | | $ _____ | |

Payable in U.S. funds (no cash orders accepted). $15.00 minimum on credit card orders.

*Postage & handling: $2.50 for 1 book, 75¢ for each additional book up to a maximum of $6.25.

Enclosed is my ☐ check ☐ money order
Please charge my ☐ Visa ☐ MasterCard ☐ American Express

Card # _____ Expiration date _____

Signature as on charge card _____

Name _____

Address _____ City _____ State _____ Zip _____

Please allow six weeks for delivery. Prices subject to change without notice.

Source key #42